THE WAR ANIMALS

THE
WAR ANIMALS

ROBERT E. LUBOW

DOUBLEDAY & COMPANY, INC.
GARDEN CITY, NEW YORK
1977

Excerpt from *The Pigeon,* by W. M. Levi, reprinted with permission of Mrs. W. M. Levi.

Excerpt from *Animal Behaviour,* article entitled "The discrimination by the nose of the dog of individual human odours" by H. Kalmus, reprinted with permission Bailliere Tindall publishers.

Excerpt from "Pigeons in a Pelican" by B. F. Skinner, which originally appeared in *The American Psychologist,* 1960, Number 15, reprinted with permission of the American Psychological Association.

LIBRARY OF CONGRESS CATALOGING IN PUBLICATION DATA
Lubow, Robert E
The War Animals.

Includes bibliographical references.
1. Animals, War use of. I. Title.
UH87.L8   355.8
ISBN: 0-385-11458-3
Library of Congress Catalog Card Number: 76-50779

First Edition

Acknowledgments

This book owes its being to the help of many people. To Dr. Eugene E. Bernard, close friend, and co-founder, with me, of Behavior Systems Inc. To Elizabeth Carr-Harris and Lynne Siebert, two of my first and best graduate students, who came to work for BSI, and later to run it. To Richard and Cathy Thal, who joined us a little bit later and who were also instrumental in the growth of BSI.

To all of the young people around Raleigh, North Carolina, who helped in the care and training of war dogs, who were strong enough to be passionately against the war in Vietnam and still to want to save the lives of soldiers, even Americans.

To the personnel of the Limited Warfare Laboratory, John Romba, Dr. Max Krauss, and in particular to their chief, Milton Cutler, who could overlook (most of the time) the fact that we were a motley band of peace protesters, hippies and professors, because we could also produce something that the Army needed.

To Dr. Mildred Mitchell, who was at the Air Force Avionics laboratory and was an early advocate of the use of animals for military purposes.

To Colonel Mike Kaplan of the Israel Police, who, more than anyone else, has been interested in developing animal sensor systems that are firmly based on laboratory investigations (and, even more important, who introduced me to my wife, Mali).

To my assistants in Israel, Moshe Kahn, Reuven Frommer, Norman Naftali and David Sandberg, who worked with me on developing

the explosive-envelope-detection dog. To Ina Weiner, who read the manuscript and made many constructive suggestions.

Finally, to Beverly Gordey of Doubleday for her advice, encouragement and enthusiasm.

Contents

Introduction

By all common standards, I imagine that most people will find this book unusual, for the good or bad. In addition to the unique nature of the subject matter—training and using animals for war—the book combines elements of autobiography and science, with the emphasis being clearly on the latter. Most of the chapters are based on my own experience. Some, however, are taken from the published reports of other investigators and some from stories that have been told to me.

I had several goals in writing this book and in using the particular format mentioned above. The first was to put together, in one volume, most of the very fascinating research on the uses of animals for purposes of war. Prior to the publication of this book these materials were scattered over scores of different articles and were inaccessible to most people, laymen and professionals alike. Secondly, I wanted to show how the basic, theoretical psychology of the laboratory could be applied to real-world problems and, as such, to provide a case study for the interaction of applied and theoretical science. In addition, it was my intention to illustrate, to the sometimes skeptical public, that a hardheaded scientist, one who may even at times work on military problems, may also be interested in humanity.

The reader might well ask why the author chose to introduce a few sections based on undocumented conversation. First of all, these chapters are all realistic extrapolations of what could be done with our current knowledge and technology. Secondly, all of these chapters are based on talks with "responsible" people who were, at least, thinking along the lines of action that are described.

Finally, I wanted the experience of writing a book that might be of interest to the general public. Both the practice of science and the writing of fiction are creative behaviors, and both are deeply rooted in the past experience of their creators. Both are also social enterprises. Few people would write without intending that it be read by the public. Similarly, science is completely without meaning if data and theories are not publicly accessible, even if intelligible only to other scientists. Good science, like good fiction, poses questions and attempts to find answers to those questions. As human beings we are always asking questions of ourselves and of others. In writing, at least literate fiction, these questions are large ones, the ones that are central to our existence and to our understanding of the human condition. The successful novelist is able, from his own experiences, to distill the essential elements from these questions and to present them in dramatic form so that the reader at least feels, and, with effort, can hope to understand, the issues with which the author is coping.

The scientist, based on his experience with the material that he is studying, phrases his questions in terms of hypotheses, reasonable guesses as to what would happen if ———, and then proceeds to get the answer by means of an experiment, or by some other technique which can reliably be repeated. Although most scientists ask questions about the inanimate world, the world of atoms and molecules, compounds and genes explored by physicists, chemists and biologists, there is also the science of psychology, which concerns itself with empirical investigations of behavior. Not mind, not soul, but behavior.

Psychology is the science of behavior. It is precisely that definition of psychology that ties together otherwise disparate explorations. The study of dreaming, of smoking, of intelligence, of schizophrenia, of consumer preferences in the supermarket, of the rats' performance in a maze, are all subsumed under this definition of psychology.

The two great unifying themes in psychology, at least as it is practiced today, develop from answers to the question of *what* is studied and *how* it is studied.

WHAT: Psychology is the study of *behavior* of organisms. Such a simple statement is seemingly incontestable. But the history of psychology is strewn with conflict and bitterness over the deceptively simple question of what should the psychologist study. Even today the arguments are still with us, albeit the zealous frenzy has subsided. The history of the problem is worth reviewing, however briefly, if only to suggest that today's orthodoxy may be tomorrow's anachronism. (The reader may want to substitute "heresy" for either orthodoxy or anachronism.)

Sometime during the middle of the nineteenth century there occurred a convergence of influences that gave rise to experimental psychology. To understand the nature of this new science which culminated with Wundt's creation of a laboratory of psychology in Leipzig in 1879, and strongly influenced the entire conception of experimental psychology for the next generation, one has to examine the intellectual background of Western Europe during the earlier part of that century.[1]*

Experimental psychology developed directly from experimental physiology, which itself was a new endeavor and grew from progress in the so-called exact sciences of mathematics, physics and chemistry. The first point to be noted is that the experimental method, based on observation, manipulation and control, had been very successful in the natural sciences. The contributions of Gilbert in magnetism and Galileo in optics and mechanics had been accepted, built upon and, perhaps even more important, given practical applications.

As Boring,[2] the great historian of psychology, notes, the concept of experimentation, based on observation and control, had a long history and "was quite obvious once the renaissance had turned men's thought from theological fiat[3] to experiment." However, I suspect that the history of experimentation is probably as long as that of man himself, with only techniques being refined and a greater proportion of his activities being taken up with experimentation as opposed to divination. Certainly one can find good examples of experimental method in Archimedes' writings.

The early experimental psychology was modeled after the successful physical and biological sciences of the mid-nineteenth century. This modeling extended not only to adopting the methodology of these sciences, namely the experimental method, but also to accepting their implicit assumptions. These implicit assumptions included a mechanistic conception of causality and the simplifying idea that un-

* Superior figures refer to the notes and references at the back of the book. These are arranged according to chapters.

derlying all complex events are elementary principles. Indeed the demonstration in Leipzig's laboratory that an organic compound, urea, could be synthesized from simpler inorganic materials, gave psychology a considerable impetus for conceiving of complex perceptions as being composed of simpler sensations.

Psychology took as its province the study of the contents of the mind—i.e., perceptions and thoughts—and assumed that these were composed of simple elementary sensations bound together by certain primitive laws of association. The method that was chosen to reveal these contents was that of introspection. Trained, highly skilled subjects were induced to make observations on their own sensations. This was an experimental science in that manipulations were made, as for example the amount of force on the skin, and responses, in the form of verbal reports of sensory impressions, were taken. The difficulties of this approach lay in the unreliability of the report because of its inherently private nature, and, of course, in the false assumptions concerning the nature of mind. Mind is not a passive receptacle for sensations that become associated as a function of contiguity in time, and which can be again separated by, in a way, turning the mind's eye in upon itself.

Nevertheless, during its time, the introspective approach of the structuralist psychologists had considerable influence. Today almost nothing that is considered of substance is left from all of the work of those decades around the turn of the century. The most lasting mark that introspective structuralists had on psychology was to provide a point of focus for the Gestalt and Behaviorist revolutions. Each rebelled against a different aspect of the older tradition—the Gestalt psychologists against the idea that mind was composed of simple elements and the Behaviorists against the introspective methods.

This book is not the place to delve into the differences between the two new approaches. However, it should be noted that with time, at least for certain early differences, the clear distinctive qualities that they once had have become obscured. Some will argue still that psychology is the study of mental processes. To that I would say yes, it is that too. But these processes are explanations and not data. They are inferences that are made from the study of behavior.

To repeat then, psychology is the study of behavior. All science is the study of behavior. In this respect, psychology is to be differentiated from other sciences only in that it is the study of the behavior of organisms. It is no accident that all sciences are concerned with behavior, because implicit in the meaning of the word "behavior" is that it is observable. It is only the observables that provide the data of science. The physicist may study the behavior of falling bodies, the astronomer the behavior of the stars, the cellular biologist the behavior of cells. Each one has as its starting point observations which are public and repeatable. In the same manner, the psychologist studies behavior, and is committed therefore to the methods of science. This brings us from the first question of WHAT to the second question of HOW. The study of behavior is accomplished by using the scientific methods.

What is science? First let us strip it of those vain affectations that allow people to dismiss an opponent's argument with the almost thunderous conclusivity: "But that's not scientific." To label some activity or verbal statement as being "scientific" does not endow that behavior with any more virtue than calling an apple "red" or a man a "Republican." Likewise, the labeling of an activity as being "unscientific" should not be a term of opprobrium. Like virginity, it is either there or not there; it is a fact. The value, positive, neutral or negative, that is attached to that fact will depend on the purpose for which it is used, the culture that is lived in and a variety of other considerations. There are many scientific activities that are commendable and others that are condemnable; and similarly for nonscientific activities. In fact, as an exercise one can construct a fourfold table enumerating examples of all four types. However, it should not be forgotten that the contents of these cells have a number of degrees of freedom, and depending on the century, the occupant of one cell may be found to have changed residences. This is more true of the commendable-condemnable continuum than the scientific-nonscientific continuum because the first is a matter of judgment, and the latter of fact. It is easier for a person to be transfigured from saint to sinner than an activity to be transformed from scientific to nonscientific.

In defining psychology as the scientific study of behavior, I will have irritated and even offended a number of people. There is no purpose in defending the position, since it is basically a matter of definition. What I will defend, and this is one of the purposes of the book, is the belief that the methods of science provide the keys to the secrets of the human condition, which unless unlocked may result in tragedy for all of us.

The last decade has given rise to two movements which have gravely affected experimental psychology. For convenience I will label these Political Nowism and Personal Nowism. The first movement has resulted in limiting the growth of basic research in almost all areas of science. Perhaps this was an expected reaction to the unprecedented growth of basic science in the two decades following World War II. But, at least in part, it was a concession to the political hedonists who, when faced with problems for which science had not yet provided solutions, attacked further expenditures in the theoretical sciences as being wasteful and frivolous. It certainly is true that scientists had no answers to Vietnam, to campus riots, to urban disorders. (But could it also be that our legislators were reacting to the fact that some of the university recipients of congressional largesse were outspoken against governmental policies in these areas, and many others, although quiet, were completely without sympathy for the formal government positions, particularly in regard to Vietnam?)

These governmental legislators and administrators concerned with solutions NOW, and working with finite budgets, placed the emphasis first of all on defense expenditures and secondly on remedial social action programs. This was accomplished, to some extent, at the expense of funds for basic research.

It is one of the ironies of this book that most of the research to be discussed was supported by monies from the U.S. defense budget. But it will be quite clear that these researches were funded only because they were applied and the investigators pledged to provide usable answers to pressing military problems. The irony is that the answers would not have been forthcoming had the research not been preceded by years of basic, theoretical investigations. From what base will we be able to answer other applied questions, ones that might be asked ten years or fifty from now? It is an act of political hedonism and irresponsibility to have today's satisfaction at the expense of tomorrow's survival. What is not recognized by most people is that basic and applied research can be mutually supporting, rather than separate and conflicting entities.

The scientist is often viewed as concerning himself almost exclusively with the realm of ideas and theories, building abstract models of esoteric behavior, while his nonscientist counterpart in the real world is busy with the practice or application of knowledge gained from the scientists' laboratory many years earlier. This is the distinction between the physicist and the engineer, physiologist and physician, experimental psychologist and clinical psychologist. Like many caricatures, there is both truth and falsity in these images. There is a dynamic interaction between theory and application such that each endeavor supports and enriches the other. However, the lines of interaction are exceedingly complex and somewhat confusing. It would require several volumes in a History of Science Series to explicate the relationships and to establish some useful generalizations. Suffice it to say here that the exchange between theory and application exists, and it exists in both directions; though it is more obvious that theory affects application than that application affects theory. The existence of these bidirectional exchanges need only be established by examples, several of which are presented below.

The classic example of the influence of theory on application is, of course, the Manhattan Project, the development of the atomic bomb. Completely theoretical efforts of such renowned scientists as Einstein, Bohr and others were applied by other theoretical scientists such as Oppenheimer and Libby to create a weapon. Other applications evolved into practical ways of generating energy for peacetime uses. Indeed, it is one measure of the strength of the theory that from it such diversity of applications were developed. Both in war and in peace the impact of these applications has been enormous. It is quite clear that the current technology in nuclear power could not have been built but upon the strong theoretical base that preceded it, and which itself took decades to establish. So here, in one case, theory led to application, and application strengthened theory. It is possible to conceive of application as a prediction from theory. Thus, every time an application derived from a theory works, it must necessarily strengthen that theory from which it was derived.

This is not a simple effect. Theory need not always precede application. Fires were built and stones hurled long before the animal skins were replaced by white laboratory coats. And the Wright brothers, experts in bicycle mechanics, knew nothing of theories of aerodynamics.

Some examples, within psychology, further clarify the interrelationship between theory and application. One set of such examples is presented in the investigations reported in the main body of this book. Another example is that of the use of laboratory-developed learning principles to change undesirable human behavior.

In many respects the two endeavors, behavior modification and war animal training, are quite closely related. This is true not only in the manner in which they both represent an intersection of theory and application, but also in specific techniques employed, in general philosophy and in the history of their development. That one is concerned with changing the behavior of humans to make it more acceptable to the individual and to the society, and the other is concerned with shaping the behavior of lower organisms so as to make them of use to man in war, reflects both the general power of the training principles and the ingenuity, if not the irony, of man.

The application of principles of learning to problems of maladaptive behavior did not derive directly from theory, but rather, for the most part, was conceived of by people who were actively engaged in doing basic theoretical research. One has a suspicion that the behavioral sciences are more prone to the effects of serendipity in translating theory into practice than are the physical scientists. Perhaps this is because theories are not as well developed in the behavioral sciences as compared to the physical sciences, or because people are basically conservative and fear behavioral change that is perceived as being externally manipulated. This latter assumption is especially relevant in understanding the objection to behavior modification.

The behavior modification techniques which have been developed and successfully tested are numerous. A few of the maladaptive behaviors which have been treated within this framework include bedwetting, stuttering, a variety of phobic behaviors such as fear of snakes, of small places, various specific ward behaviors which are disruptive, as for example aggression and head-banging. In addition to the extinction of these undesirable responses, there are the many instances of shaping new adaptive responses, which might include, for example within a hospital, toilet training, self-feeding and even language behavior on the part of previously mute inmates.[4]

I do not want to give the impression that the behavior modification approach is an unqualified cure-all. It is not. In many cases the evaluative research has been poor and we cannot adequately assess the treatment effect; furthermore, even if we could, it would be difficult to isolate the cause, the independent variable.

The question now, for the purposes of discussing the relationship between pure and applied science, is how did this radically new applied approach to problems in clinical psychology develop from basic research? During the 1930s and 1940s, following World Wars I and II, there was a burst of activity on the part of those psychologists involved in the area of tests and measurement. This activity can be partly accounted for by the large-scale successes of the testing movement in the placement and training of soldiers. Here it can be noted that, apparently for the first time, behavioral measures (test scores) were being used to predict other behaviors (e.g., success as a rifleman, or as an officer).

Physicians, on the other hand, charged with the responsibility for the care and treatment of the mentally ill, were meeting with little success. And, at least in the hospitals, their functions became primarily custodial. These physicians, I suspect, became intrigued with the measurement and quantification mystique of science. They noted their failures with the so-called mentally ill, recognized that other branches of medicine, more successful, used measurement techniques to assess a patient's condition (e.g., the *thermometer,* white and red blood *counts,* heart *rate,* etc.). From that it would seem to be a logical step to adopt the idea that psychological test scores could be used to identify an underlying "mental disease." And sure enough, test after test appeared to fill the apparent need: the Rorschach, TAT, Szondi, Draw-a-Man, etc., etc., and with them thick manuals to explain how to get numbers, the quantitative quality of science.

The business of constructing tests, scoring tests and interpreting tests was given a vast push forward by the physicians attending the mentally ill who were looking for science to help them. Aiding this movement was the cultural *Zeitgeist.* Only recently had society shed itself of the notion that the causative agents for mental disturbance were demonic spirits, and a sure cure burning at the stake. And perhaps during the period of time that we are now talking about, the three decades between the 1920s and 1950s, there was an overreaction to the primitive belief systems of earlier centuries. The once inherently evil person, exhibiting strange behaviors, was relieved of all responsibility for his behaviors; and even more important, the members of his family and the society in which he lived were also kept guiltless—all of this by defining the causative agent for the abnormal behavior as a disease. Thus, just as society, or the individuals in it, could not be considered to be responsible for a case of measles (also you might want to compare earlier histories of the Black Plague) in a member of the family, they were also free from any burden of guilt associated with having a schizophrenic in the family. With this change in perspective came a change in terminology—from madhouse and lunatic asylum to mental *hospital,* currently on its way to the more neutral designation, institute or center.

It was during that time, 1920–50, that the clinical psychologist was absorbed into the "mental health system," under the guise of being a scientifically trained technician, to serve as an adjunct to the medical professionals.

However, the training of clinical psychologists continued to be in the academic departments of psychology, and not in medical schools. These academic departments of psychology were run (and many of them still are) by experimental psychologists. Without question, the prestige and status of psychology emanated from these men, who, in turn, shaped the training programs for all graduate psychologists. In these departments there was the insistence, zealously proclaimed, that psychology was an empirical, experimental science, whose goals were to develop laws and theories of behavior, with the almost categorical imperative that all of the graduates of these psychology departments had to be at least exposed to, and even better, trained in, the methods and contents of experimental psychology. It is to this end that the "core" programs were developed. Every student—clinical, industrial or experimental—took courses in History and Systems, Sensation and Perception, Learning, Motivation, Statistics. Each student was required to do an empirical dissertation. This model has only recently been modified, though many of the original elements, some of questionable validity, still remain in most clinical programs.

The graduate clinical psychologist with his Ph.D. readily found employment in mental hospitals. But he also found himself in a most dissatisfying situation. With the same amount of training as the psychiatrist-physician, the psychologist played a distinctly minor, even subservient role in the hospital system. The responsibility for decision-making was in the hands of the physicians. The right to do psychotherapy, as opposed to testing, was jealously guarded by the medical doctors. Only the physician through some mysterious initiation rite could be allowed to practice what then seemed like priestly arts. Deprived of the role of healer, the psychologist with his more rigorous scientific training began quickly to question the validity of many of the treatment procedures that were being employed.

This combination of frustration, skepticism and training in the techniques of experimental psychology, particularly in the learning laboratory, led the psychologists to discover their "own" method of treatment. The flavor of the resentment and hostility that psychologists developed is illustrated by a recent comment by a clinical psychologist in regard to behavior modification: ". . . its application is not contingent upon the approval of psychiatric jurisprudence. . . . A psychiatrist wishing to use the method would have to learn from, and be supervised by, a psychologist."[5]

The behavior modifier readily accepted Victor Raimy's pronouncements that "psychotherapy is an undefined technique applied to unspecified cases with unpredictable results. For this technique rigorous training is required."[6] There are the Bad Guys and the Good Guys: ". . . since the technique can be taught to many persons . . . [it] allows for a broadening of the base of people that can help such patients. The Behavior Modifier stands ready to train nurses, hospital aides, volunteers, Gray Ladies, parents, physicians, teachers, social workers, secretaries, psychiatrists, playmates or siblings in the methods . . ."[5] To which this writer will simply comment that it is characteristic of successful revolutions to be imbued with an excess of optimism, at least in the early post-revolutionary period.

Regardless of future evaluation, it is clear that a new approach in the treatment of abnormal behavior did develop from training in basic experimental psychology. It should also be noted, however, that this was only one current of the dynamic interaction between basic and applied psychology. What has been described until now were the conditions for creating a receptive buyer for the behavior modification technique.

There was also a second current, which flowed from the faculties of psychology and the prestigious experimental programs, which reinforced and further propelled the behavior modification movement. As mentioned earlier, since World War II, basic-research budgets in all sciences, including psychology, had increased yearly. However, at some point in the middle of Johnson's presidency, perhaps as a response to the mounting social pressures, as illustrated by rioting in the black slums, student unrest, the general rising rate of violent crime, the discontent with the Vietnam War, and the associated budgetary pressures created by these events, there was heard across the land the cry of "relevance" (that is, application). Priorities and funds were shifted from basic research to applied research, from theorizing to practicing.

Twenty years ago, when I was studying psychology in the classroom, the most prominent figures in psychology were the theorists of learning—Hull,[7] Tolman[8] and, to a lesser degree, Guthrie.[9] Hull, especially, was esteemed. He built a hypothetico-deductive system of behavior. In so doing, he mimicked the physicists who were regarded as the model scientists of the time. He identified the key problems of psychology as being in the area of learning, adopted, as Watson[10] before him, an almost complete environmentally deterministic posture and attempted, as the physicists had done so well, to create a system of postulates and empirical laws from which one could deduce new testable hypotheses in regard to learning.

Hull's attempts to construct a theoretical model of learning behavior were quite successful, at least as measured by: the number of experiments that were developed from it; the controversial issues that it crystallized; the number of presently prominent psychologists that were influenced by his teaching and research. The typical course in learning proclaimed the virtues of the Hullian approach and concentrated on a comparative analysis of contemporary learning theories. While extolling theory, the atheoretical work of Skinner[11] and that of applied psychology were dismissed. Here, a distinction should be made between atheoretical and application-oriented work.

Applied research has a stated goal, to develop information for an interested nonscience consumer. Research to determine the melting point of the metal titanium may be commissioned by an aerospace company or by the government to determine whether such a metal would be useful as a skin for a recoverable space capsule. This is applied research. Or, a candidate for political office might commission a social psychologist to measure the intensity of public opinion on a particular issue. Again, applied research.

Skinner, on the other hand, does atheoretical work in a different sense. He does not believe in the usefulness of theories in which the excess meaning of explanatory concepts is detrimental to the lawful exposition of the relationships between behavior and environmental events. The basic-research psychologist should concern himself with simple descriptive relationships of system inputs to system outputs—and in this manner create an interlocking pattern of laws from which will emerge larger generalizations, but completely based on the original data. Thus, Skinner can be described as being atheoretical but still concerned primarily with basic research. Although in his special case he also has made enormous efforts to show the implications of his basic research on everyday problems—from designing machines to teach reading[12] to redesigning societies.[13]

Let us return now to the older tradition of Hull, in which scientific value and prestige were measured by the degree of theory construction. The assumption was that it was possible to produce a complete theory of behavior or at least of learned behavior. That theory would stand by itself as an ultimate achievement of the behavioral sciences and result in useful applications in the real world. But the most precious goal was the theory itself.

The years passed and experiment after experiment, meticulously derived from theory, were designed and executed. These studies concerned what appeared to be, at that time, basic differences between opposing theories—e.g., the role of drive reduction as exemplified in studies of latent learning, or the necessity of a stimulus-response association for learning (as opposed to stimulus-stimulus as exemplified in the sensory preconditioning studies). Studies of this type mushroomed in the 1940s and early 1950s, but then faded away, and left little impact on the theories with which they were concerned.

On the other hand, the studies concerned with obtaining more parametric data—e.g., the effects of different schedules of reinforcement or the effects of the magnitude of the unconditioned stimulus on learning—also grew, and, I think, quickly made obvious that there were so many qualifications for any simple statement of law that the entire theoretical enterprise took on the character of Sisyphus. For every stone added to the theoretical edifice, another stone fell out of place.

Finally, it was recognized that the creation of a global Behavior Theory, or even a general Learning Theory, was beyond immediate reach. The direction of theorists then changed to the construction of micro-theories—e.g., a theory of extinction, a theory of avoidance learning, a theory of discrimination learning, etc. During this time there were no applications coming from the basic-research laboratories. The dominance of the white rat as the king of experimental subjects no doubt contributed to this state of affairs.

Even before this period of disenchantment set in, Skinner, as noted earlier, had taken a position exactly opposite to that of the prevailing trend. He dismissed the role of theory in explanation. He recognized that psychology, if it did resemble physics, was at the Galilean and Newtonian stage of development (descriptive) rather than at the Einsteinian stage (theory construction and testing). The breaking of the paradigm was both a revolution and a regression.

It was a return to an older tradition of psychology: the simple descriptions favored by Wundt and Titchener. The difference, of course, was that they were describing what they believed to be the contents of mind, sensations. The underlying assumption was that if one knows the "elements" of mind one can predict the "compounds." This was a reductionist attempt at explanation, one that followed the model of the successful organic chemistry of that era.

Skinner's reversion to simple description chose another domain for analysis. Instead of verbal reports of sensations, where the focus of interest is on the sensation itself rather than the report, the Skinnerian approach is primarily concerned with the executive behaviors.

It is the malfunctional executive response that is the concern of the behavior modification psychologist. His task is to change the stimulus control of that response. The head-banging of the infant responding to the appearance of the mother is to be extinguished. The urination of the child in response to stimulation from the bladder is to be changed to urination in response to bladder stimulation plus stimulation from toilet facilities. It is this approach, emphasizing description of executive responses in terms of controlling stimuli and the history of reinforcement that has caught the current imagination of psychologists. And, at least, it has borne some fruits of application.

One final point should be made in regard to the interaction of theory and application. The review of the history of the Behavior Modification Movement as a countermovement to the traditional psychotherapies would indicate quite clearly that the traditional psychotherapies ultimately failed because they suffered from inadequate theories. That individual successes were achieved cannot be doubted; but were they because of the theory or because of the analyst? The priest and the rabbi also meet with success in dealing with interpersonal problems. Their particular approaches are guided by religious tenets; do their successes confirm the validity of those tenets? The same type of argument can be applied to the various forms of psychoanalysis where theory is stated in such a way as to be incapable of being validated. Behavior modification avoids this problem by avoiding theory, but creates other special problems—namely, how, without theory, to develop generalizable laws that are useful.

In summary, it has been shown how the fortuitous combination of basic, theoretical experimentation in psychology and political-social circumstance led to the development of new and useful treatments for behavioral disorders.

Although in the above example the political-social NOWISM had positive effects in fostering the development of behavior modification, the overall effects, in the long run, must necessarily be negative. If general theoretical interests are not actively cultivated with governmental funds, even if no immediate payoff is visible, then in the future there will be no kingdom from which the Princes of Serendip can sail forth to make their new, albeit unexpected, discoveries.

In addition to the political-social NOWISM, there is yet another aspect of the NOW movement that has had a detrimental effect on experimental psychology. It is not only the minions of government that are impatient and want quick answers to questions that have histories as long as that of man. This impatience has a more general manifestation among individuals in society.

Personal NOWISM has expressed itself in a variety of forms, all characterized by one common element, best described as an inability to suffer delays in gratification, to postpone immediate satisfactions. These states are typical in the normal development of children when visceral needs cannot be quieted by cerebral action. And perhaps, too, these behaviors might be adaptive in a more primitive, less complex society than the one in which we now find ourselves. But the continuation and progressive development of society depends on the ability to use individual experiences, the experiences from our cultural history, the new experiences distilled from experimentation and science, as well as the experience passed on to us through our biological heritage.

Without question there are conditions in our civilization that ought to be destroyed: war, racial and religious prejudice, poverty and many other disordered behaviors. One could make a strong argument that these conditions are but reflections of our biological state, products of the evolutionary history of our species, rooted in adaptive mechanisms which served the goal of individual survival in a primitive world not graced by man's own intervention. The world of natural elements, of limited food supplies, of predators. The primitive man of Thomas Hobbes would, indeed, fit well into such an environment, while it would be difficult to imagine Rodin's Thinker or Hamlet surviving for very long.

How ironic that today, when basic biological needs can be satisfied as a result of man's ability to use his brain, to be creative, to problem-solve, these very attributes have also allowed him to create the means of destruction of the species. And at the same time we become less and less patient of rational solutions, or solutions that can be constructed from knowledge imparted from science.

The personal NOWISM movements to which I am addressing myself, the Drug Culture and the Radical Left, are essentially reactionary ones. Reactionary in that they conceive of amelioration of the human condition, not through pragmatic social efforts, but through individual acts, NOW. These are essentially biological, gut responses to societal problems, often perceived correctly, but to which the responses are inappropriate.

These movements are reactionary in that they are biologically primitive. Adaptive and successful for the infant and for the prehistoric man, but counterproductive in the twentieth century. Drugs and radical political movements are but extreme examples of this more general reactionary trend.

Another example, for which I am sure a label of reactionary NOWISM will appear to be ill-fitting, is the New Humanism, as expressed particularly in psychology. On the one hand, I cannot help but have sympathy with the humanistic cause, which, after all, is an expression of the desire to allow the human potential to reach its maximum level. The modern pioneering writings of Carl Rogers[14] and Abraham Maslow[15] are to be recommended to any serious observer of the human scene. But to those "groupies" on the psychological scene who use the banners of "self-actualization" and "individual uniqueness" to promote an antiscientific parade of ignorance dressed in a costume of concern, I have only contempt. A contempt made no less bitter by their efforts to vilify the experimental psychologist, to make science and human values antithetical, and in particular to evoke specters of fascism when discussing issues of prediction and control in psychology.

It is the layman's belief that the scientist has the power to predict and control events in the real world, and that this ability may border on the awesome. It is not difficult to understand the sources of this stereotype, nor should the scientist be too quick to dispel this fantasy completely.

As human beings we are all concerned with prediction and control. Indeed, this may be one of the characteristics that distinguish between the inanimate and the living and between the so-called lower and higher forms of life. Life continues because an organism is capable of prediction and control. This capability may be attained genetically or it may be acquired during the lifetime of the individual organism.

For the human, we can see the operation of prediction and control behavior in numerous everyday occurrences, from the most simple to the most complex. One looks, hopefully, both ways before crossing the street, and even if a car is coming, with amazing accuracy one can judge whether or not to attempt to cross the street, and with what degree of haste. On a higher level of behavior we have learned what to expect (to predict) if we fail to obey laws, to do what the boss says, etc., and to modulate the consequences by doing what we want anyway, but in such a manner that it is accepted by the other party (control). The entire process of socialization is based on the ability to understand or at least to utilize prediction and control. Within this framework of analysis, Skinner, in *Beyond Freedom and Dignity*[16] and *Walden Two*,[13] has presented the penultimate applications of these devices as manipulated through principles of reinforcement. That Skinner's works are at once so popular and so controversial may well indicate that he is tapping a fundamental aspect of human nature.

We are built to predict and control. We behave in such a way as to predict and control behavior of ourselves as well as that of others. When we do it subtly we are successful politicians and diplomats. When we bare the mechanism of our artifice we become a Rasputin, a Svengali, or a Skinner. And when the mechanism of control is both obvious and oppressive, the controller takes on the guise of a dictator such as Hitler or Stalin.

Skinner appears to be correct in his implication that as psychology becomes more successful in predicting and controlling, it will also become more feared and abused. However, Skinner would contend that appropriate application of reinforcement principles will negate the fear. In this regard I do believe that Skinner's monolithic approach is but an extension of the naïve environmentalism of Watson. Perhaps an alternative is to recognize the fear of control as a species-specific defense reaction[17] or as an easily attained association[18] (irrespective of whether this fear is justified or not) and to continue from there, even under the most benevolent of auspices, to apply the controls in a latent fashion—and with that also to accept the responsibility of being labeled "cynical."

Nevertheless, since every individual also assigns a positive value to the ability to control (as long as he does not see *himself* as being controlled), the scientist must walk a careful path. If control of environmental events, as in physics and chemistry, is to gain power and to elicit fear, how then is the psychologist to practice his science?

That this has not been, as yet, a critical problem may merely reflect that the psychologist is not perceived in the public eye as being a scientist; he is not seen as having the ability to predict and control. He is seen as a healer, a physician-priest. An image that he, rightly, is not too eager either to destroy or to transform into that of the scientist. Perhaps the two images represented by the two different activities cannot be compatible in the same practice of psychology. It should be no small surprise that one psychologist, the "warm," friendly Rogers, "heals" patients, while another, Skinner, the "stern controller," practices science. Could their roles be reversed successfully?

In summary, there are fundamental issues that should be examined. Rhetoric and rage will not substitute for reason and experimentation in providing the answers that we all so desperately need. This feeling of desperation cannot be soothed with NOWISM dogmas, but must receive patient and careful examination by the behavioral scientist.

During the last several years the effects of NOWISM have been felt within departments of psychology all over the country. In particular, the number of graduate students who choose to study experimental psychology has been dwindling. The hard-core, basic, theoretical areas are spurned. These areas are seen by the student as the last stronghold of the uninvolved nonhuman scientist. Many bright students in psychology, turned off by their perception of failures of systems based on science, have moved toward the individualist mode of response, and want to help other individuals through some mystical power of personal communication, rather than through the application of laws of behavior.

It would be foolish to deny that, in fact, there are a few people who can accomplish major feats of individual rehabilitation. The point is that the number is few, and that the ability does not depend on special training but can probably be found in equal proportions in all areas where the practitioner is given the required status by society; where it is expected that he will be instrumental in curing. But in society today, with the traditional authoritarian institutions breaking down, can we afford to wait for ameliorative happenstance, whether it be from priest or psychologist? Or will we invest the resources and develop the attitudes that will allow for the full development of a basic behavioral psychological science, and the subsequent imparting of clinical technique through reliable, reproducible means which can reach almost any practitioner?

These then are some of the goals that I have set for myself in this book. To portray experimental psychology as a science with fascinating and relevant questions to answer, and to portray the experimental psychologist as a human-problem solver, sharing the concerns for continuing *and* improving our human condition even as he experiments with animals for war.

But in addition to the avowedly didactic and even propagandistic aspects of the book, I hope to be able to bring to the reader the sense of adventure, humor and frustration involved in conducting these researches and in pursuing the various ancillary activities inevitably associated with projects involved in military defense, tactics and espionage. And throughout, providing the glue on the book's binding, is the personal story of an experimental psychologist whom many people will no doubt see as being the unhappy progeny of a miscegenous marriage between a hawk and a dove—a duck. A feathered symbol for only a human feast.

I

Some Stories
from the Past

The history of the use of animals in combat probably dates back to the time of man's first war. When this occurred is in part dependent on one's definition of war, as well as some clear notion of the origin of man. It is reasonable to assume that wars preceded man's first written accounts of himself and therefore the beginnings of this animal-man partnership are probably lost.

Nevertheless, it is interesting to try to reconstruct what may have occurred. One can imagine an early cave-dweller, primitive in means but yet immeasurably more intelligent than the animals sharing his environment. A wild boar is surprised while nursing its young. After considerable snarling, pawing the earth and a growling attack on the intruders, it is driven away from its nest site. The baby boars are easily captured and brought back to the cave. A fire is prepared and the piglets roasted. The group hastily consumes the catch. Meanwhile the hyenas and the wolves, having whiffed the aroma of what they too have, on occasion, lustily consumed, converge on the source of the odor. Having reached the entrance of the cave, they find the still warm bones of the suckling pig. When the meal was consumed inside the cave the remains were thrown out. Past experience had shown, to even this primitive group, that if the bones were not discarded, all types of vermin and insects would be attracted and would make their cozy enclave quite uncomfortable.

The leftovers, thrown outside, are soon picked up by the scavenging animals. The result is that the wild animals' approach to the cave has been reinforced. Previously he had probably avoided man; perhaps because of man's attempt to make him into a meal, or because of a generalization from other large animals which indeed might have been frequently successful in bringing down a member of his pack. The evolutionary advantage for survival in having the relatively small, defenseless doglike animal avoid larger animals is quite clear.

But, of course, there is also an adaptive advantage in having one's behavior changed as the result of changing conditions. In this case, the appearance of man, and the introduction of a new source of food to satisfy the ever present hunger of the prowling scavenger, provided the necessary conditions of reinforcement to change the response of fear and avoidance of humanlike creatures to friendliness and approach.

Wild dog and man, by contingencies of reinforcement, were forced into proximity with each other. The area around man's cave became a highly probable place for finding food. The animal now spent much time there and soon learned that the bones and morsels of food did not appear on the ground spontaneously, but rather were associated with the presence of a man who came to the mouth of the cave and heaved the bones outside.

Man's behavior toward the wild dog was also shaped by the reinforcement conditions. Even for early man food and sex were not the only conditions of reinforcement. Variety and change were also instrumental in shaping his activities, and above all, the ability to control the behavior of another object or organism. How satisfying it must have been to make a fire, not only because of the warmth and light, but also because man could make it, extinguish it, and make it again.

At first the bone was thrown out in a random direction. However, man was quick to notice that as soon as the bone hit the ground several dogs appeared from the surrounding bushes and fought for it. No matter where he threw the bones the dogs chased after it. The more clever dogs associated bones and man. Now they made their appearance when the man emerged from his cave. Even before he threw the bone, they scampered out from behind the bushes and, ears pricked high, alertly followed his movements. The man too learned to appreciate an association. He came to know that his appearance was the cause of the dog's coming out of hiding. He, in a sense, controlled the behavior of the dog, and reciprocating the favor, threw a bone to the dog. Perhaps the bone fell a little short of where the dog was sitting. The dog therefore had to come closer yet to the man before consuming this new morsel of food. This was the first time that the dog ventured to come so close. Again the man's behavior of throwing a bone to the dog was reinforced by the dog's exhibiting some new behavior never before witnessed by the man. Because it was new and because it had an aspect of control to it, the approach behavior of the dog became a powerful reinforcer for the man's bone-throwing behavior. Thus the frequency of the bone-throwing behavior was increased and both the dog and the man ended up in a circle of reinforcement. This sort of unbroken chain, where each element supports the other, is usually referred to as a vicious circle, but in this case, where the effects are positive, it is perhaps more appropriately labeled as a mutually beneficial reciprocative chain of reinforcement. Each element, man and dog, provides reinforcement for the other, and changes a once neutral, perhaps even negative social bond to a positive one. Friendship and love, which are concepts used to describe relationships between two people, can probably be analyzed in the same fashion. I suspect, though, that such an attempt might cause one to lose a number of friends and, at a very minimum, to gain the anger of one's wife. In living the relationships, romanticism seems to be preferable to behavioral analysis, but it does not mean that it is the preferred mode for understanding the behavior.

Returning now to the primitive man and the dog who was close by, the cycle of mutual reinforcement continued and the dog finally reached the side of the man, who placed the bone directly in his mouth. Only those dogs that overcame their fear of man did this, and therefore it is only these that were fed by the man. The tamer dogs were therefore isolated from their original companions and interbred among themselves. With each succeeding generation, the tamer ones remained in closer contact with man, creating conditions of separation from the wilder animals, and again bred among themselves. In this manner reinforcement shaped the direction of evolution and the result was a new breed of animal called the domestic dog whose natural habitat was at man's side.

Who knows how many generations this process may have taken? But once concluded, the dog became man's constant companion, accompanying him wherever he went, including to the hunt, where success meant not only food for man but probably some immediate reward for his four-footed friend.

I will not speculate further on how man came to use the dog as an aid in hunting, to track, chase down or retrieve the prey. Nor can we identify when the first dog, perhaps still in a wild state, alerted the cave-dweller to the danger of a human trespasser in his territory by barking loudly in the night. Perhaps even consciously early man chose to throw bones out for the animals just to keep them in the vicinity of his home so as to provide an early warning of the presence of an intruder.

Let us now try to trace the historical development of man's use of animals in warfare. However, it should be recognized that an orderly elaboration of use, from primitive hominid to space-age man, is quite impossible. The best that can be done is to cite examples, without making an attempt to determine whether the earliest examples were independent inventions or products of a diffusion process centering on a single source or a very few multiple sources. Nor within any one culture can we display an orderly evolution of the animal-for-war system, as one could make for the development of most machines, such as the gun or the automobile. If anything, the later history of the use of war animals exhibits a curious cyclical pattern of development, disuse, redevelopment, disuse, etc., with very little information being passed on or used from one system to another. For example, within the last forty years, systems for mine detection based on the olfactory capability of the dog were laboriously created several times, both in different countries (England, the United States, Germany, Russia, Israel) and within the same country.

These systems were successful. Yet somehow they always managed to disappear, and when the need again arose for such a system it had to be redeveloped, almost from the very beginning. Later we will return to the question of why the war-animal systems are so prone to extinction. In the meantime let us examine some of the early attempts to use such systems.

Several examples can be found in the Old Testament. One may consider the tribulations of Noah as part of a larger scene representing, if not a battle between man and God, at least one between man and the environment. After forty days and forty nights of continuous rains, Noah and his floating menagerie were drifting on an endless sea. In order to determine exactly how precarious was his lonely position,

> . . . he sent forth a dove from him to see if the waters were abated from off the face of the ground. But the dove found no rest for the sole of her foot, and she returned unto him into the ark, for the waters were on the face of the whole earth: then he put forth his hand and took her, and pulled her in unto him into the ark. And he stayed yet another seven days: and again he sent forth the dove out of the ark; and the dove came unto him in the evening; and, lo in her mouth was an olive leaf pluckt off: so Noah knew that the waters were abated from off the earth. And he stayed yet another seven days; and sent forth the dove, which returned not again unto him any more. (Genesis 8:6–12)

The story of a great deluge also can be found in the literature of other peoples, and in many of them the dove appears as a bearer of good tidings. The Hebrew version is very similar to an earlier Akkadian one, in which Utnapishtim released a dove only to have him return, then a swallow, which also returned, and finally a raven, which failed to come back. Failure to return was the signal that the flood waters had receded and that the animals on the ark could be released.

It is interesting to note that Noah, before releasing the dove, also released a raven, which did not return. This was interpreted by him, not as a training failure, but rather as a casualty of the weather. A comparison of these two stories makes a lovely point in regard to the design of information systems. For Utnapishtim the absence of a signal (the bird not returning) was used to conclude that the waters had receded. For Noah the presence of a signal (the bird returning with an olive leaf) was used for the same purpose. Noah was clearly on safer grounds in drawing his conclusion than his more primitive fellow sailor, Utnapishtim.

The ancient Egyptian version also employs a fail-safe device:

> . . . on its second visit to the ark, the red appearance of its feet proved that the red mud on which it had walked was already freed from the waters; and to record the event, Noah prayed that the feet of these birds might forever continue of that colour, which marks them to the present day.[1]

Why did Noah's dove finally choose to fly toward land and why did she return to the ark? It is quite possible that land was to be found close by, on all sides of Noah, that he was not in an open sea but rather in a large lake. The dove, soaring to heights well above the ark, could see landfalls that from the point of the ark were over the horizon. I would guess that even a modern pigeon released in an ocean from a not too distant coast will head for the land rather than out to sea. It would be interesting to try this little experiment. Who knows what form the next holocaust might take?

As for understanding why the dove returned to the ark, simple reinforcement theory can account for it if we assume that she was within a reasonable distance from the boat; or, one can invoke some of the more complex mechanisms suggested to account for the homing instinct in pigeons. Since reinforcement is a tool that we will use many times in this book to develop all types of latent capacities in animals, it is only consistent for us to suppose that Noah was also aware of these techniques, albeit by other names. Noah was, after all, the master animal psychologist of his day, perhaps of all time. Just imagine trying to get all those animals marching in paired parade precision up the gangplank. Unfortunately our sources do not inform us how many were lost in rehearsals. Even Konrad Lorenz would find himself presiding over a tumultuous panic when trying to get zebras and lions, snakes and rats and birds to organize for salvation.

All safely aboard, the ark was set afloat. Noah must have sent his doves up to scout around a number of times. Each time, with no other place to go, they returned to the ark and were fed. In this way the response of returning to the ark was reinforced, and on that one time when the dove did find land she still returned to her roost on the ark. The modern homing pigeon exhibits the same behavior.

Samson knew much less about animal behavior, especially that of women. Nevertheless, he too was able to exploit an animal for purposes of war. His system was based on the not too astonishing observation that foxes' tails will burn, and that the burning tail will send the fox scurrying madly around the fields much like a wild Fourth of July sizzler.

And Samson went and caught three hundred foxes, and took firebrands, and turned tail to tail, and put a firebrand in the midst between two tails. And when he had set the brands on fire, he let them go unto the standing corn of the Philistines and burnt up both the stocks, and also the standing corn with the vineyards and olives. (Judges 15:4–5)

And thus ends the tale of how Samson outfoxed his enemies.

Another story of success, at least from the point of view of man, as the animal casualties again were also high, can be found in the historical account of the Peloponnesian War (431–404 B.C.), in which the Greeks fought the Corinthians. Of one of the many engagements it is told that:

The Corinthians, too, used dogs for purposes of defence, and the citadel of Corinth had a guard of fifty placed in boxes by the sea-shore. Taking advantage of a dark night, the Greeks with whom they were at war disembarked on the coast. The garrison were asleep after an orgy, the dogs alone kept watch and the fifty pickets fell on the enemy like lions; all but one were casualties. Sorter, sole survivor, retiring from the conflict, fled to the town to give warning and roused the drunken soldiers, who came forth to battle. To him alone were the honors of victory, and the grateful town presented to him a collar with the inscription, "Sorter, Defender and Savior of Corinth," and erected a monument engraved with his name and those of the forty-nine heroes who fell.[2]

This sorter thing would have been a great hit two hundred years later in the Punic Wars.

In about 386 B.C., when Gallic invaders laid siege to Rome, the Citadel was placed in extreme danger. Somehow the Gauls had found a way to climb the rocky mount. Then, according to the Roman historian Livy, telling the tale more than three hundred years afterward:

Having first sent an unarmed man to reconnoitre the route, they began the climb. It was something of a scramble: at the awkward spots a man would get a purchase for his feet on a comrade below him, then haul him up in his turn—weapons were passed up from hand to hand as the lie of the rocks allowed—until by pushing and pulling one another they reached the top. What is more, they accomplished the climb so quietly that the Romans on guard never heard a sound, and even the dogs—who are normally aroused by the least noise in the night—noticed nothing. It was the geese that saved them—Juno's sacred geese, which in spite of the dearth of provisions had not been killed. The cackling of the birds and the clapping of their wings awoke Marcus Manlius.[3]

Rome, although mostly in ashes and ruins, was saved.

Over two thousand three hundred years later, the beleaguered hamlets of South Vietnam were said to have used geese to warn its citizens of approaching Viet Cong.

Although Noah's use of the dove suggests that the bird was domesticated, the earliest evidence for such domestication dates back to 4500 B.C. in Iraq and to the fifth Egyptian dynasty (c. 2494–2345 B.C.).[4] In 1150 B.C. the Sultan of Baghdad was supposed to have developed a postal system using the pigeon. Capsules containing small papyrus sheets were strapped to either the leg or the back.

As a messenger service, the birds were also employed by the Romans, and they relayed the news of Caesar's conquest of Gaul to Rome. Pliny, the Roman historian, writes that Brutus and Hertius were able to keep in contact with each other at the siege of Medina (43 B.C.) by using pigeons. Much later, during the Christian Crusades pigeons again found employment, this time by the Saracens. Gibbon writes of their use at the siege of Acre and Monsourah, and Fuller reports that pigeons were flown at the siege of Jerusalem.

In 1574, during the War of Independence in Holland, the city of Leyden had been under Spanish siege for six months. It was the pigeons, returning from friendly neighbors at great distance, who brought them messages that relief was on its way. It is said that these messages bolstered the morale of the beleaguered citizenry to such an extent that they could continue holding out against the Spanish enemy. Alexandre Dumas, in *The Black Tulip,* used these events in writing about one particularly successful pigeon.

Much later, the English defeat of Napoleon at Waterloo was communicated via pigeon carriers. Similar activities were accomplished during the Revolution of 1848 in France. In 1849, when the telegraphic service between Brussels and Berlin broke down, the pigeon took over its function.

However, it was at the siege of Paris (1870–71) during the

Franco-Prussian War, that the pigeon reached the climax of its fame. Levi[5] describes his researches about this period:

Balloons were released from Paris containing, among other things, Parisian pigeons. These birds were then taken to London, Tours and other cities and subsequently released with messages to the besieged Parisians. In the beginning, paper messages were simply wrapped up tight, waxed over, and attached to a feather of the bird's tail. Many messages were lost. Subsequently, the dispatch was inserted in a small goose quill and tied by waxed silken thread to the strongest feather of the tail. By the aid of micro-photography, original messages were copied, greatly reduced in size, upon thin films of collodion, each of which contained, on an average, 2,500 communications. As many as 12 of these films were carried by one bird. On one occasion, a single Homer bore 16 of these minute films, the equivalent of 40,000 messages.

During the 4 months of this siege, 150,000 official and 1,000,000 private communications were carried into Paris in this manner.

This marvelous story was not lost on the military planners and strategists. The Germans were among the first in modern military history to capitalize on the possibilities of this reliable messenger service. They established as many as eight military pigeon lofts throughout the country. In 1887, they were said to have about 400 trained birds in each loft.

In World War I the trained homer pigeon was used extensively by both the Germans and the Allies.

The Belgians, the French, and the Germans, from the inception of the war, recognised the value of the pigeon as a messenger in many situations. The Germans, as soon as they occupied Belgian or French territory, ordered all pigeons destroyed. Any enemy, combatant or non-combatant, found owning or selling them was punished for possessing contraband of war . . . it has been estimated that 1,000,000 Belgian pigeons were taken by the Germans during their occupation. How many pigeons actually served in the war will probably never be known. Their number for all forces has been estimated as varying from 20,000 to

500,000. At Lille, in France, a monument has been erected to them, commemorating the birds killed in action (estimated at 20,000).[5]

Great Britain, for a time, lagged behind in the use of messenger pigeons. It is reported that all pigeons along the Channel coast were ordered to be destroyed or relocated. The fear was that these birds might be in the employ of the enemy spies who were relaying messages from England to Germany.

However, British mine sweepers did make use of the homer, and a formal pigeon service was established. Several different modes of operation were employed. In one, pigeons were dropped in baskets from airplanes into friendly areas. Local inhabitants would pick them up, load one of the message containers with information that might be of interest to the Allied military authorities, and then release the bird. The homer, after circling the area one or two times, would head straight for his home loft, perhaps hundreds of kilometers away.

A second type of mission also involved carrying the pigeon aboard a plane. This time the pigeon was released if the plane crashed. He carried information about the crash location. According to Levi, the records of the British Air Force indicate that 717 messages were delivered by pigeons from British planes which had fallen in the seas. The British Admiralty reports that of several thousand messages carried by pigeons 95 percent were received.

The United States, like Great Britain, was late in entering the pigeon race. Nevertheless, the stories of successful use and of individual heroics are many. J. L. Carney wrote enthusiastically about the military value of the pigeon during the prolonged and bloody battle of the Argonne Forest. As quoted by Levi:

Barbed wire entanglements, machine gun nests, and Boche-filled trenches that honeycombed the scrubby woods from end to end made this pivotal point a Gibraltar. Nothing could live above ground and the trenches and shell holes were filled with dead and wounded. Time after time the attack was on and almost as often repulsed. Division after division was thrown into the line to face the most deadly of modern weapons, the machine gun. With small artillery firing incessant, high explosive shells dropping everywhere and the gas attacks on hourly, there was little

wonder that man-made lines of communication should wither
and break.

Into the breach went the little racing pigeon—the most gallant
little bird the world knows. And they came through—came
through with messages of weal and woe; came through when
shattered troops were crying for aid—when every other line of
communication had failed.

Among the official war records is the following:

. . . during the Aisne-Marne offensive, with mobile lofts in use,
72 birds carried 78 important messages without failing to return. In the St.-Mihiel drive, 90 important messages were delivered by pigeons. Twenty-four of 202 birds used were lost or
killed, but every message delivered as the messages were sent in
duplicate. In the Meuse-Argonne offensive 442 birds delivered
403 messages safely, the distance varying from 12 to 30 miles.
Not a single important message went astray.

These impressive but dry statistics are made more tangible by accounts of individual actions, which, had they been performed by a
human, would certainly warrant the label "heroic."

Cher Ami, an English bred bird (N.U.R.P. 615, blue check
cock), is perhaps the best known of our Racing Homers, having
received credit for saving the "Lost Battalion," though a number of other birds performed services equally as outstanding.
During his military service, he delivered twelve important messages from the Verdun front to the loft at Rampont, the average
distance of which was thirty kilometers. He was attached to a
New York battalion of the 77th Division, commanded by Major
Charles S. Whittlesey. On October 27th, 1918, the battalion had
advanced too far ahead of its own lines at Grand Pré into
enemy territory and the men found themselves entirely surrounded by the enemy. Cut off from support and with inadequate rations, they were in sorry plight. Every endeavour to
make liaison had failed. Soldier couriers could not penetrate the
line, rockets and flares were of no avail; all wires were down or
left far behind. Their condition was desperate and, unless their
location could be conveyed to Division Headquarters, hundreds
of men would perish or have to surrender. Several pigeons

released with messages were unable to get through the hell of shell and shrapnel, and fell to the ground mortally wounded soon after being released. Only one bird, Cher Ami, remained to be released with the vital message advising their location . . . up he rose, the instinct of returning to his home loft uppermost in his throbbing heart. Through barrage of shells and bullets he rose, circled, and, like a dart, headed for "home." There was a sudden burst of shrapnel and Cher Ami was hit. He straightened out and, with one leg utterly shattered, reached his home loft at Rampont in twenty-five minutes, covering a distance of forty kilometers, although the missile which carried his leg away had also passed through his breast. The message holder was attached to his wounded leg, hanging by a few shreds of sinew. Cher Ami that day saved the members of the "Lost Battalion." His body has been mounted and placed in the Smithsonian Institution, U.S. National Museum, Washington, D.C.[5]

It was during World War II that more sophisticated uses of the pigeon were attempted.

The Germans were reported to have strapped small automatic cameras to the bodies of pigeons and to have taken many photographs of the French emplacements along the Maginot Line. One can assume, however, that the basic mode of operation for these birds was similar to that of the homers in World War I. The pigeon, with camera attached, was released over the target area. A timing device triggered the camera's shutter after an initial delay of perhaps twenty or thirty seconds, and as the bird headed home a series of photographs accompanied him. This was exactly the same sequence of behavior and training as was required for the messenger pigeon. The only novelty was that now the pigeon had a camera attached to him as opposed to a message container.

A truly novel approach, and one that is exquisitely simple, was said to have been employed by the British. As anyone who lives near the seashore knows, flocks of sea gulls will congregate around refuse dumps, fishing boats unloading their catch, or any other easy source of food. It is a common sight, for instance, to see several gulls trailing a ship waiting for the garbage to be dumped overboard, or for some passenger to amuse himself by throwing crusts of bread into the air which the agile gulls will then catch in their beaks.

It is reported that British submarines submerged off the English coast released large amounts of bread. The bread, floating to the surface, would be spotted by local gulls, and soon an entire flock would be circling and diving in the area of the bread and the submarine. There is no information available as to how many times this association of events, bread and submarine, had to be repeated before the sea gulls began to appear at the sight of the submarine alone. However, it is told that when the gulls spotted a long, dark shadow moving beneath the surface of the waters, they would proceed to flock to that place. Wheeling and screeching, they were observed by human spotters on the shore. The location of the swarming gulls was reported, and if that location did not coincide with the known position of a friendly submarine, the appropriate military countermeasures were initiated. It is not known how many German U-boats became victims of the scavenger gull's insatiable search for food.

It was a Harvard professor, the chemist Dr. Louis F. Fieser, who was associated with another unique bio-military project. During the early 1940s Dr. Fieser was working on methods to increase the range of flame throwers. It was this research group that was responsible for the invention of napalm. How ironic that he should also be involved in another satanic scheme using the devil's own agents, bats, to deliver a fiery holocaust. As described by Hersh[6] it was:

. . . a weird scheme to equip bats with tiny incendiary bombs. Theoretically, the bats were then to be air-dropped over Japan where the bombs—with delayed fuses—would trigger hundreds of fires. Fieser and his associates developed a satisfactory bomb weighing less than one ounce, but the bats never cooperated. The bombs were to be attached by surgery with a piece of string to the chests of would-be bat bombers. As the Army envisioned it, the bats would be dropped over large Japanese cities, quickly find hiding places, chew their strings, and leave the bombs. After two years of research, a trial run was made in Carlsbad Caverns, New Mexico. On the first day, some bats escaped and set off fires that completely demolished a general's auto and a $2 million hangar. The Army project was abruptly cancelled. The

Navy then took over with a new approach; it theorized that if the bats could be artificially cooled and forced into hibernation they would stop gnawing and thus would not immediately chew through the string. By this time scientists from the Massachusetts Institute of Technology and University of California at Los Angeles, along with Harvard, were involved. The hibernating bats were packed like eggs into crates, flown to New Mexico and dropped. Theoretically, the bats would tumble out at a certain altitude and begin to awaken in the warm lower air over the desert. But, as one report less than adequately put it, "most slept on"—and fell to their death. By this time it was August, 1944, and the macabre project was finally scrapped.

A similar fate of laboratory success accompanied by the inability to convince the potential customer of the value of application occurred more recently in the civilian industrial area. Verhave[7] in 1966 described the advantages of using a bird in a factory line operation:

Many of the operations involved in the quality-control inspection of commercial products consist of monotonous checking jobs performed by human operators. In addition to monotony, these, usually visual, inspection jobs have several other characteristics in common: (1) they require little if any manual skill or dexterity, (2) they require good visual acuity, (3) they require a capacity for color vision, and (4) they are extremely difficult to automate. There is, however, an organic device which has the following favorable properties: (1) an average life span of 10 to 15 years, (2) an extreme flexibility in adjusting to its environment as well as an enormous learning ability, (3) a visual acuity as good as the human eye, and (4) color vision. The price for one such device is only (approximately) $1.50; its name: Columba livia domestica, or the pigeon. Because of the characteristics listed above it is quite feasible to train pigeons to do all the visual checking operations involved in commercial manufacture.

Verhave was successfully able to train pigeons to discriminate "defective" gelatin capsules from nondefective capsules. The defective capsules, called "skags," had one or more of the following characteristics: off color, dented, piece of gelatin sticking out or a double cap. Normally this job of quality control is done by human sorters on "a group bonus schedule employing error cost." The results of Verhave's preliminary exploratory study were quite encouraging. However, the pharmaceutical company sponsoring the research decided to abandon the project for a variety of reasons unrelated to the efficiency of the technique. The major deterrent to continuation was, as one might expect, the concern about public reaction. What consumer would be confident in the reliability of a drug part of whose quality control was supervised by a pigeon? Verhave's study provided impetus for another exploratory study, by Cumming,[8] who trained pigeons to inspect diodes. This quality-control task also required the pigeons to sort into two categories, defective diodes and nondefective diodes. A defective diode was characterized by an imperfection in the paint. In general, the project was quite successful, but once again was terminated by management. In addition to the general success on the sorting problem several other interesting pieces of information emerged.

The data indicated that pigeons could be expected to reject about 5 percent of the good diodes, while rejecting over 98 percent of the bad ones.

The pigeons, for the most part, could perform at a rate of 1000 inspections per hour (the task was self-paced).

The pigeons could operate for at least four hours at a stretch and probably considerably longer. Four hours was the maximum session duration attempted and there was no decrement in performance as compared to the first hour; and, in fact, some improvement.[8]

To give but two examples of both the high rate of inspection and the accuracy of the categorization: "Bird 119 inspected almost 6000 diodes and failed to detect defects in only four cases. . . . Bird 117's second session, it averaged only one percent errors during the entire session while inspecting at a rate of more than 1000 inspections per hour. There is no reason to suspect that performance would have deteriorated quickly had the session been longer than four hours."[8]

These latter two studies, by Verhave and Cumming, already employed sophisticated training techniques—procedures that owed their existence to the earlier pioneering efforts of B. F. Skinner.

2

Pigeon-Guided Missiles

In the spring of 1940, while war was raging in Europe, B. F. Skinner, then at the University of Minnesota, began Project Pigeon. German bombers were taking a heavy toll against both civilian and military targets, and there was an urgent need for an effective guidance device to be used in a surface-to-air missile. Skinner conceived an idea for using an organic system to direct ground-launched missiles against enemy aircraft. Early in the program, perhaps because of the development of the ground-based radar to control antiaircraft guns, this direction was switched to an air-to-ground missile.

The particular missile for which pigeon guidance was contemplated was called the Pelican. That cumbersome bird very nicely describes the state of the art of American missile-making at that time. "Its detecting and servomechanisms took up so much space that there was no room for explosives: hence the resemblance to the pelican 'whose beak can hold more than its belly can' ";[1] and hence the title of Skinner's well-known article describing his adventures and misadventures in trying to convince the military of the value of a pigeon-controlled missile-guidance system, "Pigeons in a Pelican."

The unwilling subjects were common park-variety pigeons, the kind that hang out on statues. After capturing several of them and acclimatizing them to the laboratory, including being hungry most of the time, the first tests were conducted.

The pigeon was attached to a block in such a way that, except for its head and neck, it was completely immobilized. The block was attached to a moving hoist. The hoist could be moved by the pigeon with an appropriate motion of its head. If the bird lifted its head, the hoist was raised; if the bird lowered its head, the hoist was lowered. Left and right movements of the head resulted in similar movements of the hoist. The pigeon thus served as the control system for the hoist, with head movements sending the appropriate motors into action which in a turn affected the hoist's position. The entire device could be pushed across a room toward a wall on which was mounted a bull's-eye target. At the center of the target was a dish filled with the bird's favorite grain. The pigeon's task was to reach the position of the food and thus the target center. To accomplish this the bird had to use its head. The experimenters changed both the position of the target on the wall and the starting point of the hoist. After sufficient training, the pigeon could reach any target that was within striking distance of the hoist, even if the hoist was moved rapidly across the room.

In spite of successful demonstration of this somewhat primitive device, the defense establishment did not encourage continuation of the efforts. However, on the day after the Japanese attacked Pearl Harbor, Skinner and a young graduate student, Keller Breland (who later with his wife, Marion Breland, went on to form Animal Behavior Enterprises, and to continue a long series of researches and projects applying laboratory-based techniques to animals for civilian and military problems), started to think about the problem again.

If a missile or bomb could be rotated while descending, then the pigeon could steer it by simply moving its head from side to side. They designed a harnessing system for the bird, and set up moving targets on a large revolving turntable. The rapidly descending pigeons were trained to "hit" models of ships.

Again the project failed to gain support from the military. This time, apparently, because there was no missile in the defense arsenal which had the capability of being guided toward a target. That is, even with a perfect sensing head which could detect targets and give a signal that was related to the deviation between target position and projected missile impact point, there were no operational devices for converting this error signal into corrective missile movements.

According to Skinner's account,[1] the project languished until the summer of 1942, when a young man, whose name Skinner has since forgotten, walked into his laboratory looking for an animal psychologist who would provide expert witness for yet another harebrained scheme. The idea was to place dogs in antisubmarine missiles. The sensitive ears of the dog would pick up the faint acoustic signals emanating from the submarine. The dog would use these signals to steer the torpedo toward its target. Although the project was rejected, the unknown inventor did bring the tale of Skinner's work to the attention of General Mills (the food manufacturer), which offered to support the project through its initial stages of demonstrating feasibility and until the government could be interested in taking over funding for the work. The project was moved from the University of Minnesota to the top floor of a flour mill in Minneapolis.

One of the earlier problems had been to get the pigeon to respond to the visually small movements of a distant target. The birds had a tendency to withhold responding until close to the target, when target movements were conspicuous. This type of behavior, although suitable for a normally slow-moving bird, was quite inappropriate for generating useful corrective signals to a high-velocity missile. To overcome this, Skinner and his associates designed a new system in which the target image was projected onto a translucent screen. The pigeon was constrained so that he was always within pecking distance of the screen and was reinforced with grains of food for pecking at the target image on the screen. The screen was mounted in such a way that information as to the quadrant location of the peck on the screen could be detected. This information was then conveyed to the control system, which moved the "missile" in such a way that the target was recentered on the screen. Since the target, a ship for example, was always moving, it would soon go off the screen unless the necessary corrective signal was forthcoming from the pigeon's pecks.

By using long intervals of time between reinforcements the pigeon could be kept continuously tracking for several minutes. This was long enough so that in a real combat situation the missile could be effectively controlled from launch to impact.

Once the basic concept was shown to be workable in its pure laboratory form, it was necessary to determine how many special variables of the real missile environment might affect the tracking behavior of the pigeon. A whole host of these and other variables were investigated.

"We ascertained optimal conditions of deprivation . . . studied the effect of special reinforcements . . . tested the effects of energizing drugs and increased oxygen pressures . . . of extremes of temperature, of changes in atmospheric pressure, of accelerations, of increased carbon dioxide pressure, of increased and prolonged vibration, and of noises . . ."[1]

Armed with new data, and the arguments that the pigeon guidance system was superior to all other existing systems because it could selectively respond to pattern (that is, it could discriminate, for example, between a boat and a buoy), and that since it used a visual image rather than radio frequencies it was less capable of being jammed, Skinner again set off to try to sell his idea. This time, in June 1943, he succeeded. General Mills was given a small contract to develop a homing device for the Pelican missile.

The operational problems were both real and compelling. They introduced considerable complications into the neat simple system that had worked so nicely in the laboratory. The pecking performance of the bird had to be matched to the performance characteristics of the missile. The signals for controlling the Pelican had to be proportional to the error. If the missile was way off the correct track, it had to make a corrective response that was stronger than if the deviation were a minor one. It was no longer useful only to know in which of four sections or quadrants the bird was pecking. The distance of the peck from the screen center was required. Thus if the target was at the periphery of the screen, the location of the peck had to be sensed and converted into a strong corrective response. On the other hand, a small deviation of the peck from the center of the screen would be converted into a mild rate of change of missile course.

The engineers associated with the project designed a pneumatic system that resulted in a graded response, with the further away the peck from the midpoint of the screen, the stronger the response. The key problem had been solved, and without using any of the strategic war materials in short supply. In spite of this, there was considerable resistance to the project. In particular there was concern in regard to the reliability of performance. After all, how much trust can you put in a bird? Repeated demonstrations and hard-nosed data did not assuage the fears that a bird-based system was inherently unreliable.

To overcome these trepidations, a multiple-bird system was designed. There was room in the nose of the Pelican for three birds and their equipment. If one pigeon was reliable, then taking the average response of three pigeons would make the system a very reliable one indeed.

A simulator was built which would mimic the flight characteristics of the Pelican missile and which would contain the three pigeon bombardiers. Targets were presented on a far wall and the entire closed-loop system was studied in detail. The results were, once more, very promising. In December 1943, a mere six months after the project was started, the product was ready to be demonstrated. Again success. Again failure.

After what appeared to be much wrangling over whether the signal strength was proportional to the amount of error, Skinner and his group were given the opportunity of presenting their case to a committee of the country's top scientists. In order to convince these physical scientists that it is possible for an organic system, even a pigeon, to perform in an orderly, reliable manner, they brought a demonstration pigeon to the meeting to supplement the dry data of numbers and graphs.

A small black box had a round translucent window in one end. A slide projector placed some distance away threw on the window an image of the New Jersey target. In the box, of course, was a pigeon—which, incidentally, had at that time been harnessed for 35 hours. Our intention was to let each member of the committee observe the response to the target by looking down a small tube; but time was not available for individual observation, and we were asked to take the top off the box. The translucent screen was flooded with so much light that the target was barely visible, and the peering scientists offered conditions much more unfamiliar and threatening than those likely to be encountered in a missile. In spite of this the pigeon behaved perfectly, pecking steadily and energetically at the image of the target as it moved about on the plate. One scientist with an experimental turn of mind intercepted the beam from the projector. The pigeon stopped instantly. When the image again appeared, pecking began within a fraction of a second and continued at a steady rate.

It was a perfect performance, but it had just the wrong effect. One can talk about phase lag in pursuit behavior and discuss mathematical predictions of hunting without reflecting too closely upon what is inside the black box. But the spectacle of a living pigeon carrying out its assignment, no matter how beautifully, simply reminded the committee of how utterly fantastic our proposal was. I will not say that the meeting was marked by unrestrained merriment, for the merriment was restrained. But it was there, and it was obvious that our case was lost.[1]

The project was sidetracked. However, with further developments in the field of guided missilery, accurate homing systems again became a focus of attention. Franklin V. Taylor, of the Naval Research Laboratory in Washington, undertook the task of promoting Skinner's scheme, as well as continuing the work in his own laboratory.[2]

The repeated evaluations of the system all pointed to the same direction. It was feasible to use the pigeon as the basis of a missile guidance system. Nevertheless, in spite of all of the success, or perhaps because of the rapidly expanding engineering technology, the Pigeon in a Pelican never got off the ground; nor did the pigeon in any other missile.

From its conception, at the beginning of World War II, to its demise in the early 1950s, a period of over ten years, the sporadic work must have consumed many tens of thousands of dollars. Yet not one missile hit its target as a result of a pigeon. One might well ask, of this and the many other such projects, in all fields of science and technology, which have not resulted in field application, was it all worthwhile?

Each case, of course, has to be judged on its own merits. This one, the Pigeon in the Pelican, did make several valuable contributions, albeit indirectly. On the practical side there was the achievement of a transparent electroconductive sheet. To accommodate the need for knowing where the bird was pecking on the target projection screen, the engineers at the Naval Research Laboratory developed a translucent plate which when contacted with a conducting wire transmitted an electrical signal with information that could be converted to target position. The pigeon, outfitted with a gold electrode at the end of its beak, could thus communicate directly to the control system. This became the basis of a radar display system used by human operators. The operator no longer had to give a verbal report of the position of a target. He merely had to touch the displayed target with a special pencil-like probe, and the target position was automatically communicated to the next relevant position in the system. This device is still used today. The Golden-Beaked Pigeon did lay one golden egg.

Also important are the indirect contributions that such a project made. Contributions that are not easily specified, but are concerned with changes in direction of thinking, elaborations of general philosophies, that reinforced certain ideas which otherwise might never have been developed.

In meeting the stringent requirements for developing an applied organic system, Skinner had to sharpen his techniques for shaping behavior and for bringing that behavior under stimulus control. And, to the degree that it succeeded, it strengthened his own convictions as to the importance and generality of these methods.

In the year which followed the termination of Project Pigeon I wrote *Walden Two,* a utopian picture of a properly engineered society. Some psychotherapists might argue that I was suffering from personal rejection and simply retreated to a fantasied world where everything went according to plan, where there never was heard a discouraging word. But another explanation is, I think, equally plausible. That piece of science fiction was a declaration of confidence in a technology of behavior. Call it a crackpot idea if you will; it is one in which I have never lost faith. I still believe that the same kind of wide-ranging speculation about human affairs, supported by studies of compensating rigor, will make a substantial contribution toward that world of the future in which, among other things, there will be no need for guided missiles.[1]

It is only a little more than fifteen years since Skinner's statement of faith. Although the time is certainly short, there still is no evidence that there is any decrease in man's reliance on guided missiles. If anything, there appears to be a movement to accept aggression, and even war, as the normal state of affairs, as an intrinsic part of the human heritage. Konrad Lorenz, Robert Ardrey, Desmond Morris and a host of other ethologically oriented commentators on the human condition have argued for this point.[3]

On the one side, there is Skinner, the optimistic behaviorist, who believes that most behavior is determined by conditions of reinforcement and is therefore plastic, subject to change by changes in the environment. On the other, the pessimistic biologists see behavior as the product of an evolutionary history, relatively unmodifiable because of genetic determinism.

The arguments are ancient, and historically can be separated into two distinct streams. There is the tradition from philosophy and religion which is concerned with answering fundamentalist questions in regard to Man's Basic Nature, Good or Evil. Quite apart from that, there is the tradition within psychology and biology which is concerned with determining the relative importance of heredity and environment for shaping behavior.

It is only to this second tradition that my comments will be addressed. The position that I have adopted is one of compromise, which recognizes the contributions from both nature and nurture, and rather than seeking to assign relative weights of importance, accepts that the two are in a dynamic interaction. An organism, man included, ceases to behave when there is no body, and ceases to behave when there is no environment.

As a speculative proposal designed to integrate the two positions, and to suggest a fundamental paradox of our existence, consider the following:

1   To control the behavior of others is positively reinforcing for the controller.

2   To be controlled is negatively reinforcing for the controllee.

Put another way, we enjoy controlling but resist being controlled. The problem is that in a complex society there must be an allocation of functions which do not necessarily coincide with the demands of the individual. Society does impose many controls on individual behavior. These controls are found in the religious codes of conduct as well as in the legal codes. The Ten Commandments are quite specific, and so are the secular laws, in describing which behaviors are allowed and which are prohibited or even proscribed. Most of us, most of the time, accept this type of control. We do not kill, we do not steal; we do pay our taxes, do drive on the right-hand side of the road. We are being controlled but we do not object. This control is accepted because it is not perceived as being directed by another person. It is something coming from God or from Government. It is, in other words, institutionalized. We will readily do for an institution what we would deny to a man. How many went to fight in Vietnam only because the government ordered them to? To the extent that these orders were perceived not as coming from an institution, the government, but rather personalized as coming from, for example, Lyndon Johnson, or the generals in the Defense Department, then they were not responded to. We despise, even fear, being controlled by mere people. It is the art of the clever politician to make it appear that his desires are but reflections of what the party or government want, or more broadly what all of the people, collectively, want. The political leader who is said to have charisma is the one who achieves this perceptual unity between himself and the larger institution. This is beautifully illustrated in the Kennedy rhetoric, "Ask not what the country can do for you, but rather what you can do for the country," where clearly the word "country" is a symbolic unification of Kennedy, the President, and the people. It is "we" and therefore not the source of feared control which emanates from the third person "him."

This is exactly what Skinner fails to appreciate. Reinforcement can be used to change behavior and, if applied on a large enough scale, to change the institutions that are, after all, products of man's behavior. But people will resist these changes not because they fear control, in the general sense, but rather because they resent control applied by another person.

Now that we have a technology for reinforcement we have to face the task of finding appropriate conditions under which it can be made to work. Who would have predicted that this applied research with pigeons would raise fundamental questions regarding the nature of man and his future survival?

3

A Bird in the Bush

Following World War II, the pigeon made a brief reappearance, if not as a bird of peace, at least as an instrument of negotiation. This occurred during the long-drawn-out debates at Pyongyang after the cease-fire in Korea in 1953. The North Koreans, aware of the fact that the dove is a symbol of peace, trained scores of white pigeons to perch on top of the buildings in their compound, thus proclaiming to the world that they, the North Koreans, were the ones that were truly desirous of peace. It is to be wondered why, given this unexpected sense of the theatric, they did not follow through with the almost obvious second step, to train a fleet of bald eagles, or even better, vultures, to promenade on the top of the American and South Korean headquarters.

The peaceful uses of the dove were, however, short-lived. The military pigeon, like the phoenix, was reborn; this time from the kindling of the Vietnam War. In the early 1960s a number of projects were initiated which were relevant to American participation in a counter-insurgency, anti-guerrilla war.

Dr. Richard Herrnstein, a Harvard professor and former student of B. F. Skinner, in consultation with the General Atronics Company, embarked on a series of studies to develop the pigeon as part of an ambush-detection system. This work was continued later at the Limited Warfare Laboratory in Aberdeen, which together with the Advanced Research Planning Agency of the Department of Defense (ARPA) funded the early investigations, and at Animal Behavior

Enterprises, Inc. This latter company was also run by two former students of Skinner, Keller and Marion Breland. The work of these different groups is described in a series of documents, many of which, for some unknown reason, still have not been declassified.[1]

One of the first tasks was to determine if the pigeon is capable of differentiating the human figure from a variety of other stimulus materials. The general problems of discrimination and concept formation are classical ones in psychology. The human figure is a complex visual pattern, and one that can take on a wide variety of representations. Not only does the stimulus pattern differ from one person to another—short and tall, thin and fat, etc.—but even more critically the same person, as represented in the pigeon's eyeball, has a different configuration depending on the angle from which he is viewed. In fact, there is an almost infinite number of transformations that the human figure can cast on the eye's retina. Higher organisms such as the human being can, of course, identify an object as a human being irrespective of these normal transformations. We possess the concept of "human," although as yet we cannot with certainty identify the stimulus properties which all of the transformations have in common that allow us to reliably identify humans in assorted sizes, shapes and positions.

But what about the pigeon? Does he have this concept? Normally not. But can he be trained to acquire the concept of "human"? This is the program of research that Herrnstein and his associates undertook as the first step in designing a pigeon system that could detect ambushes. After all, what is the definition of an ambush? One or more people in a place where no one ought to be found. A patrol moving down the road in an unfamiliar guerrilla-infested area can come to only one conclusion if it receives information that fifty yards down the road there is an unidentified group of people. This is the type of operation in which the ambush-detecting pigeon was to work. But first it was necessary to show that the pigeon would tell a person from a tree, or more precisely any person in any position from any other object.

The subjects for Herrnstein's experiment were five male racing pigeons which they obtained from a local breeder. For those who read the scientific literature with an eye for what the experimenters might be doing that they are not reporting, this choice of subjects should have raised a few brows. The report in which the study is described appeared in the journal *Science* in 1964.[2] This was well before the public was aware that there were programs to use birds for military purposes. However, the standard pigeon subject in the psychological laboratories at Harvard, as well as most other places, was the White Carneau, a thoroughly domesticated breed that often finds its way onto elegant restaurant menus. That the scientists chose a hardy, outdoor relative should have suggested that the capabilities which the experiments were designed to confirm would eventually be employed in the field.

The birds were reduced in weight to 80 percent of normal, after which preliminary training was begun. The apparatus was the familiar Skinner box, a small cubicle enclosing the animal and isolating him from the surrounding environment. On one wall there was a translucent disc, and below that a food hopper filled with grain. The hopper was normally out of reach of the bird's beak but could be raised with an appropriate electrical signal delivered either by the experimenter or by the bird's pecking on the disc above the hopper.

For the first several days, the bird was trained to eat from the hopper. This was accomplished by periodically raising it, illuminating it and allowing the pigeon three seconds of access to the grain. The sound of the feeding device being elevated and the illumination of the food area soon became conditioned stimuli for eliciting approach and eating responses. Even if the bird was in the back of the box when the sound and light occurred, the pigeon swiftly waddled to the vicinity of the feeder, poked his head into the hopper and consumed as much as the three seconds would allow him.

Following this stage of training, the pigeon was taught to peck at the hinged disc. This was accomplished by using the method of successive approximations. The feeder is raised only when the animal's head is close to the disc; and then only when it is close to the disc and the beak is pointing at the disc; and then on each successive occasion the beak has to be closer to the disc than on the previous occasion in order for the experimenter to trigger the feeding device. Finally the bird is virtually forced, by the contingencies of previous association of responses and reinforcements, into the disc, and he emits the correct response. The peck on the disc closes a small switch, and the grain is delivered. Very quickly the bird is producing a fairly high rate of pecking response, limited only by the fact that he stops to eat for three seconds after each peck.

After two such sessions, the pigeons were placed on an intermittent schedule of reinforcement, designed to produce a relatively high, steady rate of disc-pecking without stuffing the bird. The particular schedule of reinforcement that was used is called a variable-interval one-minute schedule. With such a procedure, the pigeon receives re-inforcement only for the first disc peck which follows, on the average, one minute from the previous reinforcement. In this situation, it is quite normal for the pigeon to peck at the disc one to two times per second for fairly long, continuous periods of time.

The final stage of the preliminary training was to get the pigeon to peck at the disc only when the disc was illuminated. This is easily ac-complished by withholding all the reinforcements during the time that the disc is dark and, conversely, having the reinforcement schedule, as described above, operative only during the time that the disc is lit. The pigeons learn quite quickly not to respond to the disc when it is dark, and to limit the high disc-peck rate to that time when the disc is illuminated.

The critical portions of the experiment involved projecting images from slides onto the disc. For this purpose, the experimenters had available to them over 1200 35-mm. color slides with a wide variety of content, including country and urban settings, woods, fields, large expanses of water, meadows, lawns, etc. Before each session, the Carousel magazine of their slide projector was loaded with 81 slides, approximately half of which contained photographs of humans in various settings and positions, and approximately half of which were devoid of all human form but also contained a variety of scenes.

Many slides contained human beings partly obscured by inter-vening objects: trees, automobiles, window frames and so on. The people were distributed throughout the pictures: in the cen-ter or to one side or the other, near the top or the bottom, close up or distant. The people themselves varied in appearance: they were clothed, semi-nude or nude; adults or children; men or women; sitting, standing or lying; black, white or yellow. Light-ing and coloration varied: some slides were dark, others light; some had either reddish or bluish tints, and so on.[2]

The procedure for training the pigeons to discriminate between the two sets of slides, one set containing human figures and the other not, was exactly the same as the procedure for training the birds to discriminate between the illuminated disc and the dark disc. The reinforcement schedule was in effect when a human slide was projected onto the disc but not in effect when a no-human slide was presented.

Although the same slides were used throughout training, the large number and the fact that the order of presentation was changed daily, prevented the pigeons from learning specific stimulus-response connections. If the pigeon was to reliably get food in this experiment he had to learn the concept of "human form."

Within five to seven sessions all of the five pigeons learned something about the concept. In other words, they exhibited a higher response rate to the human slides than to the no-human slides. After 70 sessions, when presented with a set of slides that they had never seen before, the five pigeons responded with remarkable accuracy. Two of them were presented with black-and-white slides, to which they also responded well.

The evidence seemed quite clear. The pigeon was capable of forming the abstract concept of "person." An analysis of the type of errors that were made during training gave additional support for this contention. Frequently, if the human figure was severely obscured, the pigeon failed to peck. In addition, especially early in training, the pigeon often emitted pecking responses to pictures which did not contain a human form but which did have objects usually associated with the presence of a human, such as cars, boats, houses.

Herrnstein and Loveland believe that the racing pigeons entered the experiment with the concept already formed. They reached this conclusion as a result of the rapidity with which the birds learned this very complex task. The evidence for this is, of course, quite weak. Nor does it matter. At least in theory one could count on the racing pigeon to identify a potential ambush.

Once it was shown that the pigeon could learn the concept of "human being," it was time to consider some of the practical problems of field use. First of all, it was necessary to demonstrate that the person-identification ability that the pigeon had displayed in the laboratory was also demonstrable under field conditions. Secondly, it was necessary to find a way to control the bird's flight path in order to make certain that he surveys the area through which the patrol will move. Finally, there was the problem of devising a system whereby the pigeon could report back to the patrol that an ambush had been detected.

The birds were given training so that they would fly out from their loft and return. This was accomplished by having the hungry pigeons find food at increasing distances from the loft, and also upon their return to it. In some of the experiments, the feeding apparatus was mounted inside a garbage can. When the bird landed on the can and pressed a disc with his beak, a small portion of grain was delivered to him. A similar technique was employed in the loft. In this manner, with a minimum number of people involved in training and recording responses, the distances between loft and "target" could be increased. By also getting the pigeon accustomed to eating from the hand of any person on the designated route, it was possible to test the bird's ability to find partially hidden targets. As an example, a target person may be set 100 yards down the road from the loft. He crouches behind a bush, simulating an ambush position. He cannot be seen from the road, but he is quite visible to a pigeon flying overhead. When the bird is released he follows the road. This is what he has been trained to do previously by having all targets and feeding stations next to a road. Upon sighting the crouching man the bird lands next to him and is fed by the target. A number of variations of this sequence with different roads and different conditions of camouflage indicated quite clearly that the pigeon was capable of identifying partially hidden human figures under real-life field conditions.

When the roads were familiar, the pigeon could achieve outflight distances, loft to target, of about one mile. With unfamiliar roads, difficulties were experienced with even 300 yards. In fact, when the training sites were moved daily, many of the birds were lost. This was one of the insurmountable problems. In order to achieve reliable flight control it may be necessary to rely on continuous experimenter-controlled guidance signals or direct stimulation.

Since in the real situation it was quite unlikely that the ambush-detecting pigeon would be fed by the potential targets, nor would the enemy radio back that they were being visited by a bird, a reporting device was designed. This device consisted of a miniature radio transmitter with an air-pressure switch. When the bird decelerated for landing the change in air pressure closed the switch, which actualized the signal that was transmitted over the radio. This signal was the cue that the bird had landed, a response that should be made only when a human target was found.

A test to assess the military usefulness of the pigeon ambush-detecting system was planned for September 1966. Unfortunately, most of the birds became infected with pigeon pox and were incapacitated. The military-potential test was canceled and all work by outside contractors was halted.

There was a continuation of the program at the Limited War Laboratory with particular attention being paid to the problem of extending and controlling outflights over unfamiliar territory. Although some improvements were obtained, it is doubtful if that approach will ever achieve the degree of reliability required for a military system. Later, in the chapter on Project PAPP, some alternative procedures for constructing such a system will be examined.

4

Pigeon Intelligence

The Russians launched the world's first successful artificial satellite, Sputnik, on October 4, 1957. A little less than a month later, they showed that it was not a technological accident, and triumphantly repeated the astonishing feat. It was quite clear at that time that this was a major Russian victory, one that would have dramatic consequences all over the world, and for many decades. The first reactions of the Western world to this bold innovation were surprise and fear. Suddenly the weak partner of World War II, the huge but backward giant in the East, gave signs that it too had mastered a sophisticated technology and was capable of achievements not yet even reached by its Western neighbors.

The fear engendered by knowing there were Russian-made moons orbiting our own skies was initiated by thoughts of the possible uses for these satellites. Two main areas of utilization were of concern, to both the military and the public. There was the possibility of using the satellites as platforms for missile launches and, less drastically, using them as observation platforms in order to have permanent eyes and ears in the sky. Unlike the American Lockheed U-2, these satellites literally would be above the law. No one had yet contemplated the legal proprietorship of the space above the atmosphere. There was no equivalent of national air space or twelve-mile limits which determined jurisdiction out in space. Nor was there any means to enforce such laws had they existed.

The fact that the following year saw the Soviet Union achieve a workable intercontinental ballistic missile (ICBM) made the threat from above, in terms of an armed platform, superfluous. At the same time it made the potential intelligence-gathering capabilities of these satellites of even greater concern, and increased the American need for a similar system to monitor Russian ICBM development and deployment.

The U-2 was only a temporary solution to the problem of collecting information. The long-wing, high-altitude Lockheed jet reconnaissance aircraft had been capable of flying out of reach of Soviet antiaircraft guns. With a top speed of 494 miles per hour flying at 70,000 feet, it was thought to be beyond the range of existing Russian guns. But in May 1960 it was revealed that one of the U-2 pilots, young Gary Francis Powers, aged thirty, was sitting in a Moscow jail. Premier Khrushchev used the situation to full political advantage by denouncing the United States for conducting secret intelligence operations over Russian territory. Khrushchev announced that Powers had admitted that he had taken off from Peshawar, Pakistan, and was to fly across the U.S.S.R. in a northwesterly direction to land at the military airfield in Bodö, Norway. To the extreme embarrassment of Western diplomats, Khrushchev emphasized his feelings of self-righteousness and betrayal by using this incident to terminate the Summit Meeting in Paris.

This event highlighted the legal and political consequences of flying over a foreign land. Nevertheless, the U-2 continued to be used, and it was photographs taken from a U-2 that served to validate the presence of Russian missiles in Cuba in 1962.

The political consequences of having another U-2 incident over Russia were severe enough so that these overflights probably were discontinued. Although I have no direct knowledge to support this statement, it is a reasonable conclusion that is based on the fact that no other U-2s were reported brought down over Russia. Apparently the penalties of not collecting the data were less than those of being caught at it. Nevertheless, as a good experimental psychologist I should caution the reader that the null hypothesis (i.e., the hypothesis that something did not happen; in this case, that the planes did not fly) logically cannot be verified.

Efforts in America quickly turned to producing a U.S. satellite, one that could replace the endangered aerial-reconnaissance activities characterized by the overflights. One of the earliest of these "spy in the sky" systems was SAMOS (Satellite Anti-Missile Observation System). This relatively small intelligence-gathering satellite was equipped with a twenty-foot-focal-length camera which was optically folded into four feet. The system was capable, even then, in the early 1960s, of resolving objects as small as one foot in size at a distance of 100 miles. By examining photographs taken with this equipment, the photo-reconnaissance expert could obtain a remarkable amount of information: not only the presence of a missile, the number of missiles, but also their state of readiness. By comparing photographs taken at different times, it also was possible to ascertain whether or not new sites were being prepared. Many other types of information could also be obtained: construction progress at airports, industrial complexes and highways, and even the monitoring of production from particular factories by counting the number of railroad cars on the sidings or large trucks next to the warehouses. The sophisticated photo-reconnaissance operator could, from the most meager of information, deduce a story enriched with significant military conclusions.

Two classical incidents from World War II emphasize the value of photo-reconnaissance information, not only for the planning of aerial assaults and for damage evaluation, but also for discovering unexpected developments in the enemy's technological capability. Early in 1940 the inspection of a series of photographs taken over France revealed that the Germans had deployed a radar surveillance system, thought to have been known only to the British. Later in the war, an almost chance photograph revealed, for the first time, that the Germans, at Peenemünde, were preparing rockets for use against England. Some of the key German scientists involved in the V-1, V-2 rocket development program were instrumental in developing the rocket boosters that would put into space optical and electronic reconnaissance systems many orders of magnitude more powerful than the relatively primitive device that first detected their own activities.

As elaborate and sophisticated as these systems may become, one essential key to the utilization of the information which they can detect is the human photo-reconnaissance operator. Electromagnetic signals of all varieties may be sensed, decoded and even interpreted by machine. But the richest source of information is in that portion of the electromagnetic spectrum that we label as the visual bandwidth, between 450 and 750 millimicrons. Even translated into simple black, white and tones of gray, the visual image contains the vast majority of information useful for military purposes. It makes little difference whether the pictures are first sensed by extra-visual means such as infrared or radar. The conversion of this information such that the topological relations, the relations of parts in space, remain true to that of the real world, give the human operator the key to unlock the intentions of the enemy.

Vision is often said to be the queen of the senses. Certainly, for the human organism it is true. If we measure the amount of the human cortex involved with visual function as compared to the functions of any of the other senses, we find that vision dominates. But more importantly, if we measure our daily activities in terms of the total amount of time that each sense modality is used, as well as the amount of information received through that modality, again we would find that vision takes first place. It is no wonder then that the most valuable source of military intelligence still comes from those sensors that can re-create, in picture form, the data that were sensed.

It is yet another irony of progress that our military technology, as exhibited by SAMOS in the early 1960s, could develop a system to see from distances and directions undreamed of by naked man, but in the final analysis needed a man to tell it what it saw.

This then was the situation when, as a member of the General Electric Bionics Unit, I was consulted about the problem by personnel of the Avionics Laboratory at Wright-Patterson Air Force Base. A number of satellites in the SAMOS series had been launched, each with its own particular orbit. The reconnaissance systems were operating on an almost continuous schedule, and either by telemetering or by capsule ejection were returning the valuable images to earth. Unfortunately, on the earth side of the operation a bottleneck had developed. There simply were not enough skilled photo interpreters to process the many thousands of feet of film that constantly were being returned.

Somehow, an error of oversight had occurred in the SAMOS systems analysis. The mechanical aspects were superb, but no one planned on not having enough trained operators. Nor, once discovered, could this obstacle be quickly overcome. The training for photo reconnaissance is both rigorous and time-consuming and calls for personnel qualifications that were not easily obtainable in the U.S. defense forces in the 1960s.

Almost immediately after recognizing the problem, a solution was suggested which called for the design and development of a recognition computer—one that would automatically and rapidly process the increasing backlog of photographs. The problem would be solved, then, by eliminating the necessity of the human operator. A computer would be designed to function like the human, to make target-recognition responses.

Although this solution had a certain amount of appeal, the implementation, as we shall see in a moment, was not a simple thing to accomplish. To design a computer to recognize certain classes of targets means that the designer must be able to specify, in terms that eventually can be translated into electronic circuitry, what are the physical stimulus characteristics of that target class. If, for example, the requirement is to recognize airplanes, this in effect means that one must specify, in advance, the common physical characteristics that airplanes share. And, since we are limiting ourselves to photographs, these characteristics can only be those that are reflected in the two-dimensional static array of different gray values that we call a picture. Thus whole classes of possibly useful information are denied to us. The contents of the interior of an object are also not available to us. The altimeter, the parachutes, the hundreds of other items that might provide clues to the function of the object are all hidden from view, as are the roar of the engines and any of the specialized electromagnetic emissions that might be used in flight, such as radar. What remains, then, is a raw shape, about which we *might* have some additional information in regard to its composition. For instance, the general shape of a bird and a plane are quite similar, and given a low-resolution system one might easily mistake a large bird for a small plane. On the other hand, if the source of the pictorial display is from a radar rather than a camera, the soft nonreflecting bird would present a very low-contrast signal, if any at all, as compared to the highly radar-reflecting plane.

Putting these factors aside, and returning to the main question, what are the invariant physical stimuli on a photograph that characterize an airplane? The first answer given to this question is usually that a plane has wings that are, more or less, at right angles to the fuselage. But this is true only if you are looking down from above. It is also not true of helicopters and not true of small swept-wing fighters as seen through a low-resolution camera. On the other side, that de-

scription also fits highway intersections and many apartment buildings, as viewed from above.

For even a single relatively simple target class there are difficulties
in specifying target characteristics. When the reconnaissance mission
is a very general one, meaning that all military information may be of
significance, the problems of design are multiplied manyfold. Finally,
one should remember the incident of Peenemünde, where a vital and
significant interpretation was made while the photo-reconnaissance
operator was *not* looking for that type of target. The interpreter was
responding to an unexpected configuration. Theoretically, of course,
it would also be possible to have a computer store all of the inputs of
its working history, and then compare each current input with its
memory to determine if a unique event has occurred. This depends
on the form in which the material has been coded and stored. Completely raw information, a bit for every resolution dot on every photograph, would result in gibbering nonsense. Whether the correct
code could be designed would in part be based on the designer's ability to predict the nature of the unexpected event.

The ability of the human organism to recognize an object as being
the same object even though he is looking at it such that the physical
stimulation falling on the retina of his eye changes from moment to
moment is called object constancy. It is this capability that one would
like to reproduce in a recognition computer.

"A rose is a rose is a rose . . ." In this redundant but precisely
metered phrase Gertrude Stein pinpointed form or object constancy.
Within limitations, viewed at any angle, at any distance, under a variety of colored illumination, the form is categorized as a rose. That we
categorize objects as similar under a variety of different and unusual
conditions is a necessary condition for survival. How else could we
walk down an unfamiliar street, or read the idiosyncratic handwriting
of a friend who rarely writes? In order for the same response to be
elicited by a variety of different proximal stimuli, these stimuli must
have some common property. The common property which elicits the
same response is called the *invariant stimulus*.

After hours of discussion it was decided that man could not be removed from the system. Instead, a computer would be designed that
would reduce the man's work load. The operators would not have to
look at every picture that came back from space, only certain preselected ones. The preselection would be computerized. Thus we

hoped to have the best of both worlds. The computer would quickly eliminate the many photographs which did not contain useful information, and the man would utilize his recognition capability on the remainder.

The validity of the invariance hypothesis has a practical consequence in the design of a form-recognition machine. Ideally one would desire a form-recognition machine that gives the same response to a form regardless of the magnification, rotation, translation, or projective transformation of that form. If an invariant-stimulus property were not present under all of these conditions, then the machine would have to store all possible perturbations of the form. This would be truly formidable, due to limitations in storage capacity. An alternative method is to predetermine and store the invariant properties for purposes of comparison. But this, as we have seen, requires the accurate identification of the physical-stimulus dimensions that are characteristic of the different classes of objects. The spelling out of these characteristics is a necessary prerequisite to the design of the pattern-recognition machine.

With incisive logic, we concluded that there would be enormous savings if we could just throw away all those pictures that did not contain man-made objects. After all, the minimum requirement for a photograph to be of significant military interest is that something in the photograph should have been constructed by man. That is, of course, not to say that all man-made objects will be of military interest. In fact, most of them will not. But the converse is inexorably true. If there is no man-made object, it is not of value for purposes of military intelligence. As it happens, the majority of the earth's surface, filled with oceans, deserts, uninhabitable jungles and mountains, does not contain objects that are man-made. Therefore most of the photographs can be thrown away.

Now the problem was reduced to coming up with a system that was capable of working on only one concept, "man-made." This single concept might now be handled by an appropriately designed machine. But first, the same question raised earlier, now for only a single concept, had to be answered. What are the stimulus properties that define "man-made"? Or, even more generally, are there stimulus properties that all or most man-made objects share?

To this question one might reply, too quickly, "yes"; and support this affirmative position by appealing to everyday experience. For instance, no matter where you, the reader, are now, raise your eyes from this page and look about. Do you see any objects that you cannot easily identify as belonging to one or the other of the two concepts "man-made" and "non-man-made"? I would daresay that the answer is "no"; that, indeed, you can very quickly make the decision as to which of the two categories any item belongs.

However, this does not provide the kind of proof that can be used for our purposes. All of the objects at which you had been looking are familiar to you. You have seen them before, used them before; and acquired, through a variety of sources, information as to their origins. Therefore your ability to appropriately categorize the materials into man-made and not man-made *might* be a function not of the immediate visual stimulus but of other factors available to you that could not be made available to the computer. When the computer looks at a very straight pole sticking out of the earth, it can only respond to the pattern of dots in a straight line, and not to the fact that this straight line was a flagpole bought at the neighborhood hardware store.

Yet, it might be argued, one could enter a foreign culture with artifacts unfamiliar to the observer, and still be able to make correct categorizations. To some extent this is true. A tool used by a South Pacific Islander to open up coconuts, if it were indeed made by the native and was not a natural object, would, I am sure, be recognized by us as being man-made. It is even likely that one would correctly identify the function of such a tool, at least in its general form—for example, that it is used for cutting or cracking. That we are capable of such an abstract categorization, man-made, even when unfamiliar with the detailed form, indicates, again, that perhaps these forms share a common stimulus property with other forms with which we are familiar and from which we can generalize. Alternatively, experience or familiarity may play only a limited role. Might it not be possible, for instance, that the human organism is biologically constituted in such a way that it can directly perceive man-madeness, independently of past experience and associations? There are precedents for this type of innate classification system in lower animals. The best example can be found in the now classic article by Lettvin, Maturana, McCulloch and Pitts, "What the Frog's Eye Tells the Frog's Brain."[1] The retinal cells of the frog's eye—i.e., that portion of the eye that responds to light—are organized in such a way that different groups of cells are sensitive not only to the punctate series of differences in brightness in the same manner as the film in a camera, but also to *properties* of objects. Thus there are groups of cells that only respond to the *movement* of light across their receptor surface, others that only respond when that pattern is within a certain size range, and still others that only respond if that pattern has a generally convex shape. When one adds up all of these properties and asks the question what is small, round and moving, it is discovered that this corresponds to the items on the frog's dinner menu, insects. If the retina is artificially stimulated so as to simulate these properties, then, as expected, the frog's tongue flicks out, appropriately, albeit in vain.

There are numerous other examples that can be cited to support the contention that lower organisms possess an innate capability to utilize some fairly complex concepts. But this does not solve the problem. It only emphasizes more strongly that concepts are defined by an identification of common stimulus properties. As for the frog, he does not have to learn that small, round, moving objects are food. Nor does the frog have to learn any concept during its lifetime in order to survive as a species.

Without doubt the human, at least in modern Western industrialized societies, must be capable of learning concepts for his survival. Even though it is quite possible that primitive man, eons ago, could utilize raw information to discriminate between edible and inedible objects, we are so estranged from our natural environment that many of these correct identifications are no longer appropriate. In the Paleolithic jungle or savanna, a large moving object, if not one's own relative, would invariably be a source of protein. Primitive man might well have been wired, like the frog, to respond with similar gustatory delight. The same response to those same stimuli today would probably find man breaking his teeth on the fender of an automobile.

Whether a concept is learned or innate, it still requires that the stimulus properties be specified, regardless of whether this specification is made manifest through the peripheral neuronal organization of a retina or through so-called higher cognitive processes mediated in the cortex of the brain.

Returning to the original problem, the practical task was to develop a target-classification system for man-made objects. The very first step on the way to a solution was to become aware that animals might be of some help. The capability for form constancy is not only present and highly developed in humans but also occurs in many other animals. That is, an organism can recognize an object even though it is varied in a number of different ways, even though the organism has had no previous experience with a particular transformation.

I was prepared to advance the idea that one might use pigeons as an integral part of the system, and that research should be undertaken to check out the feasibility of this proposal. However, I had a change of mind. The change was not precipitated because I had stumbled on theoretical or technological problems of which I was not previously aware. Rather, I recalled that first time when animals were to be used in a military system and were to be trained using modern behavioristic methods, Skinner's Pigeons in a Pelican.[2]

I did not want this program to suffer the same fate. It is one thing to fail because of an intrinsic error in a design. It is another to have a workable design rejected because of stereotypical, biased thinking. I have often wondered what underlies the hearty laughter and knowing smiles that almost inevitably greet a project that proposes to use an animal in a task heretofore reserved for a human. Do we provoke some theological demon that stands guard over certain self-designated inviolable distinctions between human capacities and those of the lower animals; a natural loathing by which man seeks to preserve his uniqueness and superiority in all contests? Whatever the source of these emotions, there is no denying their presence. Nor was I prepared to defend the increased effectiveness of a combined man-animal system by rational discourse. The sources of objection were too deeply rooted to be severed by even the sharp knife of logic. I discarded the idea, or at least the presentation of the idea, for utilizing the organism directly in series with machine components. Instead I went in a different direction, but one that still allowed me to experiment with animals and to utilize their special capacities to help solve human problems.

That morning I argued that we should study the shape-constancy process in pigeons, particularly in regard to determining whether pigeons were capable of making the discrimination between man-made and non-man-made objects. If they could do this, then perhaps by examining their behavior we could determine the stimulus properties on which they were operating. Even more basic than that, if pigeons could be trained to attain this high-order concept, this would provide proof, an existence theorem, that the concept of man-made does depend on stimulus characteristics within the image itself, and not on prior knowledge of function. If this were true, then the computer designer would know that, at least theoretically, a solution was available. Furthermore, from the study of behavior during the discrimination training it might be possible to discover the stimulus properties that elicit the designation man-made. This would further facilitate the task of the computer engineer. The goals then were to use the pigeon as a tool to inform us whether the concept man-made can be specified in terms of present physical events; and, if yes, to determine the nature of these physical events.

I remember the first meeting quite well. Most surprising was the lack of resistance. Even with the revised form of the suggestion, I had expected to meet considerable opposition. That such opposition failed to appear was a result of the audience being staff members of the Bionics Unit of the Air Force Avionics Laboratory. These people had been instrumental in developing the field of bionics.[3] Bionics is a technology that attempts to develop new, artificial systems based on the functions and principles found in living organisms. Whereas bionics seeks to emulate biological function, the approach that I took with the pigeons was to use the entire organism as a simple tool. Just as the microscope is used to enlarge images to give us a view of reality on a different spatial scale, the pigeon project was designed to use the organic and culturally unencumbered visual system, from eye through brain out to beak, as a lever to pry open a different type of secret of nature. It was to tell us what information our own systems can use, the inherited biological system or a newly devised artificial one, in order to be able to comprehend such complex high-order concepts as man-made. Although I did not look at it in this way at the time, it is quite evident, in retrospect, that the particular manner in which the pigeons were to be used was quite unique.

After several more discussions with the Air Force personnel in the Bionics Unit, and exchanges of letters, agreement was reached on the general direction of the pigeon program and the method of attack. The expressed intent of the program had to be stated in terms of using a living organism, the pigeon, as a research tool to help us extract the invariant-stimulus properties in photographs containing man-made objects. If, by the way, we might be able to convince the military to also look into the possibilities of using pigeons directly, well that would be a bonus for us.

Once having decided on the classification category that would be most valuable for the SAMOS operation, man-made versus non-man-made, and hypothesizing that this dichotomous concept could be expressed as a binary choice, we were faced with the problem of choosing appropriate stimulus materials for training the birds. To begin with, we scoured the library for books containing aerial photographs, and also contacted some local photographers who did aerial surveying. From both sources we accumulated a collection of several thousand aerial pictures of almost every imaginable type. Two young assistants and I spent several eye-burning weeks sorting these photographs into the categories on which the pigeons would be trained. The three of us had to agree, independently, that a given photo was representative of one of the two categories before it was finally used.

Photographs for the man-made category included everything from cities, isolated roads and farmhouses, to airstrips and oil depots. For the non-man-made category there were included various types of natural terrain, desert, mountain, jungle, sea, anything at all as long as we agreed that it did not also contain a human artifact. Photos from both classes were originally taken from a variety of altitudes and angles using many diverse types of cameras and lenses. In addition, the climatic conditions were quite variable, bright sunny days, hazy days and days with heavy cloud cover. In short, we tried to get as many transformations and varieties of samples from the two classes as possible. One might compare this approach to that of the traditional experimental design where everything is kept constant (controlled) except the variable that the researcher is manipulating (in this case the two stimulus categories). Although this is not the place to discuss the relative merits of these two approaches to experimentation, it should be clear that the former, using random variation of the background against which the stimuli are presented, allows for greater certainty that the results are generally valid. However, real differences between the experimental and control groups are more difficult to detect with this procedure.

In attempting to get as many of the natural variations of background as possible, a practical problem arose. Depending on the sensitivity of the subclass-categorization scheme, there can be an almost infinite population of types. A photograph of an oak forest taken at 12:01 P.M. is in some measurable way different from an oak forest taken at 12:05 P.M., with larger differences in the same forest appearing when the photographs are taken in summer and winter, in snow and in sunlight, etc.

But this difficulty is only an apparent one and, in fact, points up the advantages of using a living organism for this task. This requires exactly the special organismic capability on which we wanted to capitalize: the organism does have form constancy and, therefore, does not have to learn each stimulus permutation. We, therefore, only have to teach it to respond to some sample of the population, and it will then respond in a similar manner to other members of the same population. Thus, we could reduce the number of photographs from an almost infinite population to a sample of that population. However, there was yet another problem. To how many types of photographs must the organism be trained, in order to generalize to all specimens within that class? The answer to this question was not known. It was, therefore, decided to randomly select a number of photographs from the man-made population and a number of photographs from the non-man-made population, and to train the subject on these two finite sets. Whether or not we were lucky enough to select the right photographs and a sufficiently large number of them, would, in part, be told to us by the results. Let us then examine how we trained the pigeons to discriminate between man-made and non-man-made.

The pigeons that were to be used in the experiment were ordered from a company in Georgia with the unlikely name of Palmetto Pigeon Plant. Most of their production, I believe, goes toward satisfying the gustatory needs of those diners that have developed a taste for squab under glass. Nevertheless, they are also one of the major suppliers of pigeons for research. Since in many laboratories of experimental psychology the pigeon has come to replace the white rat as the standard subject, I can only assume that the Palmetto Pigeon Plant profits nicely from catering to both the stomach and the head. The decision to use a bird was based on the fact that most birds have excellent vision. And although the best vision is to be found in such carnivorous creatures as hawks and eagles, practical laboratory considerations dictated that we use a bird for which standard equipment and know-how was already available. Even reducing our options to the pigeon still left a wide variety of choices. There are about 285 species, ranging from the common park pigeon to exotically beautiful and expensive blue-crowned pigeons of New Guinea to groups specialized for homing and racing competition and special ways of tumbling in midair. Two characteristics distinguish the order Columbiformes, to which the pigeon belongs, from other orders of birds. One, the members of this group produce a cheesy, milklike substance in their crop to feed their young. Secondly, they drink water by sucking, as through a straw, rather than completing the act of swallowing by throwing back their heads, as do all other birds. Although these are peculiar traits of the pigeon group, they in no way are related to our research. There is, however, another characteristic of the pigeon, shared with a variety of other birds from other orders, that does enhance its value in the type of research commonly practiced in experimental psychology laboratories. The pigeon is a voracious eater. In its natural habitat it can spend as much as 95 percent of the day pecking and picking at bits of food. It has been estimated that the wood pigeon may emit pecks at the rate of 60 to 100 per minute, and that during the course of the day may collect as many as 35,000 clover-leaf fragments. What could be better for the behavioristically oriented psychologist than an organism that emits such a large number of easily observable responses, and whose rate of responding can be controlled by turning on and off the availability of small tidbits of food? Thus, without hesitation, we chose the pigeon to be our experimental subject. Although for the sake of economy one could simply have taken a bag of popcorn down to the park and lured enough experimental subjects into a sack for several experiments, this procedure was not attempted. First of all, the feral urban pigeon is thought to be the possible carrier of a number of diseases quite harmful to man. But more important, he is common. If we were to have a problem with the general acceptance of our first idea, to use pigeons to replace some human operators, why not soften the disgrace by at least using a more regal member of the pigeon family? And so we ordered six White Carneaux from the Palmetto Pigeon Plant.

Within several days they arrived, air freight, special delivery, at our laboratory. About twice the size of the ordinary variety, they are tall, haughty animals, completely white except for the pink rims of

their eyes and the darker pink legs and claws. One of the first tasks
that faced the laboratory assistants was to find names for each of
these six white beauties. By convention every name is supposed to
have some basis in scholarly antiquity. One could always make
points with one's colleagues or even a visiting dean by introducing an
experimental subject as Salamandre or Titus, and then knowingly
explaining the relationship between the name and the significance of
the research. I discovered that for two whole days my entire laboratory staff was engaged in trying to find such appropriate names. (In
this case, no doubt, noms de plume.) With the power invested in me
as Principal Investigator, I arbitrarily christened the new subjects:
Sam, Jack, Mary, Louise, Marx and Philby. Taking heed of the
women's liberation movement, I bestowed the names quite indiscriminately of the sex of the subject. Marx, by the way, was Groucho
and not Karl, although I was not beneath passing him off as the co-
author of the *Communist Manifesto* if, on a particular visit from the
military sponsors of the research, he was not performing to my satisfaction.

Each bird had his leg banded, and was given separate quarters
with his name prominently displayed on the front of the cage. The
feathers from the trailing edge of the wings were snipped with scis-
sors. This simple and painless procedure saves many hours of chasing
a loose bird around the laboratory; or, worse still, of climbing out
on the windowsill, in white lab coat, butterfly net in hand, while
being gaped at by hundreds of students below.

After this rather rude introduction to the laboratory, the birds are
allowed to eat and drink as much as they would like. For ten days
food and water are constantly available. Rather than fattening them
for the kill, we are preparing them for the experiment. By the end of
ten days their weight has reached an asymptotic level. It is relatively
unchanging from day to day. Then by carefully controlling and limiting the amount of food eaten on the following days, the body weight
of the bird is gradually reduced to 80 percent of normal. This provides the experimenters with a subject who is certain to have a keen
appetite, who will appreciate the value of a few grains of food, and
who will respond in the manner deemed appropriate by the researcher. Reduced to 80 percent of his normal weight, the bird is still
sleek and vigorous. Except for the rapidity with which he will engage

in food-seeking behavior, he appears to be quite similar to other members of his family.

It is in this state that he is introduced into the experimental apparatus which is called an operant-conditioning chamber or, more briefly, a Skinner box.

Reinforcement is the key to the training program. In fact, it is the cornerstone of almost all modern learning theories, although these theories may differ in their explanation of how reinforcement operates. However, for purposes of the experiments to be described, it is not necessary to explore the theoretical differences. The pragmatic definition of reinforcement, employed by Skinner, will be sufficient. A reinforcer is any event which, when it follows a response, increases the probability of that response occurring again. If, for example, I make jokes about ASPCA women, and these jokes are followed by laughter, then I am likely to continue making those jokes. On the other hand, if laughter is not provoked, then I will most likely cease to make the jokes. From these two conditions one can conclude, by definition, that, at least for me, laughter will reinforce the joke-telling response. Reinforcers may be specific or general; that is, they may work in only very special situations or in a variety of different situations. Certainly laughter would not serve as a reinforcer if it followed statements meant to be taken seriously. Nor could laughter be used to increase an eating-related response, such as the frequency of picking up a fork. Food, of course, would be a most suitable reinforcement in that situation, providing, however, that the subject was hungry.

The hungry pigeon, the one that is reduced to 80 percent of his normal body weight, can be taught to emit a number of different kinds of responses using food as reinforcement. One such response that is particularly convenient is that of pecking. The response has a natural relationship with the ultimate act that serves to reinforce it, namely eating. In general, it would appear that consummatory acts, those that bring a natural chain of responses to some state of closure, are extremely powerful as reinforcers for those responses that precede them. The pecking response and the ingestion of grain by the pigeon are in just such a relationship. This relationship is strengthened enormously when the pigeon is hungry. There are many other examples of a strong relationship between a response and a reinforcer. The orgasm following sexual activity is certainly a prime example. Who can doubt that the achievement of the orgasmic response serves to increase the probability that the particular sexual activity which preceded the orgasm will, under similar conditions of arousal or motivation, be repeated. Or conversely, that the failure to reach orgasm, the failure to obtain reinforcement, will decrease the probability that the specific preceding responses will be displayed again.

In a straightforward manner, using the principles of reinforcement, one can gain control over a number of different behaviors. It is this approach that serves as the foundation for many modern therapeutic procedures which were discussed in the introduction under the label of behavior modification.

It is necessary to understand one additional behavioral law before comprehending the procedure that we employed to train the pigeon to discriminate between the man-made and non-man-made objects. Responses always occur in some sort of environment. The environment can be characterized in terms of being internal or external. Both consist of a complex patterning of stimulation. We already have alluded to one set of such internal stimuli, those that occur when the animal is hungry. What are these stimuli? It is not really necessary to identify them, but simply to note that the ability to differentiate between our own states of hunger and satiety, or sexual arousal and sexual indifference, is proof that these states are mediated by different sets of stimuli. All information is transmitted by stimulation; it is the description of these conditions of stimulation that provide one type of explanation for behavior. The fact that a pigeon or a rat, or for that matter a man, when deprived of food for a period of time will eat with less hesitation, more rapidly and in greater quantities than comparable subjects that have not been deprived of food, can only assure us that these organisms are all aware of the differences in their internal states. Although it is only man that can provide a verbal label for his feeling of discomfort, he shares with the other species a similar pattern of responses designed to change the state—in this case, eating.

The external stimuli are those that impinge upon the organism from the world around him as opposed to the world inside him. These are the stimuli that are picked up by one of the sensory systems, vision, hearing, temperature, touch, taste and smell. The relative importance of these modalities differs across species and is, of course, related to the life style of the species. Those behavior patterns that are necessary for the survival of the individual—feeding, protection against predators—as well as those necessary for the survival of the species—reproduction—are all mediated by information contained in the stimulation. Different species, depending on their evolutionary history, gain this information through specializations within different sensory modalities. Thus birds in regard to feeding behavior are almost completely visual, paying little heed to the odor or taste of food.

Some snakes, on the other hand (someone else's, I hope), such as the pit viper, are completely oblivious to visual stimulation when hunting for food, but rely almost exclusively on information conveyed in the infrared radiations emitted by their potential victim and sensed by two specialized heat receptors located near the tip of the head.

Within a given species a particular major activity class will usually be controlled by information received in one sensory modality, as just described. Different activities may be mediated by different modalities, or all major activities may be governed by the same modality. For birds, in general, sexual activity as well as feeding activity is visually mediated, as witnessed by the importance of plumage color for the differentiation of sexual roles and special displays of feathers and visually monitored behaviors such as strutting and preening. The omnivorous rat seems to use taste as a guide to food selection, while sexual behavior, at least the onset, is controlled by specific odorants exuded by the ripe female. In the sense that man is a predominantly visual animal, he seems to be closer to the birds than to the rat. A recent study indicating that man can smell the different phases of a woman's menstrual cycle and the success of perfume manufacturers notwithstanding, a good visual pornographic film is more exciting than any odor. Can you visualize (or smell, if you will) paying money to sit in an olfactorium (an auditorium for the nose), eyes closed and nostrils flared, enjoying the latest production of *Deep Nares?* We don't even have the appropriate vocabulary to describe such an event. On the screen, an actress "appears," but what does an odor do? It wafts, it hangs, it sits, it smells. Only the last, "it smells," is not a phrase with visual connotations. Clearly, olfaction has a low order of behavioral control for humans. It would be interesting to do a word count in several different languages to determine the relative proportion of words derived from the different sensory modalities; or to explore the relative frequencies of these words as a function of age.

Let us now return to the pigeon whom we left surrounded by an external environment of visual stimulation, and surrounding his own internal environment of hunger-produced stimulation. When the pigeon emits a response, this response occurs in the presence of some particular set of external and internal stimuli. These stimuli, to a large extent, are controlled by the experimenter. On the internal side, it is the experimenter who controls the bird's food supply and keeps him reasonably hungry. On the external side, it is the experimenter who puts the bird in the Skinner box, where he can see only what the experimenter deems to be important.

Stimuli that occur when an emitted response is reinforced become important for the future elicitation of that response. In technical language the stimulus that is paired with the reinforced response becomes the controlling stimulus. It becomes the occasion for the response to be given again.

In the Skinner box, for example, the pigeon may be reinforced for pecking at a translucent plastic disc that is set into one end of the box about beak high. Behind the disc is a small switch. When the bird pecks at the disc, an electrical signal is generated. This signal results in the lifting of a tray of grain located below the pecking key, thus allowing the bird access to the reinforcement.

There are two procedures that can be used to train the bird to peck at the disc. One is called shaping and the other is called auto-shaping or self-shaping. Since these are the first stages in any training program, whether it be for pigeon or man, it is worth going into them in some detail. In addition, all along the route of shaping there are numerous instances of the acquisition of stimulus control.

The hungry bird is placed in the training chamber. The chamber is a relatively small cubicle about 18 by 18 by 18 inches. One wall, as already described, has the pecking key and the food hopper. A small 10-watt bulb, located in the ceiling, provides general illumination within the box. A constant, fairly loud hum produced by an interior fan, and the fact that the box is, to some degree, designed to be soundproof, tend to eliminate auditory distractions from outside the box. For the bird, the inside of the box must indeed be rather drab; there is neither color, complex patterns nor movement to engage his attention. All of this is purposefully designed to increase his receptiveness to the experimenter's manipulations.

The first goal, then, is simply to get the bird to reliably peck at the translucent disc. If the bird were a human, even a two- or three-year-old child, the task would be very simple, and could be accomplished through verbal instruction. "Press that button, please." And when the child presses you can reinforce the response with an M&M candy, a marble or a good word. The child will press the button again, very quickly, even without the verbal command. Things go a little bit more slowly with the lower animal subjects.

The shaping procedure substitutes for the verbal instruction. (Earlier in life the child also had to be shaped to respond to the verbal message.) Upon being placed in the box, the hungry pigeon appears to strut about aimlessly. The clever experimenter, knowing that the way to the pigeon's brain is through his beak, leaves the food hopper in the up position so that the bird can eat freely. A small light over the hopper makes the food readily visible against the dull background of the apparatus.

After the bird has eaten freely for a few minutes, the hopper drops back out of reach and the light that illuminates it is extinguished. The pigeon may spend a few more seconds poking his head into the empty hole where once the food had been, but he soon leaves this activity and resumes his small wanderings within the confines of the apparatus. Since the space is very limited, the bird, during his perambulations, soon returns to the location of the feeder.

All the time that this is going on, the bird is being spied upon by the experimenter. Through a one-way glass the investigator observes the bird, and when the bird approaches the area of the food hopper, the investigator presses a button which causes the hopper to be raised with a very audible thud. At the same time the grain, which now, again, can be reached, is illuminated.

The lighting of the food compartment already has been developed as a controlling stimulus for eliciting feeding responses. It will be remembered that several minutes earlier the bird had been eating from the lighted compartment and had been unable to eat when similar pokings of the head were performed into the dark food compartment. These are the conditions for creating stimulus control. The response that is reinforced reliably occurs in the company of a particular environmental stimulus; while the absence of that environmental stimulus reliably signifies that, no matter what the response, reinforcement is not available. That the light became an effective stimulus for controlling the feeding behavior can be tested by switching on the hopper light while at the same time not having any grain available to the bird. With the presence of the light the bird will repeatedly poke his head into the food compartment before the behavior is extinguished; while he will rarely, if ever, poke his head into the dark compartment. Nor would he have placed his head in the lighted compartment before the light had been paired with the food reinforcement. Clearly, then, food-seeking responses are being controlled by the light.

In the course of a half hour of this type of training, the food hopper may be presented and withdrawn as many as fifty or sixty times. The duration of each grain-availability event may be fairly long, waiting for the bird, at first seemingly indifferent, to respond. Then, gradually, as the bird learns to respond more quickly to the appearance of the grain, the time of availability is shortened to as little as one second. The bird appears to maximize the amount that he can consume in that short period by staying close to the source of food, sometimes even with his head lowered and one eye cocked toward the food well.

Since each food presentation is accompanied by the mechanical thump of the food hopper, which is then followed by grain ingestion, the thump also gains stimulus control over eating. After many occasions of the pairing of thump and eating, if the animal happens to be facing away from the hopper and unable to see either the grain or the special illumination when the food is presented, the sound of the hopper being raised into feeding position will be sufficient to cause the bird to turn rapidly toward the source of food, to approach and to eat. Again one can test this control more formally by removing the light and the grain. The thump of the hopper will be found to be sufficient to elicit an approach response to the hopper.

Now the bird is eating quickly each time the food hopper is raised. And the behavior is controlled by both visual and auditory stimuli. If the food is presented on a regular and rapid schedule, let's say every four seconds, for one second, one can observe the bird rhythmically raising and ducking his head in time to the programmed occurrence of the food. The bird, who only half an hour ago was wandering indifferently around the test chamber, is now a highly motivated goal-directed creature performing with machinelike regularity and precision.

When confronted with this accomplishment, self-styled humanistic scholars, ignorant schoolboys and the ladies of the ASPCA cry out,

"Nineteen Eighty-four," and shake their heads disapprovingly at what they see as a not too distant threat to their human freedom and dignity. But we are not mad scientists uncovering laws of behavior that should be better left buried because of the potential dangers of these laws being used by unscrupulous politicians. Politicians have tools available to them now which are many times more powerful, and which already use principles of reinforcement. The problem is that these laws are not stated explicitly and therefore the manner in which they are successfully applied is not understood. By publicly exposing these laws we make the individual less, rather than more, susceptible to external control.

The first example comes from a series of demonstrations developed by Martin Orne.[4] Orne was interested in studying the behavioral characteristics which make the hypnotic state different from the normal waking state. To do this he had to find some tasks which normally awake subjects would refuse to complete. These tasks would be administered to both hypnotically behaving subjects and normal subjects. The length of the time spent working on the tasks, a behavioral criterion, might then be used to differentiate between the two populations. One group of subjects was given the task of adding all of the two-number pairs which appeared on a sheet of paper. Each sheet contained 224 such pairs, and the subject was confronted with a stack of 2000 sheets. Subjects continued to work on this boring, meaningless task for several hours. With one subject, the experimenter left the room saying that he would eventually return. Five and one half hours later the subject was still busily at work adding the numbers.

The investigators continued the search for a simple task that subjects would refuse to participate in for long periods of time. Subjects were given the same task as described above. However, each time they completed a sheet, they had to pick a card from a pile in front of them and to follow the instructions that were written on the card. Every card in the large pile contained identical instructions: "You are to tear up the sheet of paper which you have just completed into a minimum of thirty-two pieces and go to the next sheet of paper and continue working as you did before; when you have completed this piece of paper, pick up the next card, which will instruct you further. Work as accurately and as rapidly as you can." To the amazement of the experimenters, subjects again continued to work on this meaningless task for several hours, and with little loss in speed or accuracy.

These demonstrations show what subjects are willing to do to themselves. Note that they behave very much like our pigeon, working quickly and rhythmically, in mechanical fashion. At least the pigeons were getting food. Another example will show what the human is willing, under certain conditions, to do not only to himself but to other humans.

The experiments described below were conducted by Stanley Milgram,[5] and have received wide-ranging publicity not only because of the implications of the results but also because of the ethical questions that they raised. The paradigm is quite simple. The experimental environment consists of two rooms connected by an intercom system. A confederate of the investigator, the investigator himself and the real subject of the experiment enter one of the rooms. The subject watches as the investigator straps the confederate into an "electric chair." The confederate is in the employ of the investigator and has to act out a preplanned role. The real subject of the experiment is then brought by the white-jacketed scientist into the second room. He is told that the person strapped in the chair is participating in a learning experiment. The subject is led to believe that he is required to administer shocks, at certain prescribed times, to the fellow on the other side. He is told that if the person in the other room continues to make mistakes in learning a list of words, the intensity of the shock can be increased. The experimenter stays with the subject and urges him to raise the shock level with each succeeding error. The shock is seemingly delivered from an ominous-looking box with a series of buttons indicating the intensity of shock; according to the numbers, the shock can be raised in 15-volt intervals from a low of 15 to a high of 450 volts marked "danger, extreme shock." The accomplice, of course, does not get shocked but expresses increasing discomfort as the subject raises the intensity of the shock, and finally shrieks with agony. The appalling result was that a large percentage of subjects continued to administer the shock. One cannot even argue that they realized that the setup was a fraud. The subject himself frequently exhibited signs of severe stress even while administering the shock, and some burst into tears and uncontrollable sobbing.

These subjects were drawn from a wide variety of backgrounds. Not only the usual college sophomores but also farmers, businessmen and professionals participated in these experiments. Who would have anticipated that such behavior could be obtained from an American population? From a fascist-oriented German in the 1930s and early 1940s, certainly. But from Americans? Was Thomas Hobbes, the seventeenth-century English philosopher, far from the modern mark when he described primeval man as "poor, nasty and brutish"? That these ordinary Americans obeyed the commands of the scientist ("Whether the learner likes it or not, you must go on until he has learned all the word pairs correctly. So please go on"), disregarding the pleas of the person in the next room, should make us stop and wonder. Subjects from similar backgrounds when *asked* how they would behave in a similar situation almost invariably denied that they would be willing to inflict pain on another person.

These examples, again, do *not* depend on conditioning, and show that degradation of human qualities does not necessarily derive from mechanistic models of behavior, conditioning or otherwise, but rather derives from the human condition itself, which can only be improved or made less lethal by free and open investigations of behavioral laws. We should not be scared off by the ignorant and the faint-hearted who conjure up the specter of a Master Controller imposing His will on the population. On the contrary, we should pursue, with all vigor, the investigation of the laws of behavior. It is only by exposing the laws to examination that we allow the exercise of our fullest potential and become less subject to irrational, demeaning and self-serving external control.

Milgram, in discussing the implications of these experiments, cogently quotes from Harold J. Laski's essay "The Dangers of Obedience" (1929):

"Civilization means, above all, an unwillingness to inflict unnecessary pain. Within the ambit of that definition, those of us who heedlessly accept the commands of authority cannot yet claim to be civilized men . . . our business, if we desire to live a life not utterly devoid of meaning and significance, is to accept nothing which contradicts our basic experience merely because it comes to us from tradition or convention or authority. It may well be that we shall be wrong; but our self-expression is thwarted at the root unless the certainties that we are asked to accept coincide with the certainties of experience. That is why the condition of freedom in any state is always a widespread and consistent skepticism of the canons upon which power insists."

What better way to cultivate this skepticism than by experimentation designed to expose the laws of behavioral control?

Now that we have the data from experiments such as the ones described, we must disseminate this information to the public in such a way that we become aware of the mechanisms of control and of our own fallibilities. As experimental psychologists we are not providing tools to would-be dictators, we are strengthening the resistance to tyrannical abuse.

When we left our pigeon, pages ago, in the middle of an experiment, he was found to be eating away, if not merrily, at least vigorously. Presumably, he was unaware that the psychologist was controlling his eating. The next step was to transfer control of the reinforcement to a response that was emitted by the bird. It will be recalled that a few inches above the grain hopper there was a translucent white plastic disc resting against a microswitch. The disc was illuminated from behind. A tap of the beak on the disc was sufficient to raise the food hopper. By pecking at the disc, the bird could achieve the result that previously had been initiated either by the experimenter pressing a button or by the automatic signals generated from the programming equipment.

How to get the bird to peck at the lighted disc? In many cases it would be sufficient if the experimenter exhibited patience and went away. Upon his return he would probably find the bird pecking at the key, eating, pecking, eating, at a steady pace. Pigeons have a natural inclination to peck at bright objects. Since each peck results in the light over the hopper being turned on and the clank of the hopper being raised, these controlling stimuli ensure that the disc-pecking response is soon followed by eating the food. In this way the pecking response comes to be consistently reinforced, and by that, increases the probability of the response being again emitted.

Another way of getting the bird to peck at the key is by "shaping" the response. Here the procedure is the same, in principle, as that followed for training the pigeon to come to the food hopper. With food being withheld, the animal again becomes restless and moves around within the vicinity of the food source. When his head is close to the pecking disc and facing in the direction of the disc, the food hopper is manually triggered. After consuming the food the bird is likely to assume the same pose that just preceded the reinforcement. The experimenter waits, however, until the pigeon's beak is a little bit closer to the disc than the previous time. When this occurs food is again presented. This process is repeated until eventually the beak hits the disc. Watching birds being shaped in this manner gives the onlooker the impression of some magical force gradually pushing the animal into the disc. But it is only the judicious application of reinforcement for the appropriate responses. Once the procedure is explained, even a six-year-old child can train the bird to peck at the disc.

As with the previous response, at first, when the experimenter removes himself from the situation, the animal responds to the disc sporadically. But within several minutes he may be found to be bobbing up and down pecking the key with his beak, lowering his head into the food chamber to eat, pecking, lowering, pecking. He has mastered a new response to receive food.

Having established control of the pecking response to the disc, the next step was to begin the first formal, but still preliminary discrimination problem. The disc is always present in the testing apparatus. If some additional stimulus-control procedures were not instituted, the animal would be pecking constantly at the key, thereby limiting the amount of information that the experimenter could obtain from him. However, by having the food reinforcement follow a peck of the disc only when the disc is illuminated, and never follow a peck of the disc when it is not illuminated, the animal soon learns to peck only when the circular patch of plastic is lit. The pecking response has now come under control of yet another stimulus.

All of the pigeon's attention is focused on the pecking disc. He must constantly monitor it to see if the disc light is on or off. In this way he can maximize the amount of food that he can get, and minimize the amount of effort expended. One can test to see if the discrimination has been obtained by comparing the number of responses to the lit key with the number of responses to the unlit key, taking care to make certain that the opportunity for responding is the same for both conditions. When this is done it becomes quite apparent that the bird's pecking behavior is under control of the illuminated key. Indeed after a half-hour session the bird will respond consistently to the key when lit, and withhold all responding in the unlit condition.

Now the stage was set to introduce the stimuli that are of prime importance for this study, the photographic slides containing man-made and non-man-made objects. Eighty photographs were chosen, 40 of each type. The photographs were then made into 35-mm. transparent slides. The slides were loaded into the 80-unit tray of a Carousel-type projector in an almost random order. Only one limitation on the randomness was imposed. The number of positive (man-made) or negative (non-man-made) slides that could appear consecutively was limited to two, and in later tests three. This was done to prevent the pigeons from developing sets or tendencies to respond continuously.

For thirty days, at the same time each day, the hungry birds were brought into the laboratory and placed in the conditioning chamber. The slides were back-projected onto the pecking disc from outside the chamber. From the bird's-eye view, what was seen was the pecking disc either illuminated or not, and if it was illuminated it contained a clear picture, either one with the man-made objects or one without those objects.

Each day the animal received all 80 slides on three consecutive occasions, thus being provided with 240 trials per day, 120 with each stimulus category. If we analyze the situation that the bird faced, there were only four sets of possible relationships between what appeared on the disc and what the bird could do:

1 A positive slide was presented and the subject pecked the disc.
2 A positive slide was presented and the subject refrained from pecking the disc.
3 A negative slide was presented and the subject pecked at the disc.
4 A negative slide was presented and the subject refrained from pecking the disc.

It was decided that pecking at the man-made stimulus would be followed by food reinforcement (thus the designation of this slide category as positive), and that pecking at the non-man-made stimulus would not be followed by food (thus the negative designation). One could just as well have reversed this arrangement with little change in the results.[6]

The exact contingencies for all four possibilities were as follows: For case 1, where the subject responded to the positive slide: immediately following the response, the food hopper was presented for one and one half seconds and then the next slide appeared.

For case 2, where the subject did *not* respond to the positive slide: the slide remained visible for two seconds and was thereupon followed by the next slide.

For case 3, where the subject responded to the negative slide: immediately following the response, a tone was activated and the tone and slide remained on for a total of six seconds from the time of response; at the end of this period the next slide was presented.

For case 4, where the subject did not respond to the negative slide: the slide remained visible for two seconds and was thereupon followed by the next slide.

The equipment for controlling these contingencies consisted primarily of timers, relays and a large stepping switch. The stepping switch served to correlate responses to positive or negative slides with the delivery of reinforcement or punishment. Responses were recorded on a paper-tape printout. This gave us information about which specific slides the birds responded to and which they did not respond to.

As one might expect, during the first several days of training the birds responded to the disc each time that it was lit, irrespective of whether a positive or a negative slide was displayed on it. But with each day of training there was a gradual improvement in performance. The pecks became more and more concentrated on the slides of man-made objects. By the twentieth day the performance had reached its maximum and remained at that level for the next ten days. The birds, on the average, responded to a little over 90 percent of the positive slides correctly (that is, by pecking), while they responded to 80 percent of the negative slides correctly (that is, by not pecking). Performance was considerably better than indicated by those figures since most of the mistakes were contributed by one bird. Philby, for example, over the last ten days of training made mistakes on only seven of 80 slides. He pecked at two slides containing non-man-made objects, and failed to peck reliably at five slides containing man-made objects. An analysis of the data indicated that the few slides that were responded to incorrectly most of the time, were, to a large extent, the same slides for all the subjects.

Given the fact that the subjects reliably responded to man-made stimuli as compared to non-man-made stimuli, could we conclude that the pigeon was capable of forming the high-order concept of man-madeness? It is the essence of science to be cautious in regard to conclusions, and to be open to the possibility that there are other, competing explanations that can, equally well, account for the obtained data. What are some of the other possible explanations of the pigeons' performance that can be evaluated against the explanation that we proposed? It will be remembered that the original expectation was that the pigeons would learn to *abstract out* the significant stimulus dimension that characterizes man-made, and that their behavior would come to be controlled by that stimulus.

Nevertheless, the test that was just described does afford several alternative explanations. Perhaps the pigeons learned the serial order of the slides. There were 90 complete cycles over the thirty days of training. Could the birds have learned the unchanging order of the slides within the cycle? This becomes somewhat plausible since the order was not completely random but had some internal structure resulting from the fact that we limited the number of successive positives or successive negatives to two.

Another possible explanation for the results is that, instead of learning the concept, the birds learned 80 distinct associations. That is, they learned to attach a response to each slide independent of its relationship to other slides that were presented.

Both of the above hypotheses would seem to require even more from the bird than the attainment of a concept. In the first case the bird would have to memorize the order of 80 items (although not completely independent of each other). In the second case the bird would have to memorize 80 separate stimulus-response associations. Both capabilities seem to be beyond the reach of this bird brain; but then, one might well argue, so is the capability of forming a high-order concept such as man-made.

Rather than attempt to win the argument by an indirect, rational approach, we performed the necessary experiments to test whether these hypotheses were plausible. In regard to the serial-order hypothesis, the appropriate test would be to take the same birds and the same stimuli, and then to simply rearrange the order of stimuli so that the pattern of positives and negatives was different from that encountered in the first experiment. This is exactly what we did. In fact, we did this several times, each time with a different order. The birds behaved almost exactly as in the first test. They reliably pecked at the positive slides and withheld responding to the negative slides.

In regard to the second alternative hypothesis, the learning of 80 discrete associations, the test is equally straightforward. New slides, which the birds had never seen before, were introduced. If the birds responded appropriately to these slides, then responding could only be controlled by the stimuli representing man-made versus non-man-made. Again, the tests showed that the birds were under control of the appropriate stimulus dimension. They had achieved the high-order concept of man-made.

Further verification of this finding came from results obtained when the slides were turned around, every which way, to one of the seven new positions not seen during initial training. (In addition to the 90°, 180° and 270° turn for the original training side, there are the four turns for the obverse side.) The animals' performance was again such that the man-made versus non-man-made slides were reliably discriminated from each other.

In summary, the results of these experiments indicate that the pigeons were capable of discriminating higher-order visual stimuli. They discriminated successfully between photographs containing man-made objects and those containing non-man-made objects. It would seem probable that they had isolated one or more stimulus properties common to photographs of man-made objects.

Could we now go back to the computer engineers and photo-reconnaissance experts working on the SAMOS program and say, "Here is the answer." Not yet. All we could reasonably conclude is that there were some stimulus properties, properties that lie in the two-dimensional picture (and not in the head), which serve to differentiate between man-made objects and non-man-made objects. And, since the pigeon was capable of discovering what these properties were, there was hope that we, the humans, might be able to do the same. We had provided an existence theorem for those properties. But what were these seemingly mysterious and elusive properties? How could we get the bird to tell us what information he was using?

By studying the similarities and differences in the visual composition between slides that were consistently responded to correctly and those that were consistently responded to incorrectly, one could construct testable hypotheses concerning the nature of the invariant-stimulus properties in the two sets of complex images. We asked several human judges to look at the slides associated with consistent patterns of errors and correct responses, and to attempt to derive the critical stimulus parameters from their own observations of the birds' choices and errors.

It is evident that any complex pattern or scene from the environment can be described in terms of many different stimulus parameters: distribution of light and dark areas, contrasts, intensities, uniformity of textures, axes of symmetry, etc. The slides of man-made and non-man-made objects contain instances of all of these parameters in varying combinations. The verbal reports of our human judges suggested that at least one of three stimulus properties could account for the ability of the bird to make this highly complex discrimination. The three stimulus hypotheses that were derived from these reports are presented below, followed by a more exact description of how they were generated.

1   The pigeons were responding to slides containing straight lines and/or approximately 90° angles.

2   The pigeons were responding to slides which contain *all* of the following characteristics: light and dark areas distributed throughout the slides; high contrast between the light and dark areas; and approximately half of the total area of the slides being light and half dark.

3   The pigeons were operating under both hypothesis 1 and hypothesis 2.

     Naturally, the converse of each of these hypotheses would also have to be considered.

1A   The pigeons were avoiding slides which do not contain straight lines and/or approximately 90° angles.

2A   The pigeons were avoiding slides which do not contain *all* of the following characteristics: light and dark areas distributed throughout the slides; high contrast between the light and dark areas; and approximately half of the total area of the slides being light and half being dark.

3A   The pigeons were operating under both hypothesis 1A and hypothesis 2A.

The following is a description of the process involved in deriving the first three hypotheses.

It was decided to concentrate on the properties to which the pigeons were responding. The term "responding" will be used as meaning a pecking response rather than a correct response of pecking or avoiding. First, the projected positive training slides which were responded to correctly were studied by a human observer to determine their common properties. These were examined while they were projected onto the pecking key. The majority of these positive slides contained straight lines and/or approximately 90° angles; thus, the first hypothesis.

Next the negative slides which had been responded to consistently were examined for common properties. These slides plus several of the positive ones contained light and dark areas distributed throughout the slide, high contrast between the areas, and about half of the total area of the slide was light and half dark; thus, the second hypothesis. Not forgetting the possibility that the pigeons could be operating under more than one hypothesis, the third hypothesis was suggested; namely, that the pigeons were operating under both hypothesis 1 and hypothesis 2.

To test each of the hypotheses, the 100 slides, 80 from the original acquisition series and 20 from the two generalization tests, were segregated on the basis of whether or not the slide was responded to on 70 percent or more of the trials. This was done separately for slides used with each bird. A similar procedure was followed for not responding on 70 percent or more of the trials. This division was done independently of whether the slide was positive or negative. Therefore a small number of incorrectly categorized slides were included in each sample. Following this, an independent observer, not knowing anything about the experiment, was given the description of the hypothetical properties to which the birds were responding, and asked to indicate the presence or absence of each property in the photographs.

The correspondence of the human observer's judgments of the presence of a particular stimulus with that of the birds' responding was remarkably high. The results indicate that hypothesis 1, concerning the presence of straight lines and/or right angles, was the most potent. For the three birds that were tested in this manner hypothesis 1 accounted for responding to 76 percent of the positive slides and for not responding to 92 percent of the negative slides, for an overall correct performance of 84 percent. With the addition of hypothesis 2, concerning contrast and the distribution of light and dark, less than 10 percent of the slides remained unaccounted for. It also should be noted that there was very little overlap between the slides related to hypothesis 1 and those related to hypothesis 2. Either stimulus condition could occur in the absence of the other. Furthermore, either stimulus condition alone could control the disc-pecking behavior; the presence of both dimensions together was not a necessary condition for eliciting the response.

More work is needed to refine the hypotheses into more exact physicalistic terms. One possible way to do this is to use a computer to simulate the properties being investigated while controlling for the presence or absence of other properties. This, of course, is very difficult to do with natural photographs.

Nevertheless, the approach used in the experiment provided a method for determining the presence of invariant properties in complex images. At the very least, it provided a method for demonstrating the presence of such higher-order stimuli, and at best it may provide the data for inducing what these properties are. Although the proposed inductive method for studying invariant properties is conceptually simple, experience has shown that building with the rocks of empiricism requires considerable perseverance.

Our results were not received with very much enthusiasm; in fact, for the most part they were considerably ignored, not an unusual response to this type of research. Whatever little impact they had was probably greater in the psychological community of theoretical psychology than in the military establishment which commissioned the work in the first place.[7]

The implications for theoretical psychology are clear. Evidence has been provided that even a lowly bird brain is capable, with the proper conditions of training, of forming a very complex concept. This capability might, at an earlier time, have been reserved as a specially human characteristic. This is but one demonstration, added to a variety of others, that should increase our admiration for the other members of the animal kingdom.

It has long been recognized that animals are capable of forming simple concepts, where the stimulus dimension is easily specifiable.

The concepts include: size, color, triangularity, numbers, novelty, patterns, guided-missile targets, bad parts on an assembly line.

More recently, the work on concept formation in animals has been extended to more complex stimulus dimensions, ones that the experimenter cannot specify in stimulus terms but are nevertheless highly reliable classifications on the basis of object qualities. In particular, several recent papers,[8] in addition to the work just described, have reported on the ability of pigeons to form high-order abstract visual concepts. These studies examined the ability of the pigeon to discriminate between the class of visual images described as containing a person and another class characterized by the absence of a person. Our study goes one step further, to an even more complex concept. It demonstrated that pigeons can learn the difference between creations made by man and creations that are not man-made; between cultural artifacts and natural artifacts. Depending on how you look at it, this either brings us closer to the level of animals or brings animals closer to the human level. No matter which way, it further reinforces the idea that there is a behavioral continuity from animal to man as well as a biological continuity. If this serves to evoke in us more humility, and a little more thoughtfulness as to our position in the universe, it will have performed a useful service.

It might be interesting to explore some other possible uses that can be made of the pigeon's ability to attain the concept man-made. If we agree that the pigeon, as we have trained him, is an unbiased observer of the human scene, at least to the degree that he categorizes man-made and not man-made only on the basis of stimulus properties in the environment, and not on any preconceived scales distorted by his own needs, values and expectations, then the following somewhat titillating scenario becomes possible.

Archeologists have long been obsessed with the problem of discovering whether certain objects were made by manlike creatures. What can the chipped pieces of flint or obsidian found in the cave of Stone Age inhabitants and dated as being 2,500,000 years old tell us about the nature of the creatures that used these objects? Professor Antrobus photographs the presumed artifacts, and then prepares them into slides in order to show to Philby the pigeon. Philby, impeccably trained for the Air Force, has a new job, to provide Dr. Antrobus with information about these prehistoric objects. Just as Antrobus routinely uses carbon-14 dating methods to ascertain the age of an object, he uses Philby to tell him whether or not the object was made by man. If Philby reliably pecks at the transparent key onto which the photograph is projected, then Antrobus concludes that manlike creatures existed hundreds of thousands of years earlier than the last claim for priority. If Philby shakes his head no, not pecking at the projected image, then the following possibilities emerge: (1) the creature that used it was still humanoid but he did not make the artifact, (2) the creature that used it did make it but the creature is not to be considered humanoid or (3) the creature that used it was not humanoid and the object was not manufactured. It would seem that these logical complications can be simplified by making the assumption that all manufactured items are man-made. But one has only to be reminded of a few of the hundreds of manufactured items produced by animals other than humans—bird's nests and beehives, rat mazes and chimpanzee paintings. It is an open question, to be decided by experiment, whether the products of these animals' activities would be classified by the pigeon as man-made. In some cases the answer would appear to be almost certainly "yes," as with the beautifully regular hexagonal cells composing the honeycomb of the bee. And yet it might also be possible that with further discrimination training the pigeon could learn, even here, to discriminate between man-made and not man-made. If not, the concept man-made might better be labeled organismic-made.

I suspect that, in fact, this would be the case, that only the ability to form hierarchical concepts is limited to man. A hierarchical concept is demonstrated by using a specific stimulus configuration as a representative of a number of different classification categories each of which has a different zone of limitation. Thus the stimulus configuration called Man is at one and the same time a representative of the increasingly broadly defined categories of Primate, Mammal, Vertebrate, Organism.

Another task that might be put to Philby would involve presenting him with the paintings of primates, children and artists of, for example, the Abstract Expressionist school. I am not suggesting this experiment in order to demean the artist (or to elevate the monkey). On the contrary, I am a devoted admirer of the works of Franz Kline and Jackson Pollock. But might it not be possible in this manner to get at a measure of the degree of rationality exhibited in a painting or in the style of a painter? I am reasonably certain, by the way, that it would be possible to train a pigeon to differentiate between the works of two different artists. However, it would have to be between the works of artists and not just painters, because one of the ways of characterizing an artist, as opposed to a dabbler, is that the artist has a consistent style. That is to say, there are elements in common across different paintings done by the same hand. These elements may diverge with the time between paintings. However, within a given period, these similarities allow us to identify two or more different paintings as being created by the same artist even though we do not know who that artist may be. The ability to make these judgments of similarity once again must depend on responding to common stimulus elements or patterns. Theoretically, then, we should be able to train the pigeon to do the same. Perhaps he could also be sensitive enough to detect forgeries. The art expert frequently makes this discrimination on the basis of extra-visual cues. Such clues might include the type of material of the canvas or a chemical analysis of the pigments. These cues would certainly not be available to the bird.

Man is not a man-made object, at least not in the sense that we have been speaking about him here. But the drawing, painting or sculpturing done by a human, of a man, does meet the criteria for being man-made. Would the pigeon classify such products as being man-made? Not having any experimental data on this subject, one can only speculate. My guess is that the pigeon would not be able to differentiate between photographs of real men and photographs of realistic representations of man (indeed humans themselves might find the task to be quite difficult). Perhaps that is one of the special qualities of the human condition, that it is only man that can create something man-made with the guile to make it appear natural to even the pigeon (although the rarity of pigeons alighting on people as compared to the statues of people seems to belie this conclusion).

As a final digression, what conclusions would you draw if you were told that Philby responded to certain photographs from Mars by vigorously pecking at the projection screen? He did not, but perhaps only because the experiment has yet to be conducted.

5

Project PAPP:
Planning for
the All-Purpose Pigeon

In the early part of 1966, Dr. Gene Bernard and I founded Behavior Systems Inc. At that time we were trying to convince the Air Force that if they were going to seriously pursue the use of organic systems for reconnaissance and intelligence purposes in such a way that research would have an impact on operations, then a generalized, broad-scoped development program would have to be established.

Training a pigeon is not like constructing a rocket. There are built-in time delays that are virtually impossible to overcome. It takes a certain number of days to make an animal hungry, another set number of days to train him on simple discriminations, etc. Adding more money, people and space to such a project has little effect on the overall duration. Also, with any new project there is a certain start-up period, which may last from two or three months upward, even on the order of years, depending on the nature of the project. Add to this that there were many training techniques that had not yet been tried or even developed, and one can see why a long-range development program was required.

Our first contract was to help the Air Force to define the requirements for such a development program. The specific goal was to prepare research guidelines and to identify the resources needed for a reconnaissance pigeon,[1] a bird that would go out, get information and bring it back, much like the German pigeons over the Maginot Line were supposed to have done.

The results of our efforts showed the complexities of adapting apparently simple problems of animal training for use in the field. To gain an appreciation of these problems, it is worthwhile to discuss the program in some detail.

The first step in the analysis was to describe the mission requirements in their most general, all-inclusive form. We did not want to define a system that would be limited to, for example, detecting tanks, or detecting ships. Rather, we wanted to know what were the general requirements for any usable airborne biological reconnaissance system. The multiplicity of mission goals, designated by identifying different target types, is more apparent than real. They all follow the same paradigm. The most generalized version of that paradigm employs the following functional steps:

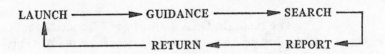

LAUNCH is the point at which the pigeon is separated from his transport and from which his guided trajectory to a search area begins. GUIDANCE is the process by which the animal moves to the area in which search will occur. SEARCH is the pattern of movement that is required over the target area in order to make the target available for detection. REPORT is the stage at which, upon completion of the detection response by the animal, a specified report response is made so that the military personnel who are monitoring the system are informed that a target has been located. RETURN refers to the animal's coming back to the launch point.

The above scheme is only a general outline. For each major function there are a number of possible alternatives for reaching a solution. An analysis of these alternatives provides the most feasible way to accomplish the mission goal. Where answers are not available either from logical analysis or past investigation, then new researches must be instituted. The goal of our project, then, was to establish the information requirements for writing a set of working specifications for a general-purpose reconnaissance pigeon.

Now let us take a look at each functional step separately, and examine the possible methods for achieving the function.

LAUNCH SYSTEM

From Ground

There are two alternatives at this phase, and they differ with respect to such variables as logistics of sensor deployment, support requirements, animal-training regime, handler training and animal-transport requirements. In terms of support systems it would clearly be advantageous to launch the sensor from a vehicle. This would facilitate carrying adequate transport cages (and, of course, more than one) and complex reinforcers. Alternatively, launch from a hand-carried system, such as would be likely to occur with use of animal sensors by combat patrol personnel, would place considerably more stringent restrictions on support capabilities. It would also require special transport design, adaptation training of the sensor to being carried on the person and corresponding changes in handler training and handler equipment.

In general, the differences between the two systems are not major, and for any ground-launch system we recommended that the system be designed with both possibilities in mind. There are two substantial reasons for this recommendation. One is that it produces a highly flexible sensor capability which covers—so far as launch problems are concerned—the majority of ground-launch situations. Another is that, within reason, divergence from extreme specificity and rigidity of environmental conditions under which training and performance are accomplished will tend to produce more stable and reliable performance characteristics on the part of the animal sensor.

From Air

Again, there are two relevant alternatives: the sensor is launched from a substantially high-speed platform or a low-speed one. From a high-speed platform the launch system requires special protection for the sensor. The most obvious possibility is the use of a launch canister which protects the sensor during ejection from the aircraft. It is only necessary to slow the canister's descent (e.g., by parachute) and arrange a release system either at a predetermined altitude or upon contact with the ground.

Launch from a low-speed platform, though airborne (e.g., helicopter), is simpler than from a high-speed platform in that the special protection requirements are minimized. For most purposes this alternative may be regarded as similar to the ground-vehicle launch system.

Airborne launching was recommended because a solution for the airborne-launch problems would also provide the answers for a ground-launch system. However, the converse is not true. Therefore, by solving the airborne-launch problem maximum flexibility is obtained.

Although it would appear that the method of launch would be dependent on the method of guidance, this is not the case. The best method of launch, and this would be true in all choices, is that which requires least training. For example, for the pigeon, some work has been done which suggested that releasing the pigeon from a tube results in the bird flying a straight-on course from that tube, much like a bullet from a gun.[2] Employment of such a basic tube-launch procedure for guidance was, therefore, recommended.

GUIDANCE SYSTEM

Pretrained Guidance

There are several variants of this type of guidance. If the bird is to be trained to go to a given type of terrain, such as jungle, it is necessary first to demonstrate that terrain discriminations are learnable by the bird. While no data exist to directly demonstrate such discrimination capability in the pigeon, it is quite likely that such discriminations are easily accomplished. Furthermore, in many reconnaissance operations one might expect that search would be most desirable in thickly wooded areas. Since in typical operations it would often be possible to release the bird over or near a wooded area to be searched, fine discriminations on terrain would seldom be necessary. Indeed, whenever the bird could be released over the area to be searched the whole guidance problem becomes trivial.

Guidance by fixed direction can be carried out in two ways: by compass direction or by direct aiming of the bird at the time of launch. Compass direction is not a likely possibility, despite its seductive relationship to the well-known homing capabilities of many strains of pigeons. Direct aiming is very likely a better alternative, due to the propensity of pigeons to fly a straight path out of a chute. It would be necessary to explore the limitations on exploitation of this phenomenon, but we may assume that facilitation of such behavior by training can probably be accomplished. Any consideration of this kind of guidance system would require close examination of many critical variables besides its susceptibility to training: e.g., the extent to which the behavior would be weak, in the sense that the animal might easily be diverted from a trajectory.

Guidance by preset route is one of the most attractive possibilities, insofar as it represents an easily learned paradigm for the pigeon. But it is only feasible where there is indeed a route to follow, such as a road or trail which is distinguishable by the organism. In many proposed applications this will be the case, as in detection of ambush installations, and in use of the animal as a homing-missile target on road intersections, dams, railroad bridges and comparable targets which constitute identifiable interruptions along distinguishable routes.

Direct Flight Response Control

Theoretically, this guidance system may prove to be feasible. It would require that the bird be trained to make ascents, descents, right and left turns to different signals which would be telemetered from a monitoring station to the bird. The monitor would have to receive information from the bird as to his current position. This information could be obtained either by direct visual contact or by radio signals transmitted from the bird. Knowing the position of the bird, the monitor would then transmit back to him a correction signal. A low-frequency tone in the right ear, for example, might be the pre-trained stimulus for a right turn. It may also be possible to use signals that are delivered to small electrodes implanted in the brain. This latter approach would probably reduce the weight requirements on the flying bird. In fact, weight is one of the major drawbacks of the approach.

At a minimum the bird must carry a receiver. In addition, he may also be required to carry a transmitter. The added weight may reduce the performance of the animal. Some studies already have investigated how much weight different species of birds can carry, and in what position it can be carried most efficiently. Strapped to the outside of the body, probably along the midline between the wings, the turkey vulture is capable of flying with a load of 250 grams; mallard duck, 100 grams; crow, 90 grams; starling, 12 grams. If the weight is implanted in the peritoneum (the body cavity surrounding the internal organs), then the load-carrying capacity becomes: turkey vulture, 160 grams; mallard duck, 100 grams; crow, 40 grams; starling, 12 grams.[3]

It is not clear why the pigeon was not included in these studies, but it is reasonable to assume that the capability of the common pigeon would fall somewhere between the starling and the crow. In terms of modern electronic circuitry, if the pigeon can carry as much as 20 grams he would be able to fulfill most mission requirements. He could carry both a receiver and transmitter with the necessary battery weight for the latter.

What remains to be investigated is whether or not the pigeon can be trained to respond to different stimuli delivered in midflight. Alternatively, one might try to stimulate certain motor areas of the brain to induce the required flight movements directly rather than through training to a stimulus.

At this point it should be noted that the Army's contracts with Animal Behavior Enterprises[3] and General Atronics,[2] as well as their own in-house work at the Limited Warfare Laboratory,[4] have all relied upon the more classical animal-training procedures for guidance. In all of these projects achieving successful guidance has been most unsuccessful, particularly as compared to the successes in the area of detection. This discrepancy can be attributed to problems of delay of reinforcement. The very nature of the problem is such that the detection response is subject to a short delay of reinforcement while the in-flight behavior must await the correct detection before being reinforced. This argues strongly for the investigation of new procedures, such as electrical brain stimulation.

SEARCH

Now that the pigeon has reached the area in which the search is to be made, what provides the signal for him to begin this new task and to maintain it over a period of time?

By Command

Active command initiation of a search pattern suffers the same disadvantages as does the "direct flight response control" guidance system, for in fact the two are similar, differing only in the flight pattern and in the location in the total reconnaissance sequence at which they occur.

By Pretraining

If the search sequence is regarded, from the sensor's point of view, as a part of the complex GUIDANCE–SEARCH, then for this method there are two possibilities: (a) The entire complex is learned as one behavior pattern. After a given time, or flight distance, or when a critical kind of terrain has been reached, the cue provided by that event is the conditioned stimulus to initiate the second stage of the sequence—namely, the search flight pattern. (b) The search process runs simultaneously with the guidance process. In this case, the sensor is searching from the launch point out until some event ends the sequence (target detection, or a RETURN sequence is initiated). For the animal there is no difference between the guidance and the search functions. Likewise, for airborne-launch systems, in which it might often be the case that the sensor will be directly released into or over the search area, differences between guidance and search can be regarded as negligible, and in that case the whole paradigm is substantially simplified.

Search Patterns

In the work done so far in this area, search patterns have been very simple: typically requiring only that the sensor follow an easily demarcated route (such as a road) and search for a target (e.g., a man) on the route or at its immediate periphery. For many applications this is an entirely adequate search pattern, especially when such sensors are used by ground patrol units. However, for targets such as encampments or supply depots in dense foliage, a linear search pattern may not be useful. The necessity to orient a search pattern on a landmark such as a road would render the sensor useless for many reconnaissance applications. One should consider training the sensor to execute search patterns such as a spiral or a zigzag grid.

Although these patterns may be achieved by methods already mentioned, the problem is to ensure that the bird is actively "paying attention" to targets while going through these flight maneuvers. Although it may appear that "attention" is not an appropriate term to use by a psychologist who considers himself to be a behaviorist, there are overt responses (behaviors) which characterize attention and give it a meaningful usage. We move our eyes to fixate on a strange person who has entered the room. We sniff at a flower in order to catch the odor. We reach for and run our fingers through a new fabric. These behaviors designed to enhance and focus the stimulation that the organism receives are not unique to humans and can be studied in animals. In the controlled environment of the Skinner box one can demonstrate attention-like behavior in the pigeon, and even condition it. In one such study pigeons learned to press a pedal in order to have visual stimuli presented to them on two pecking discs. These stimuli provided the information as to which disc to peck in order to get food reinforcement. In other words, birds learned to make a preliminary response which resulted in their then being able to make a correct detection.[5] Whether this type of behavior can be transferred to a bird in flight remains to be investigated.

The in-flight equivalent of the pedal might be electrical stimulation of the auditory portion of the cortex. If the visual portion of the cortex then responded in a manner characteristic of attention (alpha blocking), this could be reinforced by stimulating certain subcortical areas which have been shown to be reinforcement centers. With this procedure the auditory stimulation becomes the signal for making an attentional response. To ensure that the attentional response is directed at searching for the appropriate target materials, it would be necessary, early in the training, to withhold the reinforcement until a target stimulus fell on the visual field of the pigeon. But even this is a problem. The pigeon's two eyes do not have overlapping visual fields, but rather cover an almost 360° panoramic view. How can we be certain that placement of the target in the field corresponds with attention to it? This difficulty might be circumvented by assuming that just as people look before they leap, likewise the bird looks before he pecks. Three-dimensional models could be made to appear directly behind a transparent pecking disc, with the distances between the target and the disc increasing with trials. Thus the bird is forced to look down a long tube in order to determine if the critical target stimulus is present or not. This looking behavior comes to be controlled by the auditory stimulation because we program the situation such that only if the auditory stimulus is on is there ever a chance for the target to be at the end of the tunnel.

This would be followed by moving outdoors and gradually increasing the distance between the bird's starting position and that of the pecking disc and food. For distances of fifty yards or so, an enclosed flyway could be used. Later in training a large open field, with release of the bird from a tower, could be employed. Up through flyway training the position of the key and hopper are fixed and the discriminative stimulus is simply the pecking disc itself. When the bird has reached an adequate level of performance—i.e., when released from the launch canister he flies directly to the key and responds—then we introduce the stimuli of interest.

For the moment let us assume that the stimuli of interest are vehicles. Vehicles then are always associated with the pecking key and hopper. Within the flyway, we begin discrimination training such that the association between vehicle and food is consistent. It should be a relatively simple task to get the bird in the flyway to always land on a vehicle for his food reinforcement. At this point we move to the open field with vehicles at a considerable distance from the bird, then to tower release, gradually making the vehicles more and more difficult to find. Using the above procedures, it is believed that the pigeon can be trained to search, and to detect any specific targets of military interest that fall within its basic visual sensory capacities.

Such a research program, especially the part where it is later transferred to the in-flight bird, may appear to be quite fanciful, but of such fancy, progress is sometimes made.

TARGET DETECTION

In training, this phase is inseparable from that of search. Here the main questions concern the general ability of the pigeon to learn to detect the various different targets of military interest. Can they detect tanks, trucks, large concentrations of troops, ambushes, artillery pieces, naval vessels, radar stations, etc.?

It has been amply demonstrated, in work reviewed earlier, that the pigeon can make discriminations of stimulus complexes as sophisticated as those ever likely to be the objects of routine reconnaissance missons: men or man-made artifacts. The training paradigm is simple discrimination learning, and detection per se is probably the least problematical phase of the entire reconnaissance sequence.

One practical question is concerned with whether each bird has to be a specialist. Do we need different pigeons for tanks and radar stations? If not, how do we program the pigeon so that he knows that on one mission he is a tank detector and on another a radar station detector?

According to Louis Ridenour,[6] Skinner

. . . to avoid confusing the birds . . . would train each individual bird only on one class of target. Thus he had not just Tokyo pigeons; he had Emperor's Palace pigeons, and Mitsubishi-factory pigeons, and so on. He had battleship pigeons and destroyer pigeons, and pigeons trained to peck at aircraft carriers. . . . The inflexibility thus introduced into the bomb load of any given airplane worried him somewhat, but he figured that bombing missions are carefully planned in advance, and not many bombs are expended on targets of opportunity.

If Skinner had the data from our recent studies on concept formation in the pigeon, he well might have been able to reduce the number of target types, and have fewer pigeon specialists—at least somewhat. While it is said that "only God can make a tree," only man can identify so many different stimulus configurations worth destroying.

REPORT

The report is a learned response for which the conditioned stimulus is the target. When the pigeon identifies the target this information must be sent back to the pigeon-control station.

The report response can be either an active one or a passive one. In the first case, it may make use of a response that is not a part of the bird's normal behavior. An example of this approach would be to have the pigeon peck at a microswitch located on a breastplate. A passive response, on the other hand, does not require an overt muscular act from the bird. Examples of such passive responses include changes in heart rate, respiration rate, blood pressure, galvanic skin response. These responses, governed by the autonomic nervous system, would have to be conditioned to the target stimulus. Although there is ample evidence that such conditioning can be accomplished, there is the limitation that, again, equipment has to be added to the bird, devices for sensing the bird's response and for transmitting it back to the controller.

Assuming that these technical problems can be overcome, there is yet another obstacle. Typically the autonomic responses are triggered by a variety of different stimuli in addition to the target stimuli to which the subject has been trained. In general, all stimuli which evoke emotional arousal are adequate stimuli for autonomic responses. To use them as conditioned responses would require fairly complete habituation to the irrelevant arousal-provoking features of the environment. In a "natural" environment in which one may expect the occurrence of some emotion-arousing but extraneous stimuli (e.g., predators which prey on the pigeon), it may prove that the use of conditioned autonomic responses for the report function would be impractical.

A report response which is active, but which uses a motor act that itself requires no training, would be that of landing on or near the target. The sensor for this response can be similar to the one developed for free-ranging detection dogs—namely, a sensitive jiggle-type switch which opens and closes during movement but is in a steady state when the animal has ceased locomotion. Thus, when the bird is flying there is a steady clicking sound at the controller's station. When the bird lands the pattern of clicks changes, and when he stops moving, the clicks cease entirely.

The pigeon having landed, the controller knows that the bird has found a target. Now the problem is that of locating the pigeon. Once the pigeon is located, then, of course, so is the target. Direct visual location may be useful on some occasions, but it will frequently be impossible. It would be possible to implant a small transmitter in the bird which would continuously send out signals. These signals could be detected by appropriate direction-finding equipment at the controller's station. These same signals, in flight, can be used for determining guidance correction. Systems such as this have been successfully used in studying bird migration patterns.

RETURN

Again, we must consider the choice between initiating a function by command or arranging the learning experience so that the function occurs as a result of stimuli presented to the sensor from the immediate stimulus environment.

Initiating the return by command would not (unlike search) normally require visual contact by the monitor. The monitor need note only (a) that a report had occurred and the mission is completed, or (b) that within a specified period of time no report had occurred and it is presumed that no target stimuli were present.

If the return is chained to the rest of the behavior sequence by training, so that it is not initiated by active command from a monitor, it will most likely be achieved only when it follows a target detection and report response. In this case the stimuli generated by making the report constitute the conditioned stimuli for return. However, if no target detection occurs, the stimuli initiating return would be exceedingly complex for a pigeon to discriminate (e.g., passage of time or completion of an extensive search maneuver).

All this assumes that the bird has some known or detectable point to which to return. For ground-launch systems, as from a patrol or even a vehicle, this is probably a reasonable assumption since the bird will not be far from the launch point at or after target detection, and in many cases the launch platform will not move appreciably during the bird's tenure in the field. However, for airborne-launch systems the problem of return and retrieval is considerably more difficult. In a potential target area, where the bird would be launched, it would seldom be feasible to retain a hovering helicopter or slowly circling airplane. Were it safe to do so, there would be little reason to suspect the presence of the enemy in the area! Furthermore, retrieval of the bird into an airborne platform presents severe technical problems.

It seems likely, if retrieval is to occur at all, then it must be by ground forces. Such a restriction implies that the bird either know where the return point is or be able to locate a new one. From a training point of view this can be accomplished in the same manner that the target detection was achieved. Indeed it is simply another variant of the reconnaissance mission, but now the target is the launch point, and the place to which he has to return is the target. If in the costing of the eventual program, the operational bird, delivered to the target site, is relatively inexpensive, then we might be able to dismiss retrieval as unimportant.

In 1967 we estimated that it would require about $500,000 per year for two years, just in order to demonstrate the feasibility of the reconnaissance pigeon concept; in other words, to field one or two systems which would perform all of the functions described—launch, guidance, search and report, with the precision and reliability of standard military equipment. Only when this could be accomplished, would it be worthwhile to construct an operational system.

The size of the project, and the fact that it was devoted to the lowly and suspect pigeon, prevented it from ever getting off the ground. It is interesting to note that at the same time at least the same amount of money was spent for related projects, but the monies were portioned out in much smaller amounts to a variety of laboratories from a variety of different Department of Defense agencies, none of whom knew very much about the projects of the other. The results were all the same—many interesting, titillating demonstrations but never a system that could be used in the field.

The detailed, logical analysis of the pigeon reconnaissance program remained locked in the drawers of the U.S. Air Force Bionics Unit. It was given a classified rating and seemed to have officially marked the death of applied pigeon psychology for the military. It was quite an unexpected event when we took up the same problem for the Israel Ministry of Defense, together with a survey of the local bird population.[7] Indeed we even began some preliminary work to use pigeons to visually identify certain man-made stimuli.

In 1974 I published an article, in the open scientific journals, reviewing some of our earlier work.[8] This report was based on the study done for the Air Force in the context of aerial and satellite-based reconnaissance, as described in Chapter 4, "Pigeon Intelligence." Some reporters were made aware of the article and, putting two and two together, came up with something other than the correct answer. Citing the British magazine *Psychology Today* and the Manchester *Guardian,* Reuters and UPI put out press releases indicating that Israel was training pigeons to spy on the Arabs. According to the Reuters dispatch, it was being done by "equipping the pigeon with electronic sensing devices and then training them to land on likely military targets." After about a month they "can be trained to go out and flutter down on man-made installations where his [the pigeon's] attached electronic equipment can flash back information without soldiers on the spot having any idea of what is happening."

During the two weeks following these stories my telephone rang more frequently than usual and with greater urgency, including in the middle of the night with long-distance calls from curious reporters and newscasters.

"No, it's not true that my pigeons are now flying over Damascus."

I took considerable delight in giving this somewhat ambiguous reply and following it with: "That is really all I can say on the subject."

The Arab press also picked up the story. The following is a verbatim translation from a Beirut newspaper:

POSSIBILITY
THAT PIGEONS, FISH AND RATS
ARE EMPLOYED
IN THE ISRAELI INTELLIGENCE SERVICES

The inclination of the Israeli army institutions to use animals, birds and fish for espionage and intelligence purposes is dangerous and deserves to be noticed. It transfers the Arab-Israeli struggle to new dimensions. Foreign and local sources reported in English that psychological scientists in Israel have begun to use pigeons, rats and thousands of fish as a means of espionage in order to uncover vital Arab military and economic targets, and to observe the movements of the Arab armies on the front lines and within the Arab land. The purpose of the enemy is to take advantage of his superiority and progress in the fields of science and technology. In the past the enemy used to get his information through recruitment of agents, exchange of information with intelligences of countries hostile to the Arabic cause, reconnaissance flights, or spying missions. Compared to these methods, the above method gives the enemy the possibility to discover vital Arabic military targets by simple inexpensive means without endangering its soldiers. The sources reported that this research is done with white pigeons, fish and rats in laboratories belonging to the American Air Force, under the supervision of scientists sympathetic to the Zionist movement. Espionage activities by pigeons have achieved an advanced stage and have been in use for some time under the supervision of Dr. Robert Lubow of the Tel Aviv University, a teacher in the Psychology Department, who performed similar research in the United States. The training starts with food deprivation of the pigeons. They do not receive food unless they localize and classify Arab military or economic targets. The purpose of the procedure is to train the pigeon to receive food only after pecking at an appropriate picture. The sources report that the duration of training is one month, and that the pigeons easily discriminate between straight and curved lines, and man-made objects. At the end of the training, a small electronic apparatus is connected to the pigeon which transmits information on order. The purpose of this apparatus is to send the signals after the pigeon's landing on the specific target in the Arab lands, and then special apparatus of the Israeli army intelligence receive the signals and take appropriate measures.

Marking of the new targets on the military map and their employment for military actions is an important achievement. It gives the enemy the possibility of follow-up after the movements and preparations of the Arab armies with accuracy and low cost. Citizens in the Israeli embassy in Washington admitted that Israel has actually come to use the power inherent in animals and birds for military purpose. It is known that Israel has for a long time used dogs in discovery of mines. The same source said that the use of pigeons is undoubtedly the cheapest method used in espionage. And a country like Israel needs new methods to use instead of the old conventional ones.

The same sources stated that special devices in Israel send every month about 10,000 fish equipped with sensitive devices to the sea to report on movements of solid objects under the water and to spy on the shore defense installations in Egypt, Syria and Lebanon.

The same mechanism is used with rats for purposes of espionage by installing tiny transmitters in their brains and sending them to the Arab capitals. These espionage programs are undoubtedly of the most sophisticated and efficient programs used by the enemy, and are considered to be an advanced scientific development that should be paid attention to. This development shows the degree of scientific progress achieved by the Israelis in science and technology.

Our experience has taught us to expect the worst of the enemy. He will not shy away from using any means of espionage, and will use cunning, shrewd, deceitful ways in trying to frighten the Arab nations and to damage their spirit.

The fact of publishing this information does not imply that the enemy has been successful in using those complicated means. We have learned from experience that the enemy always desires to disseminate information about new weapons he received or developed by himself in order to evoke hostile propaganda to play on the nerves of the Arab citizens, and we have to be very cautious and on guard. We must learn the methods employed by the enemy to help our counterintelligence services to be prepared to foil the enemy's insane schemes.

AL V'MAHOR
Lebanon, April 10, 1975
p. 24, column 1

6

Sounds from the Jungle

It does not require a very astute observer of nature to conclude that the jungle can be a noisy place. Chattering monkeys, hooting and whistling birds, chirping insects, all contribute to the cacophony of a region densely populated by a variety of vociferous inhabitants, each characterized by its own vocal peculiarities. To remind oneself of the level and complexities of sound, one only has to recall the jungle noises in a Tarzan movie—and then the waves of silence that followed the stealthy intruder on his way to kill Tarzan. All animal activity ceased as we watched the crisp pith helmet dart in and out among the forest foliage or the shiny leather boots sloshing through a swamp.

In another time, in another jungle, the same dreamy young boys who watched Tarzan movies in their childhood grew up to take part in the Vietnam War. Some of the questions that they asked in regard to the tactical conduct of the war were much the same as those that Tarzan may have posed to himself. Sitting up in the tree house with Jane and Boy, how could he tell whether a stranger was intruding into his territory? Unlike some other animals, he did not have a nose keen enough to pick up a new scent from any considerable distance; nor could his eyes penetrate the thickets. The only sensory modality that might be of value in such a situation was that of audition. He could listen for changes in the pattern of noise that emanated from the jungle, and from that he could find the clues to whether or not an intruder was present.

The same problem was being faced in many parts of Vietnam, and

M̄ ʃVietnam
Paⁿts ᵮ

the same solution had been contemplated. In 1964 the U.S. Army Security Agency completed a feasibility study on the potential uses of naturally occurring sonic and ultransonic emissions from insects, birds and other wildlife to provide early warning of approaching enemy forces.[1] In general, the report was optimistic about the use of such a technique. It concluded that with existing equipment it would be possible to sense and record a whole range of wildlife sounds, those that are normally heard by the human ear as well as those that occur at a higher frequency than can be detected by a human.

The report suggested that it would be necessary to catalogue the normal sonic and ultrasonic emissions from different areas of interest. Those areas would contain different flora and fauna and, therefore, different normal background noise against which comparisons would have to be made.

To test the feasibility of using the vocal responses of jungle animals as an indicator of the presence of enemy guerrillas, a contract was awarded to the General Electric Company.[2] The contractor was to carry out live experiments in an environment that was similar to the heavily vegetated areas of Vietnam. Barro Colorado Island in the Panama Canal Zone was chosen for this purpose.

Barro Colorado Island was formed as a result of the construction of the Panama Canal. It resides in the Gatun Lake, which is, in fact, part of the Canal itself. Within the lake, it is the largest of several islands. Roughly circular in shape, it has an overall area of approximately 5.6 square miles. Lying in the humid region of the Lower Tropical Zone, the island is heavily wooded. The vegetation is typical tropical monsoon forest, although several variations in growth can be identified. The majority of the mature forested areas exhibit a dense canopy ranging from 75 to 100 feet above the forest floor. The trees beneath the canopy are, in general, between 20 and 40 feet in height. The floor itself is covered with a moderately thin undergrowth of woody young trees.

Although the island is quite small, it contains a remarkable variety of different animal and plant types. In addition to over 1200 species of flowering plants,[3] 56 mammal, 306 bird, 62 reptile and 33 amphibian species have been identified.[4, 5]

The small island was ideally suited for the purpose of the investigations. A wildlife preserve and a biological field laboratory were maintained there by the Smithsonian Institution. Few intruders, except for those introduced for the experiments, could be expected. In addition, many of the sources of wildlife sounds had already been investigated and described.

The technical approach to the problem was quite straightforward. In the first place, it was necessary to record the sounds of the jungle animals during a period of time when it was known that no human intruder was present. Secondly, an intruder, under various conditions, had to be introduced to the same area, and the jungle noises again recorded. Finally a comparison had to be made between the two sets of recordings.

The actual tests were run in two different locations. One was in a fairly mature forest with a canopy about 100 feet high and with sparse underbrush. For this test area, four microphones were suspended about 40 to 50 feet from a large strangler fig tree alongside a trail. Two of the microphones faced in the direction from which the intruder would enter the area, and two microphones faced in the opposite direction. Of the four microphones, two were sensitive to audio frequencies down to 10 cycles per second, and two were sensitive to ultrasonic frequencies up to 100 kilocycles.

The second area was also along a trail in a similarly forested area. Here, however, the four microphones were located close to a dense tangle of underbrush which could not be penetrated by man, and also close to a water stream and an open area. It was hoped that these conditions would attract a large variety of animal types.

At each location the ambient sound was recorded twelve times per day, from five in the morning to nine in the evening. Most of the recordings were made either in the early morning or evening, the time when animal activity is normally high.

Two kinds of intrusion tests were run. In one test, called a "pass-through," four men passed under the microphones without stopping. In the second test, ambush-type, two men entered the area of interest and remained in the vicinity of the microphones for an hour. At the end of the hour, they were met by two additional men, and all four left the area together. All together, nineteen tests, almost equally divided between test type and location, were conducted. The time of day for testing was varied.

The jungle sounds were recorded on magnetic tape. Data analysis was performed in one of several ways. Either a trained listener compared the auditory output of the tapes, or a trained observer compared visual displays of a spectral analysis. In the latter case, the data consisted of a series of photographs (i.e., film) which displayed the amplitudes of different frequency calls as they changed over time. In other words, the information that is given usually to the ear was converted to a visual presentation. This type of spectral analysis could also be fed into a computer for a fine-grain comparison of the different noise conditions. However, the most useful way of analyzing this very complex pattern of data was by simultaneous listening to the tapes and looking at the film.

The analysis was simplified considerably by some preliminary work which indicated that the most useful information could be obtained in the frequency range 0–20 kilocycles. In fact, except for the "pulsing bug," which produces a series of pulses between 30 and 50 kilocycles, no sound pattern above 20 kilocycles was found in the sampled tapes.

As an additional aid to the data reduction and analysis, each tape was divided into ten-second intervals. Each interval was then examined to determine if it contained the voice of a given animal. If the sound of an animal appeared within a particular ten-second period, then that animal received a score of one "call unit." Each animal species could get a maximum score of one for each ten-second period. In this way relative vocal activity of the various animal species was measured.

Early in the data analysis it became quite clear that the time of day during which the recordings were made had a powerful influence on the amount and type of vocal activity: "Before dawn and after sunset all the noise comes from amphibians and insects. At dawn and early in the morning the amphibians cease calling and nocturnal insects are replaced by day-singing species. Birds call most frequently at this time. As the sun rises higher almost all acoustic activity ceases or slows down, with the exception of cicadas. At dusk there is another flurry of bird activity, then nighttime conditions are reestablished."[2]

As a result of these findings it was necessary to make the comparison of "empty" versus "intruder" events for similar times of day. Using a comparison of the call-unit information for different species, and sampling this information at different periods of time, before and after the intrusion, four sets of questions were asked. The first and most basic questions were: Are there species which change their vocal behavior during the presence of an intruder? Which species, if any, show this phenomenon? And what is the nature of the changes in the vocal behavior? Secondly, after people leave an area, how long does it take for the ambient noise to return to normal? Thirdly, is it possible to differentiate between the condition of people passing through an area and that of people loitering in the area? The fourth question concerned the ability to differentiate between intruders who openly loitered in an area and intruders who attempted to conceal themselves.

The last three questions are relevant, of course, only if the answer to the very first question is affirmative. If intruders can be detected, then, to make an operational system, it becomes necessary to identify the exact conditions under which this can occur, and to clearly earmark the meaning of a change in the vocal signals.

To obtain the answers to these questions, the vocalizations of 36 different species were examined. These included all of the birds that were recorded (30), 3 frogs, and the only vocal mammal that was recorded—the howler monkey.

The analyses indicated that the most effective indicators of human intrusion were five birds: *Penelope purpurascens* (guan), *Microrhopias quixcensis* (potted-winged antwren), *Myrmotherula axillaris* (white-flanked antwren), *Myrmotherula fulviventris* (fulvous-bellied antwren) and *Hylophilus decurtatus* (gray-headed greenlet). All of these birds dwell in the lower stratum of the jungle.

In general, these birds indicated the presence of people by decreasing their rate of vocalization. Most likely this occurred because the birds simply left the area once it was occupied by a person. The indicators did not differentiate between the conditions of a human entering and leaving an area and one of a human entering and hiding. This latter finding is understandable from two points of view. First of all, if the birds leave the area upon occurrence of an intrusion, this logically obviates the possibility of differentiation until the birds return again to the area. The data seem to indicate that it takes at least a half hour for this to happen. During that "dead" time there is no sensor present which can respond differentially to the two conditions. Secondly, birds are predominantly visual animals and probably use visual information to identify an intruder. Thus, a human in hiding would not be readily sensed by the bird. This also accounts for the fact that the overall ability of the birds to supply an intrusion indication was weak.

It would appear that the general idea of using the changing voices of the jungle to tell us something about the human activity in it is quite valid. Nevertheless, considerably more effort will have to be expended to convert the basically sound idea to an operational system.

Perhaps there are some ways in which we can improve on nature. A number of novel approaches come to mind. To begin with, it is necessary to know one of the main reasons why the system was only marginally useful: the animals supplying the critical sounds were quite sparsely distributed. It appears to be characteristic of tropical jungles that although they contain an abundance of different species, the number of representatives of any given species in an area is quite low. One solution to the problem of increasing the strength of the signal is to simply seed an area with members of that species which provides the best signals. One could take, for example, several hundred *Penelope purpurascens* (which, by the way, sounds more like a character from a Henry Fielding novel than a bird) and release them in a designated jungle area. This, of course, would also upset what environmental gymnasts call the delicate balance of nature; but unless one wants to argue that warfare is simply an evolutionary device for shaping natural selection, then it seems quite justified to sacrifice a few *Penelopes,* or to tilt an ecological equilibrium.

To ensure that the *Penelopes* stay within the critical area, one might have to add some extra foodstuffs. Since *Penelopes* eat a variety of seeds and grains, this should be easily manageable. But suppose the *Penelopes,* now a Greek chorus, still did not provide the appropriate signals. There are yet other sounds that these birds make, and indeed that all animals make. The sounds of the life processes, hearts beating, lungs inflating and deflating, digestive processes working. It would be possible to implant miniature microphones and transmitters so that these noises could be monitored. It would be most surprising if one could not find a set of sound changes accompanying the physiological processes of an animal which could be used to reliably indicate the presence of a human intruder.

Also, there is the behavioral engineering approach. It would be relatively simple to train a parakeet to whistle in order to get food. The bird is put in a standard Skinner box with transparent walls. Within the box there is a voice-activated microphone which is especially sensitive to the frequency band which characterizes the parakeet's whistle. Every time the hungry bird whistles, the food hopper, filled with grain, presents itself. When the bird is satiated he is re-moved from the box and returned to his home cage. When the whis-tle response rate in the box is stable and relatively high compared to the rate in the home cage, then a second contingency is added. Now the whistle only gives food if there is a person in the room. By ma-nipulating the presence and absence of the person, it would be pos-sible to elicit whistling only when a human figure is present.

The entire procedure could be completely automated, and with enough equipment hundreds of whistling-at-people parakeets could be trained and then released in the jungle. What is more, instead of allowing these beeping-peeping toms to decide for themselves what part of the forest to place under surveillance, they could be caged and placed in predetermined positions in the wilderness. I wonder how long it will take after reading this suggestion before some Department of Defense analyst reports on the required PPSM ratio (parakeets per square mile) for reliable coverage of various jungles. When he finds the number to be excessively high, because, after all, there are a lot of jungles in the world where the United States might get involved, the analyst will no doubt recommend that parakeet deployment, at this time, is not deemed advisable. To prove the validity of his con-clusion he will point out that the number of required parakeets far exceeds the world supply.

When one is looking for animal forms that are not in short supply, arthropods immediately suggest themselves. Of all the phyla in the animal kingdom this one is the richest in diversity and in absolute numbers. There are approximately six million different species repre-sented in this phyla. Most of these are classified as insects. At least for most of the common insect species there is a virtually inex-haustible supply of members.

In 1963, the U.S. Army Limited War Laboratory, in conjunction with the U.S. Department of Agriculture, undertook a program to develop a system for ambush detection and intrusion detection which was based on exploiting certain arthropods that actively seek man.[6] The logic was straightforward. If an organism such as a mosquito can find a man, as we all know it does with considerable ease, might it not be possible to capitalize on this ability by having the mosquito re-port to another person that a potential host is available?

Once it was accepted that there was merit in this approach, then two questions were raised. First, which species of insects would be most useful? Secondly, how can the fact that an insect has detected the presence of a human be made available to an observer?

Selecting the appropriate species was made more simple by eliminating those that are not in a parasitic relation to man. Those insects that live off man must be able to find him. With this as a guiding principle, the investigators chose to study the giant cone-nose bug (*Triatoma infestans*), the bedbug (*Cimex lectularius*), the Oriental rat flea (*Xenopsilla cheopis*), several mosquitoes (*Anopheles quadrimaculatus, Aedes aegypti* and *Culex quinquifasciatus*) and the tick (*Amblioma americanum*). Although all of these distinguished characters seemed to have the appropriate credentials to qualify for the role of man-hunter, further investigation revealed that some of their references were, in fact, spurious.

Lice, for instance, seem to move about randomly in the presence of a human, getting to their goal more by accident than by design. If lice-infested clothing is hung on a bedpost next to a sleeping man, the lice will starve to death in the clothing rather than find the man.[6] This, plus the fact that these creatures require a daily meal of blood, disqualified them from the competition.

The Oriental rat flea exhibits violent jumping when breathed upon. To detect the jumping, a transducer chamber (one which converts the raw jumping to a useful signal) with a tin lid was constructed. A number of fleas were placed in the chamber, and when human breath was blown on to them, the jumping against the metal lid, amplified electronically, sounded like the popping of corn. Change in activity was easily recognizable. However, because the fleas took a long time to calm down, and required frequent blood meals, they, too, were dropped from the candidate list.

Ticks, on the other hand, are hardy beasts that can go for long periods of time between feedings. They are also quite sensitive to the presence of a potential host. Almost immediately they will go from near absolute quiet to very marked activity when a warm-blooded organism approaches. But ticks too have a fatal flaw, at least for these experiments. They wear sneakers. They are so soft-footed that movement can only be detected visually. The experimenters even tried tying weights to ticks' feet. The procedure was not successful.

After one has identified a species capable of responding to man, it is necessary to design a transducer that will allow the human operator to recognize what the bug has recognized. For this the investigators decided to use an auditory index. Most of the species that were chosen for study responded to the presence of man by increasing their level of activity. They scrambled around. Various containers and amplification devices were designed so that this increased locomotor activity could be suitably intensified for use by the human operator.

Mosquitoes qualify quite impressively in their ability to find man, and even to let him know that he has been discovered. When stimulated by the presence of a host, *Aedes aegypti* will land and give a feeding response; namely, an extension of the proboscis which pierces the skin. To utilize this response, the investigators cleverly designed a "feeding" membrane which enveloped a salt solution. A taut thread was hooked to the membrane on one end and to a phonograph needle on the other end. The membrane and several mosquitoes were placed in a small chamber designed so that air carrying the human odor from the outside was introduced into the chamber in close proximity to the membrane. When this occurred, the mosquitoes would land on the stretched membrane and penetrate it with their proboscises. The proboscises were then immediately withdrawn. The amplified signals sounded like a guitar string being plucked.

For the actual field tests the investigators chose the bedbug and the giant cone-nose bug, both of whom show excellent sensitivity to man, and whose responses can be easily detected. The first tests used a small, hand-carried system. The detector consisted of a closed cell that was mounted within a cylindrical bellows air pump. The cell contained one or more insects that were confined to a relatively small space. Loosely wrapped piano wire covered much of the space in which a bug sat. It found a resting position among the windings, usually touching the wire. A pumping action by the operator introduced an airflow over the bug's body. If the air contained human effluent, then the insect was supposed to increase his activity, thus setting the piano-wire entanglement in motion. The wire, in turn, was hooked to a phono pickup cartridge. The movement sensed by the cartridge was amplified and transmitted to earphones worn by the operator.

Field tests were conducted at Gainesville, Florida, and in the Panama Canal Zone. The first Panama tests were held on a jungle road near Fort Sherman. The trials used six cone-nose bugs and twelve human targets. The ambush party was divided into three small groups and placed in various positions about ten yards off to either side of the road.

The operator, holding the detector unit in front of him and scanning from side to side with it, slowly proceeded down the road, pumping the bellows and listening on his headset for an increase in bug-generated noise. Each time an increase in noise activity was reported, the distance to the nearest target-ambush site was paced off.

The results from the first tests were not very good. Detections were apparently made at distances up to seventy-five feet, but there was also a lot of spontaneous activity. The resulting high false-alarm rate made it almost impossible to verify the validity of the detection responses. Some of this unwanted activity was a function of the fact that the cone-nose bug exhibits cyclic activity peaks related to the dark-light cycle. In addition, the design of the chamber was such that the operator might have been blowing his own effluents into it. Finally, movement of the operator-carried chamber stimulated bug activity.

These last two considerations resulted in changing the operational requirements of the system. Instead of using it as an ambush detector—carried by an operator looking for a concealed but stationary group of hostiles—it might better be employed as an intruder detector. In this context, the detector would be stationary and isolated from the human operator, who would be at some distance from it. The detector would respond to humans approaching it rather than vice versa.

Tests conducted with this mode of operation gave results that were considerably more favorable. Also, it was found that several of the other species discussed earlier could give reliable indications of human presence. The use of such insect devices as the basis of a trail-monitoring system for instrusion detection remains well within the realm of feasibility.

A different approach to employing insects as odor detectors has attempted to pick up electrical signals directly from the neurons which respond to airborne effluents. If one could create a physiological preparation that would stay vital for several days, and intercept and monitor the electrical nervous activity between the peripheral olfactory nerve endings and the central nervous system, this might provide the ultimate in a sensitive people-detection system.

This work was carried out by the same group that was involved in monitoring insect activity. Again the giant cone-nose bug was chosen as the subject for experimentation. Most of the olfactory receptors of this bug are located at the ultimate and penultimate segments of the antennae, with between 90 and 150 receptors for these two segments.

For each preparation the insect was immobilized in modeling clay. One antenna was attached by small wire hooks to the clay. Using a minute tungsten electrode, 5 microns in diameter, efforts were made to record from individual neurons immediately underneath olfactory receptors. Unfortunately, out of about seventy bugs, only one successful preparation was obtained. This preparation lasted for ten days without exhibiting any degeneration. It was selectively sensitive to human breath. However, the investigators could not isolate the component of the human effluent that caused nerve excitation, although several possibilities, including carbon dioxide, were eliminated.

I had heard of yet another insect preparation for detecting movement in the jungle. This was based on using the very sensitive tympanic membrane of the grasshopper. The output of this membrane, which is responsive to vibrations in the auditory range, supposedly was tapped and broadcast to nearby receivers. Seeding a restricted territory with a number of these preparations would have the effect of covering the area with microphones, and would allow one to listen directly to the noises of the jungle.

7

Sea Mammals

There are two basic requirements for any biosensor system that would be useful to man. One, of course, is high sensitivity of the peripheral sense organs to those changes of energy patterns in the external world that provide signatures of the target of interest. Thus, the odor of a human in a jungle is a potential signature that an intruder is present, the sound of a propeller in the water is a signature that a boat is present, and so on. The more sensitive the organ which can respond to these energy patterns, the greater the distance at which the detection can be made and thus the more effective the system.

The second requirement for a useful detection system is some manner of converting the detected stimuli to a form of energy to which man can respond. In the preceding chapters we have examined two different types of transducers: one that is based on an untrained, reflexive response of the organism, and one that is carefully taught to the animal. As examples of the first type there are the insects responding to human effluent by increasing their activity, or birds responding to the presence of human forms by decreasing their call rate. The second type is illustrated by pigeons pecking at a disc when it contains an image of a man-made object, or dogs pressing a lever when they detect the odor of an explosive.

In general, the first class of responses are most suitable for lower animal species. After all, who would try to train a flea to do anything that does not come naturally? For more highly developed organisms, the first approach remains useful. However, we can add tremendous operational flexibility to it by training specific responses, thus reducing the dependence on equipment and gaining considerable mobility. The more intelligent the organism, the more open are the possibilities for training.

The question is raised, quite often, as to which species of animal is most intelligent. Cat lovers and dog lovers seem to be locked in endless battle over which one of their respective pets is more clever. But the answer is not readily available. Competent psychologists are still engaged in controversy about whether there are any innate differences in intelligence among different human races, and indeed over the very meaning of the word "intelligence" itself.

Sometimes the psychologist will answer the last question by giving what is called an operational definition of intelligence. Intelligence is that which is measured by an intelligence test—the Stanford-Binet I.Q. test, for example. This acquires some meaning in that the test was constructed in such a way that it is correlated with school performance. If we choose members of the same population on which the original test items were validated—that is, in general, middle-class American whites—the test is a useful instrument for predicting academic success among members of this group. It is less useful as a prediction of school grades for groups that differ in cultural background from that of the original group on which the test was constructed. Culture, then, plays an important role in determining performance on most of the standard intelligence tests administered to humans. Some of the ways that this effect occurs are quite simple. As an example of one intelligence test question, a five-year-old child might be shown a picture of a television set and asked to identify it. If the child was raised in an isolated, poverty-ridden backwoods area it is quite possible that he would not have this piece of information available to him. The tests are based on the assumption that the people taking them have been equally exposed to the relevant content, and, even more subtly, equally exposed to the behavior of test-taking—that is, conforming to the requests of the test administrator, and motivated to give answers that will be considered correct by the administrator. These are behaviors that most people reading this book take for granted. But they are culturally determined behaviors, as much as our predilection for wearing a full set of clothes to the office on a hot humid day, even to our own discomfort.

If these problems occur in comparing people of different cultural background, who, after all, do share a common biology, just imagine how complicated it would be to come up with a meaningful answer to the question: which is more intelligent, the cat or the dog?

In spite of these difficulties there is a growing consensus that there are some animals that are really very clever. Maybe we cannot choose between cats and dogs in the intellectual Olympics, but almost everyone believes that the dolphin is indeed a smart animal. Since the dolphin has been extensively exploited for military purposes, let us examine his credentials. How did he gain his reputation for superior intellect?

The dolphin, or porpoise as he is sometimes called, is an aquatic mammal that comes in a number of different species widely distributed in the warm and temperate seas. The two species that are the most familiar to us are the common dolphin and the bottle-nose dolphin. The latter are the friendly, gregarious creatures that we associate with Flipper, the television and movie star. There are numerous anecdotes describing how the dolphin has come to the rescue of drowning swimmers, either towing them to safety or holding their tired bodies afloat until help arrived. This behavior, plus the dolphin's natural inclination for investigating new objects and his perpetual "smile," has endeared him to generations of seafaring peoples. He has been enshrined on urns and temple walls of the Ancients, and appears in the writings of Aristotle, Aesop, the Plinys and Herodotus. In spite of these recommendations the dolphin also appears, not infrequently, on menus, then and now. Xenophon and his Greek army are reported to have found extensive quantities of salted dolphin meat stored in earthenware jars along the shores of the Black Sea. More recently, until a ban on dolphin hunting in 1966, as many as 80,000 dolphins per year were caught in the Black Sea. The Russians prohibited this wholesale catching in order to preserve the species for biological research.

One characteristic of the dolphin that makes him so interesting to scientists is the complex pattern of sounds that he emits. These sounds appear as a rapid burst of clicks at a very high frequency, 50,000 cycles per second to 200,000 cycles per second. This is well above the highest frequency that the human ear is capable of detecting, 20,000 cycles per second. In addition, the dolphin also gives out a number of different calls within the human audible range. These calls have been described as barks, whistles, screams and moans.

The high-frequency auditory signals are directional, being propagated in a narrow beam directly in front of the dolphin. The reflection of these signals are detected by the two ears and, much like a sonar system, are used for purposes of obstacle avoidance during navigation, and object identification. A similar system is used by bats. Both species, of course, can have only limited use of vision, as only the poorest of light conditions is available to either the nocturnal bat or the deep-swimming dolphin.

The lower-pitched noises that come from the dolphin are omnidirectional and are used mostly for social communication. There appear to be distinctively different sounds associated with play, distress, mating and even helping behaviors. Some scientists would claim that the vocal behavior of the dolphin is a true language, that it can be used to exchange information at a conceptual level. However, as yet, the vocalizations remain best classified as a series of signals rather than symbols.

It is partly as a result of this complex pattern of communication and the social behaviors that accompany it that the dolphin has been thought to possess such extraordinary intelligence. What could be more humanlike than the "helping" behaviors that are displayed by dolphins? A pregnant dolphin about to give birth is accompanied by one or two other females who swim close to her side. When the baby is born, one of the "nurses" lifts it to the water's surface for its first breath of air. Similarly, sick dolphins who might be too ill to rise to the surface by themselves to breathe air have been seen to be assisted by their neighbors.

The circuitous reasoning that bestows a high I.Q. on the dolphin runs as follows: Altruism is a characteristic that belongs to the most intelligent of species, namely ourselves. Any other animal showing similar altruistic behavior therefore must also be highly intelligent.

What tasks can the dolphin perform that would be of military significance? The answer to this question is quite simple. Everything that the dog can do on land the dolphin can be trained to do in water, and then some. The dolphin can be taught to find and retrieve specific objects, even a lost atomic bomb deep in the sea, to detect intruders, to carry various devices, instruments and tools to fixed locations.

Much of the research that went into developing these highly skilled responses has been carried out by American and Russian military research teams and is highly classified. Some of the work was leaked by word of mouth, privately by former employees or publicly to congressional committees. However, by far the richest source of information can be obtained by inference from the published reports in the open scientific literature. When a Department of Defense, American or Russian, is doing *any* kind of research, one must assume that this research is related to military needs, either current or anticipated. This is doubly accentuated when the work is on an esoteric species of animal that is expensive to maintain.

In 1965 the first published reports appeared concerning the training of dolphins to swim untethered in the open sea.[1, 2] Between that time and 1970, ten additional porpoises and nine Californian sea lions were trained for open-sea release at only *one* of several such training stations in the United States—the Naval Undersea Research and Development Center at Point Mugu, California.[3]

Obviously, to be of military value, sea mammals must be used without a leash. Basic obedience training and off-leash control are even more important for the effective operational use of these animals than for dogs. Achieving control of an untethered porpoise is not an easy task. Not only does the porpoise live in an environment quite foreign to man, but also, unlike the dog, it is not a domesticated animal. A similar problem is faced by the hunter trying to exploit the falcon or the cheetah. At what point in training is it safe to release the animal into its natural surroundings and still have confidence that he will come back? It is an expensive loss indeed if a dolphin, in which perhaps hundreds of man-hours of maintenance and training have been invested, suddenly decides to return to the open sea.

The first task, then, is to achieve firm control over the dolphin's behavior so that he will both swim to designated places and return to his controller. As with most of the training procedures that we have discussed, this one begins with a hungry animal. The naïve porpoise, in a small tank, is taught to accept a fish from the trainer's hand. During this procedure the porpoise gradually loses his fear of approaching a human, and will eventually allow himself to be touched by the trainer. This is an important achievement. During the course of training there are many occasions on which the animal is subject to human handling both in and out of the water. Routine medical examinations are conducted in a laboratory with the porpoise flat out on a stretcher. Transportation to different training areas also requires handling.

Once the animal learns to readily accept a fish from the trainer's hand, he is then required to press or touch some object before being fed. He may have to nose a hand, a paddle or an acoustical signaling device. The acoustical device is employed quite commonly in such training. When the porpoise presses a plate he can activate or deactivate an auditory signal. Since the change in sound level is followed by delivery of food, the auditory change becomes a secondary reinforcer and can be used to reinforce behaviors that are at considerable distances from the final fish reward. These acoustic hydro-beacons, or pingers, are capable of operating at depths of 1000 feet.

Initial training is usually accomplished in a series of small tanks. When the porpoise has learned to touch the acoustic device to get fed, the device is moved to various parts of the tanks. The animal is required to find it and touch it before being fed. As a preparation for open-sea release, the animal is taught to return to and enter a gate that leads to his home pen. This training receives extensive attention. The acoustic recall signal is placed in front of the gate. When the animal is in a pen adjoining his home pen, the signal at the gate is sounded. The porpoise swiftly orients toward the sound source and heads straight for it. He enters the gate, touches the beacon, which turns the signal off, and continues on to the trainer for his food. This procedure is repeated over and over in a variety of different concrete tanks. He may then be moved out to floating pens along the shore of the open sea. At the Naval Undersea Research and Development Center, these pens are located in Mugu Lagoon. There are three small ones, 21 by 38 feet, with a 7-foot depth. Each one is next to a larger pen that is 58 by 63 feet. The pens are interconnected by a series of 4-by-5-foot gates.

Typically the transfer from the concrete tanks to the lagoon pens resulted in temporary disruption of behavior. However, after three or four days of retraining the original level of performance was reached. Training continued in the larger enclosures until the gate-recall behavior was perfect.

Until now there was no risk. A porpoise that was reluctant to respond to the recall command was still within easy reach of the trainer. It must have been with considerable anxiety that the experimenters embarked on the next stage—to allow the porpoise to enter the lagoon from a pen. At first the animal was only allowed to venture several yards away from the gate before being recalled. But as the experimenters gained confidence in their ability to control the porpoises' behavior, the animals were allowed to go out for longer and longer distances. Rather than losing any of the animals, many of them were reluctant to leave the pen area and some would return before receiving the recall signal.

One more stage of training was required before release of the porpoises in the ocean. They had to be trained to return to a small boat. The animal was fed alongside a stationary motorboat next to the pens, then the boat was moved away from the home area, and the porpoise was required to follow the boat for five minutes at a time as it moved through the water at speeds up to 8 miles per hour. When the porpoise was accustomed to being fed from the boat, it was introduced to the ocean-type porpoise pen, designed to hold the animal in a restricted space in the open sea. This 17-by-17-foot-square pen consisted of 855-gallon steel drums which supported a wooden walkway. A net was suspended below the walkway to a depth of 11 feet.

The porpoises were given two weeks of lagoon training with this new pen, learning to return to it from all positions in the lagoon and to stay in it for long periods of time, including overnight. The porpoise was now ready for the ocean. The animal was transferred from the lagoon to the ocean pen anchored about 200 yards offshore. To do this, the animal was hoisted out of the water and carried on a stretcher. The entire procedure took less than one hour. After transfer to the ocean pen, he was given one or two days to recover from the moving operation. Following this he was released into the ocean and again allowed to rehearse the gate-recall behaviors that he had learned so well first in the concrete tanks and then in the lagoon pens. The transfer usually occurred without incident. The porpoise responded reliably and quickly to recall from distances up to several hundred yards.

"The success of the open ocean release work conducted at Point Mugu must be measured against the number of animals who did not return. In the course of approximately 1600 porpoise work sessions and 600 sea lion[4] work sessions in the open sea during the past five years, only one porpoise and one sea lion was lost. An adult female Pacific white-sided dolphin, Lagenorhynchus obliquidens, after being worked continuously in the ocean for 9 months suddenly swam away from the trainer, apparently to join a school of wild L. obliquidens observed to be passing nearby. She disappeared in the same area of her original capture in 1964, during the time of the year that is believed to be the breeding season for this species. In 1965 prior to the development of a suitable muzzle, a sea lion surfaced from a deep dive with a mouthful of squid. It then dived again, apparently to catch some more, and was not seen thereafter."[3]

Now that the dolphin or sea lion can be controlled in the open sea, there are several specific tasks that he can be trained to perform. One such general class of activities is retrieval of objects that are lost at sea, but whose location is known to be within a limited area. These objects can be divided into three categories: mines, torpedoes and air-to-surface missiles that are used in exercises or are prototype models; aircraft that have crashed; and moored oceanographic instruments. Although recovery of these items may be achieved using divers, and manned and unmanned submarine vehicles, these procedures are often dangerous, expensive and fallible.

In the division of labor between finding a lost object and raising it: "The consensus of some 35 persons interviewed who are concerned with recovery operations is that about 90% of the money spent to recover a lost object is spent on finding the object, and only 10% is spent on raising the object once it was found."[5] Pingers and transponders are often attached to objects that have a high probability of becoming lost. These devices emit acoustic signals which can be used as the basis for identifying their location.

On a number of occasions trained marine mammals have been used to locate pingered objects. After marking the location, human divers completed the recovery. In practice this required that the diver attach some sort of grabbing device to the object to serve as the anchor point for a line to a hoist. A more refined system was developed at the Marine Bio-Science Facility at Point Mugu. They trained Californian sea lions not only to locate the misplaced object but also to attach the recovery device to it.[5]

Much of the developmental work centered on designing a set of grabbers which could be mounted on the sea lion and appropriately released when placed in contact with the object to be recovered.[6] The equipment was made specially to fit around an ASROC depth charge, the type to be used in the final evaluation of this unique recovery system. The recovery grabber fit on the sea lion's muzzle. It consisted of a pair of rounded telescopic arms that locked together when triggered. In the open position they looked like a pair of pincers or curved antennae extending from the animal's mouth. The grabbers could be used on objects with diameters up to 12 inches and weights up to 200 pounds.

Training of these more complex behaviors began with the conditioning of target-marking responses. A small canister containing an audible pinger was placed on the surface of one of the pools. The animal was trained to swim about twenty feet, touch the canister with its muzzle and return to the trainer. Gradually, the canister was lowered to greater and greater depths, until the required behavior was elicited when the canister was at the bottom of the pool. When this was accomplished, a marking device was attached to the muzzle of the sea lion. Now when the animal made the correct response, touching the canister, the trainer could be immediately informed.

During training, the pingered canister was moved randomly to different positions in the pool. The sea lions had no difficulty in quickly finding the locations. However, these animals also have fairly good visual ability, and it turned out that they simply were following the control cables to the canister. This, evidently, was an easier task than using their directional hearing ability. After precautions were taken which would prevent the animal from using visual cues, they proceeded to solve the locating problems by auditory means.

Upon successful completion of this phase, the sea lions were moved out to open waters for training and testing at greater depths and acclimatization to the grabber device. After sixteen months, from the time of taming and captivity adaptation to controlled diving to depths of 500 feet, using simulated ASROC depth charge targets, a demonstration of the bio-recovery system was undertaken.

The sea lions, trained in Hawaii, were flown by commercial airline to Point Mugu. The test was to be conducted as part of the ASROC Quality Assurance Service Test exercise at San Nicolas Island.

After several delays because of heavy fog in the waters surrounding the island, the ASROC finally was fired. A hovering helicopter dropped a dye marker and a smoke flare in order to identify the point of impact. The recovery boat with the sea lions on board headed out toward the marked area. Because of the thick fog the recovery team took over an hour to find the site of the splash-down. After correctly locating the site, the team "proceeded to home in on the ASROC's

8

The Stalking Dog

Along the coast of Indochina about fifty miles south of Da Nang and one hundred and fifty miles south of the demilitarized zone between South and North Vietnam, lies the small fishing village of Au Can. The village, like many in South Vietnam, consists of several scores of wooden huts with dried brown thatched roofs, each one facing to the sea. In the village center, bounded by a dirt road in the dry season and a heavy reddish-brown mud wallow in the rainy season, is the *dinh,* which is the temple for the guardian spirit of the village, and the village council house.

On a dark, rainy night in October 1967, about 2 A.M., a group of six Viet Cong black-pajamaed guerrillas walked into the village. They met no resistance. As was the usual case in incidents such as this one, the safest procedure for the village inhabitants was to feign sleep.

The following morning the villagers duly reported that two of the elders had been abducted, or at least they assumed that they had been abducted. No one reported actually seeing the kidnappers or, indeed, any disturbance. But since the two elders were not to be found, it was reasonable to assume that they had been taken prisoner by the Viet Cong.

The military authorities, consisting of a lieutenant in the Army of the Republic of Vietnam (ARVN), two privates and an American captain, completed the hopeless interrogation of the local inhabitants, wrote their reports and departed. The incident was closed. The VC with the two village elders were swallowed forever into the thinly populated countryside. Later, they would reappear in another hamlet, or perhaps even the same one, in their normal peasant working clothes, the black pajamas of their night raids hidden in a plastic sack alongside one of the rice-paddy irrigation ditches.

Incidents such as this, with some few variations, were not uncommon. Both the ARVN and the American troops were incapable of effectively pursuing the intruders. The villagers, in turn, were silent, out of fear of the Viet Cong or in sympathy with them. The advanced technology of warfare, of which the United States certainly enjoyed an advantage, was of no value in situations such as the one described. Guerrilla-type warfare, what we have come to call from our vantage point counter-insurgency warfare, is relatively immune to the sophisticated electronic methodology of modern armies.

In the limited-warfare arena, the initiative is placed on individual and small-group tactics, usually designed to harass rather than to take and hold territory. For the most part these activities are random in time and place, and it becomes impossible to use routine operations and equipment as countermeasures. The main function of counter-insurgency activities in these operations is one of detection, whether it be of an explosive charge, an ammunition cache, a single individual or a band of people. However, since these events are infrequent, random in time, random in place and with an extremely low signal strength, it is economically inefficient and perhaps even technologically difficult to develop an electromechanical system for purposes of these detections.

In many ways guerrilla warfare is a return to a pattern of behavior that must have served primitive man quite adequately for his survival, both as a hunting carnivore searching for animal food and as the protector of his own lair. Indeed, we see many of these functions carried out quite admirably by different animals without the aid of fancy equipment except for what has been exquisitely developed over the millions of years of the evolutionary history of the species. These special adaptations for survival serve many of the functions that the counter-insurgent group must carry out, particularly in regard to detection.

It became quite apparent to some of us who were involved in thinking about these problems that, in fact, one might use these naturally developed systems in the primitive conditions of warfare that were to be found in Vietnam. As a cynical colleague of mine once put it, "to take advantage of Nature on the way to destroying her." But that, of course, is the dilemma in many of our modern problems. We use natural resources to develop industrial technology which in turn damages the natural environment. In Vietnam, we were proposing to use nature directly in order to intervene in, and disrupt, some might say, another natural event, a popular liberation movement. Perhaps.

At the time that I was invited to the Limited Warfare Laboratory in Aberdeen, Maryland, we had already met with considerable success in training dogs to detect a variety of objects, including mines, booby traps, trip wires and tunnels. It was on the basis of these successes that we were asked to devise a dog-based program that would allow army units to track guerrilla infiltrators from the village that they had entered back to their encampment. Although it was important to apprehend the particular group involved in a terrorist act, it was more important to trace the group back to the larger enclave from which it had started. This philosophy was based on the recognition that the VC were not so few in number that they could eventually be overcome by attrition, but rather that attacks had to be made at the very centers of their operations. Most of these centers were well hidden. What the military wanted was, simply, to track the intruders back to their base.

One of the first suggestions was to use a tracker-dog team. The origin of the use of tracker dogs in military and paramilitary operations is unknown. But the fact that these teams are currently in such service as tracking down escaped prisoners and looking for lost persons testifies to their utility.[1]

At the beginning of our research,[2] in the fall of 1968, the tracker dog already was seeing limited service in the U.S. Army. The utilization of these dogs, particularly in regard to their tactical deployment, was derived primarily from British experience and doctrine as developed in Malaya and the Asian subcontinent during the previous twenty-five years. We became acquainted with these procedures mostly through two British Army officers, Captain Hall-Smith and Major Woods, both of whom served as advisers to the U.S. Army.

The normal practice was to use a combined man-dog system, in which the dog, on-leash, is trained to track by use of odor cues, and the human is trained as a visual tracker. Of the two detector elements in this system, the human was considered to be the more important.

Indeed, many armies throughout the world employ human trackers, without dogs.

The example with which we are all familiar is that of the cowboys chasing the outlaw. The sheriff, after raising his white-gloved hand to halt the posse, climbs down from his horse, inspects the ground, finds a familiar hoof mark or a broken branch and, one foot in the stirrup, announces that the bandit went that-a-way.

It is frequently believed that members of primitive cultural groups make better trackers than the so-called more civilized white man. In addition to being able to use visual cues which go unnoticed by others, the native is sometimes also able to use odor cues. The American Indian served this function for the U.S. Army, the Bedouin for the English and later for the Israeli Army. Various African, Australian Aborigine and Malaysian peoples have all fulfilled the function of native tracker for different colonial powers as well as using their prowess for their own hunting activities. The Bushmen of the Kalahari desert in southern Africa are probably the outstanding example. During the season for hunting antelope, the Bushman will approach a grazing herd from downwind, crawling on his belly. The crude bow that he uses necessitates approaching to within twenty-five feet of his prey before releasing the poison-tipped arrow. The poison is made from the pupae of a local variety of beetle. It is relatively slow-acting, taking anywhere from four to ninety-six hours before the animal is felled. During this time the stalwart, persevering native must track and follow the wounded beast until it finally expires. The chase, day and night, continues over hot, sandy, sparsely vegetated hills. The native hunter, in addition to requiring superb stamina, must use all of the senses available to him, including odor. The survival of not only himself but his whole clan depends on his success. Is it any wonder that these natives are capable of enduring such remarkable efforts and of sensing minute variations in the visual and olfactory environment that would go completely unnoticed by the Western civilized man?

From those accomplishments alone one could conclude that need and experience can so sharpen our senses that, to an outsider, it might even appear that a sixth sense had been developed. It is need and experience, or, more technically, motivation and practice, with the addition of reinforcement, that provide the basis for most of the training procedures that we employ with animals. The problem is that of finding the appropriate combinations.

To solve the problem of tracking infiltrators back to their home base, we decided to see if we could train a dog not only to track but also to stalk. That is, the dog should be able to follow a person, but to keep a minimum fixed distance from the target. If, for example, the dog never gets closer than fifty yards to the target, then it is unlikely that the target will become aware that he is being trailed. In addition, if the dog is not being followed by a handler, detection of the trackers would be minimized even further. Therefore it was decided to train the dogs to track off-leash. They could be followed by a handler an additional fifty to one hundred yards to the rear; or in a more advanced method of operation, the dog that was tracking a man could itself be tracked by a helicopter.

In this latter mode the dog carried a small transmitter on his chest. The transmitter, fairly light, under three pounds, was fitted into a specially designed leather harness. An antenna, consisting of a straight thin wire, much like that on a car radio, but half the length, protruded from the transmitter straight up into the the the air. Later on in the program the antenna had to be modified to run along the dog's back, so as to avoid being ensnared in the heavily vegetated area in which we conducted the training. The transmitter was a standard military package designed to send a radio signal or beacon that could be received by suitable airborne equipment, and from which one could then determine distance and direction. Thus in the helicopter, a few miles behind the dog, the pilot could monitor his distance from the dog and the direction in which the dog was moving. This information could, in turn, be relayed back down to ground forces which could either be following the dog directly or waiting to be helicoptered into the designated area at the appropriate time.

The tactical philosophy was fairly simple, the electronic gadgetry standard (although in practice it gave us many problems) and the tracking training seemingly uncomplicated. The element that had to be added, and for which we needed to develop new training techniques, was that of stalking. Let's review, briefly, all of the training procedures employed, the successes and the failures.

The dogs that we chose to work with in this program were Labrador retrievers. This type of retriever can be black, dark brown or yellow-brown. However, black was chosen to give an advantage of decreased detectability during nighttime operations. The Labrador retriever is a middle-sized dog standing between twenty-two and twenty-four inches in height and weighing anywhere between fifty-five and seventy-five pounds. He has a stocky, robust physique with fairly short legs. The coat is short-haired and very dense. The large ears droop down over the side of the head, hound-like, but considerably smaller than those of the hound breeds. The most distinctive feature of the Labrador is its tail, which is otter-like in that it is relatively thick at the base and tapers to a point at the end. In temperament the Labrador is considered to be gentle, but rugged, with an even disposition. He is not easily roused to excitable peaks, but is steadfastly determined in action. Next to the German shepherd, the Labrador is probably the most frequently used dog for military and police work, as well as for guiding the blind. Not to be overlooked is the initial reason for his existence as a distinctive breed—to retrieve animals, usually waterfowl that have been downed in the hunt.

The first task that we attacked was that of training two dogs to track off-leash. One advantage of having the dog work off-leash has already been mentioned—to minimize detection of the tracking system. There are several other advantages.

The type of mission for which the system was being developed was quite dangerous. To follow a band of guerrillas at a fixed distance, at night, without the psychological support of other soldiers or, even more important, without their firepower support, is, understandably, not a task that will attract many volunteers. Without armed support, the mission most likely would not be undertaken. However, with the addition of such support the mission objectives become severely compromised. Not only are the chances of detection of the tracking team increased, but the speed of the track is greatly reduced. The off-leash dog can travel several times more quickly than the on-leash dog. In addition, working at his own pace, not being restrained by the leash, he has much greater endurance and can work for several hours continuously as opposed to a maximum of two hours on-leash in the hot climates of Southeast Asia. Furthermore, the free-ranging dog can cross terrain that would prove to be an unbreachable obstacle to the handler on the other end of the leash.

For all these reasons then, safety of the handler and efficiency of the operation, we were determined to make the system work off-leash and, better still, to have no handler at all on the mission, but rather to have the dog's movements monitored from a helicopter.

Upon arrival at the laboratory kennels, the dogs were allowed ten days to get used to their new living quarters and new diet. The latter is of particular importance since the learning procedures depended on the use of food for reinforcement. Early in our work with the dogs, the decision had been reached to use a concentrated dry food. This not only cut down on spoilage, waste and the cleaning of feeding utensils but allowed us to use the food in the field as reinforcement without the messy consequences of having to carry raw meat. In the hot North Carolina countryside where most of the training took place, this was an important consideration. Use of the same food in kennel and field also enabled us to control exactly the total amount of food that the dog ate each day. Normally we tried to give the dog his entire ration during training. If the dog's usual ration was 500 grams of food per day, and he was scheduled to run fifty trials a day, he would receive fifty ten-gram rewards. In order to do this, it was necessary to use what is called a correction procedure. If on a particular trial the animal made a mistake, he, of course, was not given the reward. The animal was recalled and rerun on the same problem until he made the correct response, and only then was he given his small portion of food. Needless to say, it could happen, especially early in training, that the predetermined number of correct trials was not reached during the course of the day. In such a case, depending on the general behavior of the dog, he might be given the remaining portion of his ration back in the home kennel. If the dog made many errors but was responding vigorously, the remaining food was served out to him. If, however, his behavior was lethargic and he appeared to be slow and unenthusiastic, the unearned food was not forthcoming. In this way he would appear at his next lesson, the next day, a little more hungry, a little more eager to look for his food.

The first days after adaptation were mainly concerned with obedience training. Since the dogs were eventually going to be trained in situations where the handler would not have a physical link to the dog, it was necessary that the dog be responsive to simple verbal commands. The obedience training followed basic techniques described in many dog-training manuals and in the Army's Field Manual 20/20.

When tracker training was begun, a special leather harness was placed on the dog. This harness was used only during the training session, and was removed as soon as the session ended. The harness, with its distinctive odor and feel, served as a cue for the dog as to whether or not he should be actively searching. This cue function, of course, was not present from the very beginning of training but was acquired slowly over the course of many days during which the presence of the harness was consistently associated with the experimental procedures and with reinforcement, while the absence of the harness was never associated with those events.

In the opening stages of training the animal was taken to a large open field. For the purposes of these exercises, we had both bought some land and leased some additional adjacent land outside of Apex, North Carolina. The training site comprised about five acres of an old unplanted squash field surrounded on all sides by pine forests through which coursed many footpaths and stream beds, the latter mostly dry during the hot summer months.

A training team consisted of the dog, his handler, a trainer and a decoy. The decoy was the object of the search, the target. Training began early in the morning when the sun was still hidden behind the trees. The dog, hungry, not having eaten since sometime the previous day, the trainer and the decoy arrived at the field about six-thirty. The three of them stood in a close group while the trainer removed the light chain collar and slipped on the leather harness, tightening it so that it fit snugly over the dog's smooth black coat. The decoy, carrying a pocketful of dry dog food, walked about ten paces away from the dog. When the trainer released the dog, it at first wandered in a tight circle around the trainer's legs. The trainer stood quietly, passively, ignoring the dog. The dog, being a friendly, domesticated creature, and not having received any reinforcement from the handler, began to move outward toward the decoy. When he got to within a foot from the decoy, the handler called the command "Sit." The animal dropped back on his haunches, and the decoy, food already in hand, reached out and fed the dog a small portion of the dry chow. As he was feeding him, he also briskly rubbed the dog on his head and neck, repeating "Good boy, good boy" or some equally comfortable phrase. The first trial of the first day of training was successfully completed. If only all of the trials would be that effortless.

Now the keen observer of these first trials will raise a skeptical eyebrow and protest that the dog is learning to find the man by vision or to find the food itself by odor. He will complain that the dog does not have to rely on the odor of the man. The objection is quite valid. There are, however, several circumstances that dictate this procedure at the beginning of training. First of all, it is of the utmost importance that the reinforcement be delivered as soon after the correct response is made as is humanly possible. This is especially true early in training. Now, if the handler were the instrument for delivery of the reinforcement, he first would have to walk the ten paces, taking a few seconds to do it, to reach the animal before feeding him. These two or three seconds are quite critical. It will be remembered that in the pigeon study, where the birds had to discriminate between slides containing man-made objects and slides not containing man-made objects, the delivery of grain reinforcement was triggered electrically. There was less than one half second between the time the bird pecked at the disc and his ingestion of the food. It is possible, of course, to prolong the time between a given response that we desire the animal to emit and the ultimate reinforcement. This is accomplished by creating a chain of secondary reinforcers, all of which have been linked with the final reinforcement.

When the dog sits by the decoy, early in training, he must be reinforced immediately—even if this means confounding the critical stimuli (the decoy odor, with which he must learn to track) with the food odor. Later in training, when there is a firm bond established between the decoy and reinforcement, other techniques can be introduced to teach the dog to track any human and not just a human carrying his favorite dog food.

The procedure in which the decoy moves out ten or so strides from the dog and reinforces the dog after he approaches and sits beside him is repeated several times until the dog responds quickly and reliably to the decoy. The dog, when he has accomplished this, will no longer circle the trainer before approaching the decoy. Instead, immediately upon release (usually accompanied by the command "Search," which like the stimuli from the harness provides a cue to execute the desired behavior) the animal darts toward the decoy and, not even waiting for the verbal command from the trainer to sit, assumes the sitting position, "eagerly expecting" the food.

Phrases such as "eager expectation" usually have no place in the vocabulary of a behaviorist. Two major reasons speak against such usage. First of all, they usually lack an operational definition. That is, they represent a state of mind rather than an observable behavior. The second objection is that such phrases are anthropomorphic. They attribute to the animal a feeling derived from the experiences of humans. There is no possible way to determine whether the animal is indeed experiencing this feeling. Feelings, after all, by definition, are private. We share them with other humans only with considerable difficulty and, even then, with much misunderstanding. Anthropomorphic responses result when the behavior of an animal or an object evokes a particular feeling in us. Since the organism evokes the feeling in the human observer, the observer is compelled to endow the organism with a similar feeling. Why this should be is an interesting but unanswered question. That such anthropomorphism is scientifically invalid, although perhaps personally appealing, is shown by the alacrity with which we make these assignments of humanlike qualities. In poetry and literature this talent expresses itself in the pathetic fallacy. Does an angry cloud feel anything, let alone share a feeling with its human observer? Of course not.

Returning to the dog, why was he described as "eagerly expecting" his food? The anthropomorphic phrase was used as simple shorthand to describe the fact that typically the dog will salivate profusely while in the process of making the correct sitting response, and will continue to salivate until the food is finally consumed. It is the preparatory nature of the salivary response, which facilitates eating the dry food, that allows us, still somewhat cavalierly, to speak about the dog's expectations. But there should be no misunderstanding. It is not believed for a moment that the dog is experiencing the same feelings as a hungry man about to cut into a charcoaled steak. Perhaps he is, but since there is no way of testing the proposition, it is better to let sleeping dogs lie, twitching their body rather than dreaming.

In addition to the salivation, and at the same time, the male dogs, while searching, will often exhibit a very noticeable erection of the penis. In spite of what one might see as being conflicting desires, the dog does not attempt to mount the decoy who is handing the food to him. Nor does the dog attempt any spectacular sexual gymnastics with the food itself. He eats it, quickly, in one or two gulps, and then continues to lick the decoy's hand, covering it with spittle.

The saliva might serve as an olfactory marker or cue for directing the animal toward the food-carrying decoy. However, there is no evidence concerning this newly hypothesized function for the spittle. Nevertheless, considering that the dog is a macrosmatic animal—that is, an unusually large portion of his brain is devoted to olfactory information processing, and much of his behavior is guided by odor—it would not be too surprising to find that the dog's own spittle odor is used for purposes of identification. It is known, for example, that dogs will mark the limits of their territory by urinating at appropriately designated places. Urine signposts are probably also used by dogs that range over wide expanses of territory to enable them to find their way back to their homes. Odor, of course, is also used by the male dog to sense a female dog in heat.

One might speculate as to the function of an odorous spittle that can be identified by its owner or by other dogs. Might it be used to tag food which has to be left unattended, either to aid in finding it again or to repel competitors from stealing it? After all, if a human spits in his food no one else is likely to partake of it!

Once the dog has learned the very small trick of going straight to the decoy and sitting, the distance between the point of release of the dog and the decoy is progressively increased. From ten paces it is moved up to twenty paces. After this change is responded to in a rapid, reliable manner, the distance is increased still further. The actual progression of distances that were employed varied somewhat from dog to dog, but approximated the order 10, 20, 50, 100 yards. All of this training was accomplished in the open field with the target within line of sight of the dog. However, it should be remembered that the dog does not have a particularly keen visual system. It is considerably poorer than that of man, although it is extremely sensitive to movement. Toward the end of the 100-yard trials particular care was taken that the decoy remain immobile. That the dogs could take advantage of movement was amply demonstrated when a decoy, in a later stage of training, assuming a half-hidden position in the brush, was startled by a hornet. As he tried to brush it away from his face, the dog immediately alerted to the position and took off after him.

To reach the final stages of the 100-yard criterion could take anywhere from two to five days of intensive training. The training was usually done in two shifts, each of two hours, early in the morning and late in the afternoon.

The 100-yard distance was the critical stage. At this point, once

mastered, two innovations were introduced. First, the food-rein-
forcement function was removed from the decoy and given to the
handler. Now when the dog sat by the decoy, the decoy vigorously
rubbed him about the head and neck and whispered "Good dog,
good dog" until the trainer arrived with the food. Since the tactual
stimuli of the rubbing and the auditory stimuli of the voice had
previously been paired with the food, they became secondary reinforcers and served to maintain the dog's sitting response in front of
the decoy until the trainer arrived on the scene with the food.

Removing the food from the decoy did not seem to cause any disruption in the dog's ability to find him. This suggests that in the previous stage, even though the olfactory cues from the food were available to the dog, they were not used.

However, the sudden increase in the delay of reinforcement, the
waiting for food, which went abruptly from a second to almost half a
minute, resulted in very noticeable agitation on the part of the dog.
At the beginning of this new stage, the dog had to be kept in place by
the decoy firmly gripping his harness. Barking and yelping were not
unusual. Gradually these undesirable behaviors diminished in intensity and then disappeared entirely. After twenty or thirty trials the
dog would sit, head stretched forward, tongue hanging out, often
drooling profusely, with the head of his wet, pink engorged penis pro-
truding from its dark sheath.

Once the problems of delivering the reinforcement were taken care
of we could proceed to the main task, that of making the decoy more
and more invisible. The two main tools for accomplishing this were
camouflage and distance. By hiding the decoy within the still short
distances, the visual cues could be obliterated, forcing the dog to rely
on odor. On the other hand, the short distances should allow the
odorous stimuli to be relatively intense. Several different camouflage
techniques were used—lying flat in the weed-filled field, hiding behind
a large rock or tree at the edge of the field and even, toward the end
of training, digging and hiding in a foxhole, on the top of which was
placed a burlap-canvased frame which supported the natural ground
cover of the particular area. These exercises were conducted within a
100- and 200-yard radius from the release point.

The positions of the decoy changed from trial to trial. This was
true for both the positions of the starting points and the positions for
hiding. It was quite early in this stage of training that yet another

very important change was introduced. Until that time the same decoy was used repeatedly. Might we not end up with a tracker dog that was superb, but could only find one very special individual?

There were, in fact, some hints that this process was already developing. When the first new decoy was introduced, the tracking behavior was badly disturbed. When this occurred, we retreated to an earlier stage of training with the decoy visible. Using as many as five or six decoys each day, we rapidly advanced, again, to the place at which our progress had been stalled. Now the dog would track any individual. As frequently as possible new decoys were introduced, individuals never before encountered by the dog.

Visitors to the field station often were enlisted for the day's activities. Most people enjoyed the idea of this cat-and-mouse game, in this case dog-and-man. More than one hole was uncovered alongside of which sat the proud dog and inside of which sat a dismayed Army major or a professor of French literature. The games became quite competitive toward the end of training. A battle-tried Ranger field commander, three weeks from Vietnam, was given a field pack and an hour's head start on one of the Labradors. He was found within less than half an hour after he darted off into thick pine woods. Later, he reneged on his bet to treat the entire staff to a steak dinner, claiming some mysterious form of foul play. He demanded a rematch on the following day.

When the animals were performing satisfactorily on the 100- to 200-yard tracks in the open field, the training was moved into the network of paths and trails that ran through the pine forests of the area surrounding the field. The four dogs that reached this point in the training were then divided into two groups. One group was given a schedule of tracking problems of increasing difficulty, while the other group was diverted to develop the stalking response.

Since the distances were such that the handler might require well over an hour to reach the dog after the detection, provided that he could even find him at all, the feeding function was returned to the decoy. We were satisfied with the evidence obtained earlier that we were not creating a food-odor-tracking dog. Nevertheless, periodically, although not too frequently, checks on the assumption were introduced. This was done by sending the decoy out on a track without food. The dog's behavior on these nonreinforced trials was indistinguishable from the behavior on the reinforced trials.

To facilitate communication between handler and decoy, two-way radio receivers and transmitters were carried. This allowed the decoy to describe his track, which was necessary for our evaluation of the dog's performance, and to signal to the handler when he, the decoy, had completed the run and was in a hidden position. The dog too carried a transmitter to accustom him to the weight of the device that would later be used to send direction-finding signals to the helicopter.

The basic procedures, with the exceptions discussed above, were the same as that employed in the open-field training. The target leaves from a predesignated area and sets the scheduled track. At the completion of the track, anywhere from fifteen minutes to almost two hours later, he radios back to the handler to release the dog. The dog and the handler go to the area at which the track began. The special harness is strapped to the dog and the dog is given the command "Search!" With nose close to the ground the dog moves quickly back and forth, almost systematically, for ten or twenty seconds and then bounds off into the woods, almost invariably finding his target in a considerably shorter time than it took for the decoy to get there. When the dog reaches the target and sits, he is, of course, fed. On the rare occasion when he fails to find the target he is recaptured and sent to the kennels without food until the next trial. On the longer tracks, of which there might be only one per day, food is withheld until the first successful trial on the following day.

At first we concentrated on merely lengthening the track while keeping it simple and straight. Then special problems were introduced within the track. These problems included turns at acute angles, backtracking, walking across streams and walking in streams. Occasionally some of these devices to foil the dog were successful and the dog would have to be trained to overcome the particular problem. In such cases, the dog, on-leash, would be given three or four consecutive problems involving, let us say, a backtrack. During these practice trials the trainer provided guidance for the dog in establishing successful casting patterns. This was accomplished by making sure that the dog did not wander too far away from the track and verbally reinforcing the correct turning response.

Training progressed rapidly with these procedures, the total time of the trial reached ninety to one hundred and twenty minutes. The two dogs did not indicate any ability to perform beyond these time limits. Although not having firm evidence, we concluded that the problem was a result of the very limited climatic and geographical conditions under which all of the training had been conducted. In particular, the densely wooded pine forests and the hot, humid conditions contributed, we suggested, to the lingering of an airborne decoy scent. Thus the animals had never been given adequate experience with ground scent.

The difference between ground scent and airborne scent is quite important and needs some elaboration. Unfortunately there is no available literature that allows us even to confirm the existence of this differentiation. Nevertheless, it is interesting to note that various breeds of dogs are said to be specialized in one or the other mode of operation. The hounds, as for example the bloodhound, supposedly uses ground scent, while the retrievers, pointers and setters supposedly use airborne scent. Watching the behavior of these animals working in the field seems to support the distinction. The hounds work with their heads down close to the earth, while the others work with their heads raised, noses pointed upward in the air.

These different behavioral patterns may be related to the different functions for which the animals had been bred. Retrievers, pointers and setters are essentially bird dogs. Although each has a different function—the pointer to identify the position of a bird in a field, the setter to flush the bird into the air, and the retriever to bring back the game after it has been shot down—they all have birds as their target subjects. Birds, after all, get to a particular place by flying through the air. Therefore, they are incapable of leaving a ground-scent trail. That is not to say that the flying bird leaves an airborne trail to be followed. An airborne scent is an odor that emanates from the target. The ground scent, on the other hand, emanates from the track that the target has laid. The sweating decoy, running through the woods, deposits a countless number of molecules along his path, on the ground and the surrounding vegetation. The series of infected points provides a highway of odorous road signs for the dog to follow. Thus, with airborne scent there is one radiating source, while with ground scent there are thousands of small sources that have been laid down, so to speak, by one big dripping source.

That the Labrador retrievers that we were training were using airborne scent is suggested by several types of behaviors that they exhibited. First of all, they frequently worked with their noses up in the air. Secondly, they often took shortcuts, not following the exact trail taken by the decoy. This was particularly true as the dog approached the decoy. Thirdly, their tracking behavior sometimes was disturbed by changing wind patterns. Although we never tried it because of the absence of a prevailing wind direction, my guess is that the dogs could have been completely vanquished if the decoy escaped in such a way as to have the wind blowing on his back, with the dog coming from the same direction. Finally, the ability of the dogs to track over water also strongly suggests that the source of information was airborne scent rather than ground scent.

Thus it was concluded that the animals were homing in on airborne odor which was available to them for only a relatively short period of time as compared to the longer-lasting ground scent. Our problem, of course, was multiplied by having chosen a breed of dog, the Labrador retriever, which already has a predisposition for utilizing the airborne scent over the ground scent. Under the circumstances, we all considered a successful two-hour track to be a considerable accomplishment.

Those people interested in the actual operational use of trackers might ask which type of dog is best suited for this task. The answer to this question depends on the terrain and climate of the area as well as the lead time that the target is expected to have. If the elapsed time between the time the target subject left an area and the time that the dog is brought to the area is short, less than two hours, it would seem logical to conclude that the air-sniffing dog is to be preferred. He will work faster and be more immune to planned distractions and decoying maneuvers than the ground-sniffing dog. However, if the track is older than two hours, the slower, more persevering ground-sniffing hound is to be preferred.

In most cases the operational requirements will be so varied as to preclude reliance on any one of the specialized breeds. Either both types should be kept on hand or efforts should be made to train a breed, not specialized on the air-ground odor dimension, to utilize both sources of information. Our experience with German shepherds in other programs suggests that they might be talented candidates for such a task.

No matter what the source of the odor, the question arises as to how the animal derives directional information from it. A complete answer to this question must be based on a comprehensive theory of odor perception. Such a theory would begin by addressing itself to two fundamental problems. First of all, what are the physical-chemical properties of molecules that are capable of causing discharges of olfactory receptors and giving rise to the sensation of smell? What distinguishes these molecules from other molecules that cannot elicit an odor sensation? Secondly, what are the differential characteristics between odor-producing molecules that result in different smells? These questions are quite basic, and with the notable exception of odor, are well mapped out for the other senses.

In vision, for example, the adequate stimulus for causing the firing of a receptor cell in the retina is electromagnetic radiation whose wavelengths fall between 400 and 700 nanometers,[3] what we normally call light. Secondly, there are particular wavelengths that are reliably associated with different sensations of color. When a beam of light composed mostly of radiations that are 400 nanometers strikes the retina, blue is perceived; with 700 nanometers red is perceived. These are fundamental facts of which we have been aware for decades.

Yet in the sensory realm of olfaction we are not even close to being able to make such statements. There is some small irony in the fact that our oldest and most primitive sensory systems are the most resistant to explanation. I suspect that the dog, in some sense, shows a better understanding of olfaction than does his human master. In man the olfactory system is degenerate. Vision and audition are the keys to man's ability to adjust to and dominate the environment. It may well be that man, who can only frame questions in terms of his own experiences, is not even on the right track in exploring the olfactory world.

Nevertheless, in regard to obtaining directional signals from odor, it would seem that the information must be contained in gradients of stimulus intensity. Let's begin by making some simplifying assumptions. The odor intensity is proportional to the number of odor molecules falling on the olfactory receptor surface. Secondly, when the source is primary, as for example the decoy, there is no diminution in the number of odor molecules produced by the source over time. In other words, ignoring the trivial fluctuation as a result of eating, defecating, showering, the strength of my body odor is the same at ten o'clock in the morning as it is at ten o'clock at night. As long as the metabolic processes of life continue, the living organism produces odoriferous substances. If anything, in regard to our running decoy, his odor intensity might very well be increasing with increased length of the chase. This would occur because one of the important sources of human odor comes from certain components of sweat.

For the moment, we will assume that the number of odor molecules of the primary odor source is constant. However, the perceived intensity of the airborne odor which comes from the primary source will be proportional to the distance from the detector to the source. This must occur because the molecules diffuse out from the source and mix with increasing volumes of air away from the source. The molecules thus become less and less available to the detecting nose. Although the geometry of the situation is complex, the net effect is that a gradient of odor-molecule density is created such that at the source there is the largest number of molecules per volume of air. Behind the source, as a function of the time since the decoy has been at a particular place, there is a decreasing density of odorant molecules. The dog, constantly moving back and forth across the true path (in an ideal, no-wind condition), is able to sample the intensities and to keep oriented along the line of maximally increasing intensity. The important suggestion here is not that the dog responds to the absolute intensity of the odorant, but rather to the direction of increasing stimulation. Isolated punctate stimulation carries only meager information as compared to the information contained in patterns of stimulation.[4] One such pattern, or rather family of patterns, which describes the rate of change of density of the odorous molecules per volume of air, is hypothesized as being the source of directional information for the tracking dog.

To clarify the meaning of the gradient concept and to illustrate how gradient stimulation is used as a source of information in other sensory modalities, let us look at an example from vision. Imagine yourself looking at an infinitely long stone wall which stretches to your right and to your left as far as the eye can see. Without any doubt you would be able to tell whether the wall was straight—that is, perpendicular to the ground—or whether the wall was tilted toward you or away from you. What is the stimulus that gives you the perception of the slant of the wall? In this case the stimulus can be described in terms of a texture gradient. If, for example, the wall is tilted away from you so that its base is closer to you than its top, then the number of discriminable texture elements, of light and dark, and the number of stones in your visual field will be fewer at the base than at the top. The number of texture elements or stones is proportional to the distance to the eye. As the eye scans up the wall, more and more of these elements fill its field of view. The rate at which the number increases contains all of the information necessary to calculate the slant, and, indeed, can be used to perceive slant under the conditions just described.[5]

The dog's nose may well be bathed in similar gradients of stimulation, providing him with a world of information and a phenomenal experience of which we, as humans, can only guess. If quantitative differences can even hint at qualitative changes, we can start to appreciate some of the possibilities by comparing the olfactory system of man with that of the dog.

Although with practice even man can learn to use his nose to perform feats almost unimaginable to the novice nose, the dog will leave man far behind in any olfactory race. Examples of the lengths to which human noses can be stretched can be found not only in the hunting, tracking Bushman of the Kalahari Desert, but also in Western industrial society among the experienced nose men of the perfume, wine and cheese industries. It is said that a skilled perfumer is capable of differentiating hundreds of odors from each other. For one like myself, who can barely tell the difference between a man's after-shave lotion and an old sweaty sock, such accomplishments smell almost of extrasensory perception.

Getting back to the tracking dog, some reasonable speculations have been proposed to explain how the dog, using airborne scent, maintains the chase in the proper direction. For the ground-scent dog the principles should be exactly the same. However, the nature of gradients becomes altered since the odorant molecules are now emanating from many small sources, each one of which is fairly close to the other, and each one of which is becoming progressively weaker over time. Unlike the primary source, these multiple secondary sources, or spoors, as hunters call them, have a finite number of odorant molecules which are being decreased with the length of time since they were laid down.

The next question is even more difficult. How does the tracking dog know that he is to pursue the odor of the fleeing decoy rather than one of the thousands of other odors that must be present in the area? Again, one can merely speculate. (And hope, by the way, that these speculations may stimulate some young researcher to actively investigate these problems. Experimental research in these areas is sadly absent. Even the work that my colleagues and I have done, does not qualify as being experimentation. We have trained dogs, and while so doing have attempted to make careful observation of behavior. But these sorts of observations are only the source of hypotheses, which in turn must be ground through the crucible of a formal experimental design before they can be accepted.)

The trained tracker dog is brought to the area from which the decoy has recently departed. In the case of the prisoner going over the wall, or the lost child, the problem of cueing the dog in on the appropriate odor is considerably simplified. There is always an article of clothing that has been conveniently left behind. How often have you seen in the movies that big bull frog of a southern sheriff, with his too small cowboy hat, being tugged at by a lop-eared, liver-colored hound? When the hound's pace slows, and the dog and his master exchange bewildered looks, the sheriff whips out a dirty T-shirt belonging to the escaped prisoner and pushes it in the dog's face. The chase resumes immediately afterward.

In the type of military situation which was described at the beginning of this chapter, the insurgents do not leave such distinctive calling cards. There is no visible, tangible evidence of their having visited the village. In such a case, the dog must be brought to an area through which the targets have passed. If the area has not been traversed by other people, the dog appears to be capable of taking the most recent, smelliest track available, and following it.

Frequently in such a military operation the swarming of troops over an area immediately after an incident will completely obliterate the olfactory trail and make it impossible to use the dog for tracking. Several countermeasures have been developed which should serve to minimize these effects. Some of these will be discussed in Chapter 10.

Thus far we have focused on simple tracking while discussion of the development of the stalking response has been postponed. The reason for the procrastination is quite simple. The work on the stalking response can best be characterized by its stubborn refusal to yield promising results. With the hope that something can be learned even from failure and partial successes, the training procedures, nevertheless, will be described.

The ultimate goal in training the dogs to stalk was to have the animal follow the target, but at a distance of 50 to 100 yards from him. In this way, the target would not become aware that he was being shadowed, and therefore he would lead the dog back to the enemy camp. The dog, of course, in turn, would be followed by a military force whose mission would be to capture or destroy the central enemy stronghold.

The stalking dogs began their training in a manner similar to that described for the trackers. This training was carried up to the point where the animals were responding correctly on simple tracks that took about fifteen minutes to set. That is, the target or decoy was given a fifteen-minute head start. He took off on a more or less straight path into the pine woods and assumed an unobtrusive position. He then radioed back to the trainer, who brought the dog to the area from which the decoy plunged into the woods, and released the dog. The dog moved rapidly over this area, sliding from right to left with nose to the ground, like a little boy pushing a marble. At the point of the target's entry into the woods the dog continued with the same behavior for several hundred yards. Then, lifting his head, apparently switching to the airborne scent, he took off at a trot in the direction of the target, sometimes, in an area free of underbrush, switching to a long-legged loping pace. Within several minutes the decoy was discovered.

When the behavior was stabilized, elicited reliably, the dog was put back onto a long leash during the tracking. The purpose of these series of trials was to familiarize the trainer with any individual, idiosyncratic behavior that the animals might display when crossing from the ground-scent cues to the airborne scent that was present when the target was sufficiently close. This crossover point was to be the cue for the animal to cease pursuing the decoy.

At the point where the trainer felt that the dog could accurately distinguish the boundary between ground and airborne scent, he placed the dog in a down position. The target would then run up and feed the dog. This was done in order to keep the response firmly tied to the presence of a target. As soon as the animal's behavior indicated that he was sufficiently target-oriented, the delivery of reinforcement was phased back. The trainer gradually became the exclusive source of reinforcement.

The above procedures proved inadequate to elicit the needed voluntary down responses. We thought that perhaps the inter-trial interval, the time between the tracking problems, was too long to promote good learning of the down response to the crossover point from ground scent to airborne scent. In general, massed practice, several trials per minute, is not conducive to good learning. But when the time between practice trials is extended, it too may be detrimental to efficient learning. In our situation the time between opportunities to practice the response was about thirty minutes. A second procedure was, therefore, attempted. The interval between trials was reduced to several minutes. This technique did elicit voluntary responses but of insufficient frequency and reliability.

A study of the problem produced the hypothesis that, whereas the decrease in inter-trial intervals had significantly aided in the establishment of a response, the stimulus to elicit it was still largely undifferentiated by the dog. This stimulus, the condition of change from ground to airborne scent, may have gained poor stimulus control of the animal's behavior (the down response) because of the unreliable detection of the boundary by the handler. It will be remembered that the handler had to decide when the dog switched from ground to airborne scent by observing the behavior of the dog. This behavior was not always unambiguous. In addition, the time between the appearance of the ground-air scent transition and the handler-delivered reinforcement may have been too long for effective learning of the response to the stimulus.

Again, we changed procedures. This attempt used an arbitrary 20-foot distance between the dog and the decoy as the discriminative stimulus. Whenever the dog reached the 20-foot mark he was placed in the down position and reinforced with some food by the handler. We did recognize, even at the beginning of this stage, that distance per se, as a stimulus, might be quite difficult for the dog to learn. An additional discrete stimulus, clear and unambiguous, might be needed as a training aid to mark the 20-foot border.

We tried to train for the desired ground-air scent boundary directly with the addition of a significant primary stimulus. The dogs first were trained by means of standard conditioning techniques to assume the down position upon hearing a whistle blow. The whistle is tooted. The dog is gently pushed to the lying position, and then fed. With a number of repetitions of this simple sequence, the dog learns to lie down when he hears the whistle, and no longer has to be helped down by the handler.

As soon as this response was reliably elicited by the whistle, the animals were put back on the ten-to-fifteen-minute tracking task. The trainer was instructed to signal the target via his radio when the dogs first picked up airborne-source scent. The target then blew the whistle, which put the dog in the down position.

Again, we failed. We rationalized that this was probably due to a combination of the reversion to long inter-trial intervals and the fact that the external signs of the dog's awareness of airborne scent had been almost completely extinguished.

The final set of procedures that we tried combined the whistle approach with the setting of an arbitrary limit of 20 feet from the target. The dogs were run for two days of 60 trials per day. Inter-trial intervals were reduced to one to two minutes. The trainer placed the dog in a down position two or three trials in succession at a distance of 20 feet from the target. On the next one or two runs, the animal was permitted to approach the target freely until he reached the 20-foot limit, at which point he was "whistled down." After 20 to 30 such trials, voluntary down responses began to appear with steadily increasing frequency. By the beginning of the third day, reinforcement was made contingent upon such voluntary responses. Five more days were spent in stabilizing the behavior and bringing it up to 90 percent reliability. The dogs were then taken off the leash and trained to work at the limits of usual contact with the trainer.

In the next step we dropped the discrete trial structure and used a continually moving target. The dogs pursued and caught up with the target, responded by going down and were reinforced. We then waited for two minutes and pursued the target again. The contingencies of reinforcement in such a situation are such as to make it to the dog's advantage to respond as early as possible. They therefore began to work back, increasing the distance between response and target without specific training. Right before we had to give a demonstration to the Army they were responding at 50 to 60 yards behind target. The response was still largely cued by visual stimuli. However, several responses were displayed beyond visual range, when wind conditions were appropriate. An accurate discrimination between olfactorily cued responses and false positive responses was impossible. That is, we could never know whether the dog was really responding to the odor or whether he was giving a response to some other stimulus which we may have mistakenly assumed was odor. Without monitoring some physiological response of the animal, the distinction between olfactory-controlled responses and responses controlled through some other sensory modality was almost impossible. This stage of training was therefore long and "sloppy." It was almost inevitable that responses made to inappropriate, nonodorous stimuli were reinforced.

Food reinforcement was phased out during the last week of training, being used only for the first trial, last trial and every correct trial which followed an error. On the remaining trials, verbal reinforcement was used, with much praise being given for correct responding, and a harsh "Bad dog" being used for incorrect (whistle down) responses.

During the last week of training prior to the demonstration, the target was given a twenty-to-thirty-minute head start on about half the trials. Every such trial contained three to six choice points at trail intersections and one open-field crossing. The dogs displayed some stalking ability in being able to follow the target in such situations.

In general, we were quite pleased with what we had achieved with the tracking behavior. With the use of learning principles derived from laboratory studies we were able to train dogs to be expert trackers. This was done in considerably less time than anyone had expected. However, in regard to the training of the stalking response we were disappointed, and were anticipating the demonstration to the Army with some apprehension.

Why were we anxious about the demonstration? After all, this was supposed to be a feasibility study. We were to determine whether or *not* it was possible to train dogs in a particular operation. But somehow the people that give money for these kinds of projects have a way of forgetting the meaning of feasibility. It is seen as being a question of "when" rather than "whether," and not producing the needed product is perceived as failing in the mission. It is "You promised us a stalking dog" rather than "You promised to see if you could train a stalking dog." Since we were doing this work under contract, and were heavily dependent on our military customers for our bread and butter, it is no surprise that we anticipated the demonstration with a certain lack of pleasure.

The demonstrations took place in mid-June 1969. It was attended by a number of representatives from the Limited War Laboratory, including Mr. Cutler, Dr. Krauss, Mr. Tomlinson and Colonel Hastings, as well as all of the senior staff of Behavior Systems Inc.

The first item on the program was a demonstration of independent tracking over a short but complex course that included a backtrack, then a stream crossing and a final loop in the vicinity of the backtrack. The dog, Kala, was released fifteen minutes after the target started. When it reached the backtrack, it picked up the source scent of the target and went directly to him without completing the track. For the second run, the target was observed from the helicopter as he traveled from a point two miles from the BSI field station to a field on BSI land. This course included rough open fields, heavily wooded areas, freshly plowed fields, streams and swamps. The dog, Luke, was released one hour after the target left and made contact within half an hour. When the dog was observed crossing open areas, it was obvious that he was following the target's track. For the third run, Kala was again run on a short track. Once more, she picked up the source scent of the target before completing the entire track.

On the next day, Luke was run on a forty-five-minute track in a large field which was situated such that the target and the dog could be observed throughout the whole trial. It was amply apparent that Luke was following the ground scent of the target.

Several days later, we made the attempt to demonstrate stalking. The dog, Nimrod, was run first on a one-mile course through both wooded and open terrain. The target was given a five-minute head start and continued to move along the trail without stopping. This allowed the dog to overtake the target 20 times during the course of the run. Out of 20 trials the dog made 19 good responses, assuming the down position as soon as the target's presence was perceived ahead.

Next, the dog, Babe, was run on a one-mile course through both wooded and open terrain. The target was given a full twenty minutes' head start. The dog had to follow the track without a handler being present and to make the proper response upon perceiving the target. Babe successfully completed both the tracking and stalking response requirements.

The dogs were indeed good to us on those days, performing much better than we had any right to expect. This phenomenon, of better performance on demonstration days than on normal working days, was something that we had repeatedly run across, much to our satisfaction, in our work with dogs for the Army. After the demonstration, we turned the dogs over to the Army. Unfortunately, we were never informed about their subsequent utilization. There is no reason to believe that they were not used in the type of operations described at the beginning of the chapter—to track guerrilla bands back to their encampments.

9

Off the Beaten Track

As we already have noted in the previous chapter, dogs have been used for a wide variety of tracking tasks; they have been employed in the hunt, for animals and for people. Whether it be a Rhodesian ridgeback tracking a wild boar, a bloodhound searching for an escaped prisoner or our own stalking Labrador retriever following a terrorist back to his camp, they all operate on the same information, information cryptically encoded in vaporized molecules.

Whether one is interested in making it more difficult for the dog to follow someone, or interested in making that task easier for the dog, depends, of course, on which side of the contest one finds oneself. In either case one must look to the olfactory stimulus, the smell, or the olfactory sensors as a source of increasing or decreasing the tracking and detection capability of the dog.

As a result of our work with the stalking tracking dog we drew the attention of the CIA. It would appear that their collective organizational nose was held high sniffing the research and development environment for new possibilities, for new solutions to old problems.

Our contact was Dr. George Hoag,[1] who strangely enough resembled a bloodhound. He was a big-boned man, in his mid-fifties, with a loose, heavy skin that caused his cheeks to hang in deep furrowed folds obscuring his jaw. A football player's chin peeked out between the drooping jowls. Looking out over these lank folds of tissue were two tired, long-lashed, big brown eyes.

Someone tried to convince me that he really was a bloodhound, cleverly disguised as a person. My own theory of the Existence of Dr. Hoag was quite the opposite. The not so clever people at the CIA had tried to disguise one of their agents as a bloodhound but were not completely successful. A telltale touch of red on his nose would always blow his cover.

One could only surmise at the history of Dr. Hoag. The more that I came to know about him, the less certain I was to be of his very existence. He appeared at our office in Raleigh several times, quietly, unannounced, always dressed in the same gray suit, badly crumpled, as though he had been circling the Raleigh-Durham airport for two days in an overheated airplane before descending on us. And always carrying a black leather attaché case. We never really knew to whom he belonged, but assumed that since he refused to tell us anything, then he must be CIA. When, after a while, a little business developed between us, we would correspond with him through letters inserted in letters inserted in letters. The outside envelope would be sent to something like "The Enjoyable Toy Company" with an address in Arlington, Virginia, while the next envelope would be labeled "For Mr. Charles Dickens." The final envelope, which may have contained some significant item such as a bill for a fifty-pound sack of Purina Dog Chow, was completely unmarked. Each time I went through the ritual of addressing the set of envelopes, I felt that I was participating in some symbolic religious act. It was like a mystical ceremony to commemorate the existence of nonsense. The more envelopes that you opened, the farther away from reality you were displaced.

Communicating with Dr. Hoag by telephone was no less of a celebration of irrationality.

"Hello, the Enjoyable Toy Company, Stuffed Animal Division," answered the telephone operator, and then continued in too good English, "To whom do you wish to speak?"

"Charles Dickens," I would say.

The reply was always the same.

"Mr. Dickens is not in right now. May I take a message or have him call you back?"

Somehow Dickens-Hoag always managed to resurface at the Toy Company within minutes of my hanging up the phone. I suspected that they sent him down to the corner phone booth with a handful of nickels to return my call. In that way he could escape the powerful monitoring devices that were undoubtedly aimed at the Toy Company from the not too distant Russian Embassy. Thus we could communicate with the utmost security.

"But I never received your bill for the dog food," he said once, and then added, "We will have to have another meeting so that I can explain to you, again, how to use those envelopes."

Dr. Hoag had sniffed around enough to know that our group might be of some help to him. Sitting in my office, attaché case on his lap, he broached the problem in the most general of terms. What are some of the ways one could evade a tracking dog? From this, the task became more and more specific until finally we had a complete description of the operational situation. Whether it was accurate, or even purposely misleading, I do not know, but the story that was given to me is described below.

Somewhere inside North Vietnam there was a prison in which several inmates of interest to the U.S. government were kept together with several hundred other prisoners. The prison was in a remote area. The main deterrents to escape were the extensive distances that would have to be covered before safety could be achieved, and the dogs that were employed by the prison warders to track and to attack. A plan had been developed that would allow the several prisoners in question to break out and to reach a safe destination. The major obstacle that stood between the prison and freedom was the dogs. What could be done, using materials available to the prisoners, to prevent the dogs from following them?

Hoag, himself, had already investigated several possibilities for concealing an odor track or for preventing one from being laid down. Using tracking dogs from one of the local municipal police forces in Virginia, he had experimented with rubber boots introduced at the beginning of the track as well as exchanged in the middle of the track. He reported that these procedures were ineffective in preventing the tracking behavior of the dogs. This was not too surprising, particularly if the dogs were air sniffers as opposed to ground sniffers; that is, if they were operating on the scent from the source as opposed to the scent deposited on the trail itself. Several other attempts also failed to disrupt the dogs' performance. Laying very hot pepper on the trail was of no avail. Nor, when the track crossed an airfield, was it effective to have the hot exhaust of a jet pass over the trail.

It seems, from other research, that the significant odorous component that the dog uses is a constituent of the fatty and oily secretions from the body. The major portion probably comes from the hairy regions of the body, particularly the scalp, but also from all over the skin and, to a lesser degree, from exhalations while breathing.

To prevent these sources from radiating their odoriferous vapors is virtually impossible. One would have to create a completely closed biological system, with the fleeing man enshrouded in a nonpermeable plastic sheet in which the vapors from breathing and sweating are captured and prevented from exiting to the surrounding environment. This would provide a perfect solution to the problem of evading the tracking dog. Of course, it was a completely impractical solution.

The best that could be recommended, at least then, with so little hard information available, was some set of procedures designed to reduce the production and distribution of the odorous materials. We suggested that, if at all possible, the prisoners should shave off all of their body hair, shower thoroughly and then coat their entire bodies with oil or Vaseline. All of this was designed to reduce the secretion of sweat. In addition, the break should be made in the coolest part of the day.

There are a number of serious problems that arise as a result of the solution. Sweating, along with the subsequent evaporation of sweat from the skin surface, is one of the major mechanisms for maintaining a constant body temperature in a warm environment. One probably cannot survive very long with this mechanism completely inoperative. But if one could endure for even an hour, and then remove the coat of grease, it would enormously enhance the probabilities of escape.

The second problem engendered by this approach is the possibility that the dog will track the odor peculiar to the grease covering. When Dr. Hoag suggested this, I could only counter with some untestable hypotheses and surmises as to the nature of the stimulus that a tracking dog uses in its pursuit of a target. The first assumption was that the North Vietnamese dogs were trained more or less like our own tracking dogs. If this were the case, then they were trained to respond to an odor associated with humans, to some common odor that all humans share, that makes their odor different from the odor of trees or cows, etc.

In addition, the dogs are trained to select from the common odor the particular odor that characterizes an individual, that makes the odor of Sam different from that of George. In fact, there are several pieces of evidence that suggest that every individual within the species has his own "odor identification number." In many lower species these tags serve useful biological and behavioral purposes. One example, from our recent work with aggression in mice, nicely illustrates this point.

Among rodents, the male odor appears to be the primary stimulus for eliciting aggressive behavior. This has been demonstrated in a number of ways. Aggression among male mice is eliminated by bilateral removal of the olfactory bulbs of the brain. Aggression also is greatly reduced if the mouse's natural odor is altered by the addition of an artificial scent, as for example dousing the mice with perfume. One experimenter actually used some Chanel No. 5 in this fashion. In addition, while aggressive behavior is rarely exhibited between members of an established group of adult male mice, it is possible to initiate aggression in such a stable population by introduction of the odor of a group of strange mice. A similar increase in aggression was demonstrated by the presentation of the urine of a single strange male mouse. By removing a mouse from an established pair of males and rubbing it with the urine of a stranger, there was an increase in aggression when the treated animal was returned to its home cage. Male mice, then, appear to have both a nonspecific odor responsible for eliciting aggression in strange males, as well as a personal identification odor. Furthermore, prolonged contact between two individuals results in a decrease in the amount of aggressive behavior between them.[2]

If habituation to the odor of a stranger results in the elimination of aggressive behavior, then prior exposure to the odor alone should reduce the amount of aggression displayed when two strange mice meet. This inhibitory effect should be greatest when a mouse encounters the animal to whose odor it has been pre-exposed. However, to the degree that all members of the same species have a common characteristic odor, there should be some inhibition of aggression in a

mouse pre-exposed to the odor of a nonspecific individual but tested
with a different individual of that species. In our study[3] we examined
the aggressive behavior of male mice following pre-exposure to one
of three odors: that of the future opponent, that of a different
stranger and that of a "neutral" substance.

The reduction in the aggressiveness of the group pre-exposed to
the odor of the mouse it encountered in the test trials was striking on
several counts. Not a single mouse pre-exposed to his opponent's
odor initiated a fight. Perhaps more importantly, none of these mice
responded to being attacked in a manner characteristic of subordinate mice. In each case the attacked animal ignored his attacker, literally turning his back. Not one of the mice pre-exposed to his opponent's odor fled or in any other way indicated fear; a "clockwork
orange" mouse. This stands in marked contrast to the behavior of
subordinate mice in other conditions who squealed, fled and cowered
in response to attack.

Although these data suggest some very interesting speculations for
reducing aggressive behavior in man, the main point for our discussion here is that the above pattern of results could only occur as a result of olfactory information which is specific enough to serve as a
badge for individual identification. Other studies using different techniques support this contention.

Among humans, it has been proposed that sweat is as peculiarly
individual, as genetically characteristic as saliva, blood and fingerprints.[4] In support of this proposal, it has been observed that, although the odor of human sweat depends on from which part of the
body it is taken and these differences are perceptible to the human,
nevertheless a dog is capable of identifying the disparate sources as
coming from the same person.[5]

If the odor of sweat is genetically determined and as characteristic
of individual differences as, let us say, fingerprints, then even identical twins should be discriminably different on the basis of odor. Sir
Francis Galton made the same suggestion one hundred years ago: "It
would be an interesting experiment for twins who were closely alike
to try how far dogs can distinguish between them by scent."[6]
Kalmus,[7] who went on to perform this experiment, quotes a letter to
Professor Penrose:

In a prospector's camp in Northern Ontario was a nearly blind

Great Dane, Silva. She was not a friendly dog, but she had a passion for one prospector and fawned on him delightedly whenever he came to camp.

One day a stranger appeared for the first time and to the surprise of those present, Silva greeted him with great affection. Upon enquiry by the camp crew it was found that the stranger was the identical twin of the particular prospector whom Silva had such a passion for, and that he never had been there before nor seen the dog before.

This anecdote, of course, suggests that the twins smelled alike, in itself a startling finding, or at least more alike than any two individuals chosen at random.

Kalmus investigated the problem more formally, using carefully controlled tracking and retrieving tasks. His results indicate that, indeed, well-trained dogs can differentiate between identical twins, although this differentiation is more difficult than that between two less genetically related individuals.

Thus the evidence seems to suggest that man, like the mouse, has an individual odor which marks him off from his fellow man. What is the biological significance or adaptive value of this phenomenon—aside from making it easier for his own pet dog to find him? Could it be that in the far-distant past there existed a symbiotic relationship between man and his dog that was developed to such an extent that the survival of a man depended on the constant accompaniment and vigilance of his dog?

The argument, then, was that the dogs would not track any new odor. They were evolved in such a way as to be more acutely sensitive to organic metabolic waste vapors than to other sources of odors. Their training had capitalized on this state of affairs, and made the effects even more pronounced. Without special training to selected nonhuman odors, including the odor of the particular grease that was to be used, one would not expect the dog to exhibit the appropriate tracking behavior. Since the prison guards would not know in advance of the breakout that the grease was going to be used, there would be no opportunity to have the dogs pretrained to follow that odor.

The logic seemed to be eminently reasonable. Nevertheless, it was founded on a number of assumptions, some of which, if proved false, could lead to disastrous consequences for the escaping prisoners. I made it quite clear, in speaking to Hoag, that I was only suggesting some possibilities and that I would not take on the responsibility of making a formal recommendation. There simply was not enough information available in the scientific literature to allow anything but equivocal suggestions. The shaving-washing-greasing was just one speculative possibility.

A second approach was developed around the idea of obscuring the prisoners' tracks by having them mixed in with other recent tracks. In this particular North Vietnamese compound, the prisoners were marched, daily, to a farming area about five kilometers away. They were marched over the same route each day, thus leaving literally hundreds of tracks, back and forth. If the band of prisoners, a few hours after their return to the prison, could retrace their steps, it might be possible that the dogs would be incapable of detecting this relatively small additional odor superimposed on the waves of tracks that had been previously deposited. It might be like asking someone to find a 1939 penny. If there is only that one penny on a tabletop, the penny is discovered quickly, with little effort. If there are a thousand other pennies, then the task becomes much more time-consuming. The suggestion was based on exactly that analogy. However, again, we recognized that the analogy might be quite inappropriate. When dealing with the qualitative differences between the odors of people, as opposed to quantitative or intensive differences, another analogy might be more revealing. Looking for the same 1939 penny, suppose, instead of one thousand other pennies, we placed on the tabletop a thousand coins from all over the world. Clearly, the task is no longer as formidable as the one previously described.

In support of the second analogy I was reminded of a story that Romanes (1885) told. As reported with additional observations by Kalmus:[5]

> Romanes described how he took his terrier to Regent's Park on a Bank Holiday, when the Broad Walk was swarming with people. When the terrier's attention was diverted by a strange dog, Romanes suddenly made a number of zigzags across the Walk, then stood on a seat and watched the terrier picking up his scent

and tracking his footsteps over all the zigzags he had made until it found him. In order to do this it had to distinguish its master's trail from at least a hundred others quite as fresh, and many thousands of others not so fresh, crossing it at all angles.

This observation is paralleled by the following experiment. Gretchen, an 8-year-old Alsatian bitch, had learned to pick out one person's handkerchief . . . She was then offered a handkerchief among others scented in the armpit of this particular person as well as in the armpit of another person, also represented by herself among the other handkerchiefs. In two experiments the bitch nevertheless twice picked out the doubly-scented handkerchief. She also picked out the correct handkerchief when the armpit smell was overlaid (for the human nose at least) with the smell of Collidine, or pentadecanoline.

With each suggestion that was presented a variety of difficulties could be listed. Hoag was becoming more and more impatient with our scholarly academic discussion. He desperately wanted to bring back to the Stuffed Animal Division of the Enjoyable Toy Company a plan that we would accredit as being workable. And, as much as I wanted to accede to his wishes, there were no clear answers. The discussion continued into the evening, first over dinner and later over the Bourbon and sodas that he liked so much.

As the evening progressed, the suggestions became increasingly more imaginative. The absence of a strong theory of olfaction, mixed together with a little alcohol, allowed our ideas to become expansive. There was ample scientific evidence that the application of a local anesthetic to the nasal mucosa, the odor-sensitive membrane inside the nose, would prevent olfaction. This was shown in a variety of studies using rabbits, hedgehogs, cats and dogs. Application of the anesthetic to the inner parts of the nose suppressed electrical activity in the olfactory lobes of the brain, a fairly certain indication that the animals were incapable of smelling. Likewise the topical application of drugs such as cocaine and strychnine, although they result in a brief period of hyperosmia (keener olfaction), shortly afterward produce anosmia (no olfaction). Gymnemic acid is said to act in a similar manner. This general approach, however, was obviously impractical. First of all, there was the problem of getting the drugs into the prison. Secondly, even if this could be accomplished, how would the drugs be applied? It was not as though anyone could just walk up to a kenneled dog and stick a cotton swab up its nose.

We briefly spoke about sneaking into the kennels at night and totally anesthetizing the dogs and then applying the nose drug. Or simply killing the dogs with poison. Both were ruled out with the argument that if the dogs died or behaved suspiciously this would increase the state of alertness around the compound. The guards would suspect that a break was imminent.

As an alternative to those crude, inelegant solutions, I offered what came to be called "The Tannic Acid Solution." One of the currently popular theories of olfaction stresses the importance of molecular structure by noting the high coincidence between those substances which are composed of large molecules and those that are inodorous. This is by no means a perfect correlation, but there does seem to be a very strong relationship. Tannic acid readily combines with many odor-producing substances. Typically the odor of the new substance is greatly reduced. It has been suggested that each tannic acid molecule combines with several molecules of odorant and produces a new molecule that is so large that it is incapable of passing through the pores of the olfactory membrane.

The solution then would be to coat either the dog's nose, the prisoner, or both with tannic acid. Readily available sources for the acid might be found in a leather factory where it is used in the tanning process or in the wild state, extracted from certain commonly found insects.

Tannic acid, of course, has a peculiar odor of its own. However, the solution that we were discussing was not dependent on the tannic acid odor masking the odor of the prisoners, but counteracting it. Some writers make a distinction between masking and counteraction of two or more odors. Counteraction occurs when the total amount of odor produced by the two odorous substances is less than the sum of the odors produced independently. Masking is a term that is used when there is an increase in the total odor level. An example of the latter occurs when in the bathroom you attempt to hide the odor of a particularly smelly bowel movement by spraying a pine scent from an aerosol can. The room becomes even smellier, but a foul smell is replaced by a pleasant one. Tannic acid, on the other hand, would presumably work in a counteractive manner.

We also considered the possibilities of employing odors that are so repugnant to the dog that he would avoid it and other, human, odors that happened to be associated with it. Unfortunately, we were not aware of any substance that would qualify as being unreservedly obnoxious to the dog. In addition, a very well-trained dog, I believe, will disregard all odors, pleasant and unpleasant, attractive and repulsive, if he also has the scent of his target. In our own tracking studies we tried to lure a well-trained male off the track by having a bitch in heat within ten yards of the track. There was surprisingly little effect on his tracking behavior.

Our final approach was to suggest the use of drugs that would affect the motivational, attentional or general sensory capacities of the dog, rather than the direct olfactory capability. This would considerably increase the number of candidate substances and provide even the possibilities of finding the substances locally, around the prison camp. Some of the suggestions included substances for producing sensory distortion such as the cannabinal drugs, the most common example of which is marijuana, or drugs containing indolethylomine, such as LSD-25. On the motivational side we considered drugs which depress central nervous system activity, barbiturates, tranquilizers, any of a large variety of substances that one might hoard from a local dispensary.

Here, the problem again was one of delivery. How to get the drugs inside the dog. One simple way, of course, was to spike the food. This could probably be accomplished by the prisoners, but had the drawback discussed earlier, of making the dogs' behavior, in the kennel, peculiar and therefore arousing the suspicion of the guards.

I cannot reconstruct through what chain of logic or free association we arrived at the final suggestion, DMSO. But we were all cockily pleased at the cleverness and elegance of the solution. DMSO (dimethylsulfate) is a colorless, odorless liquid that achieved some degree of notoriety several years ago when it was prescribed as a miracle cure for a variety of ailments of the bones and joints. The unusual property of DMSO is that it not only combines easily with many other drugs, but when applied to the skin surface it is absorbed into the tissues, carrying the drug with it. In this manner it is possible to introduce drugs into the body without using a hypodermic needle and without ingesting the material through the mouth. The drug, in other words, can be delivered without the subject's being aware of it—a sort of Mickey Finn through the skin.

By this time, late in the evening, the discussion was beginning to ramble. We had really forgotten about the quite serious purpose of the meeting, and were simply enjoying our own fancifully creative solutions. But Hoag evidently kept one channel clear. He started to pump for serious answers. How much DMSO is needed? How can you synthesize it from common materials? When he was satisfied that we did not know the answers to these questions, he stood up abruptly and announced that he was tired and was going back to his hotel room.

The problem of the prisoners' escape from some military compound somewhere in North Vietnam was never raised again. Whether Hoag took the DMSO idea, or any of the others, and brought them back for more careful discussion, analysis and experimentation to the very sophisticated CIA laboratories, I do not know. Nor did I become any wiser from reading the newspapers. I had not seen any news items about a small band of prisoners escaping from North Vietnam.

10

Smelly Sneakers, Squalene and Cockroach Perfume

In the previous chapter we examined the problem of a group of prisoners inside a dog-guarded compound who wanted to escape. In this chapter the view is from the other side of the fence—keeping the convicts in, or at least not letting them get too far away. For many years, the dog, and in particular the bloodhound, has been a valuable tool for this type of law enforcement. Bloodhounds are used extensively in prison systems throughout the United States. There is even a National Police Bloodhounds Association, which coordinates efforts to maximize the efficient use of these animals.

A recent article in the *FBI Law Enforcement Bulletin*[1] describes some of the general procedures employed in training and using the hounds. A more vivid picture can be obtained by watching Paul Muni attempt an escape from Devil's Island.

As keen a detector of lost persons or fugitives as the dog might be, there is always the possibility of improving his performance. Not only by using superior training techniques but also by artificially enhancing the odor of the potential fugitive—either intensifying it or, better still, making it more qualitatively different from the odor of members of the nonprison population. It is well known, for instance, that what a person eats very noticeably can affect his body odor. The smell of members of minority groups has often been described as being characteristically different from that of the majority. Many a white New

York subway passenger will complain about how Negroes smell differently, and then gratuitously add how terrible it is to stand next to them. While the more suburban white New Yorker might recount, with either pride or embarrassment, how his dog always barks at any black person that passes the house. When I lived in the western part of the United States I heard the same stories about Indians, and in Israel about Arabs. It would not be surprising to discover that Tokyo subway passengers have similar stories to tell about white Americans.

If different cultural groups have characteristically different odors which are dependent on diet, one can think about imparting a special odor to the members of a prison population. For instance, prison meals can be heavily seasoned with a special garlic. The dogs can be trained to follow the particular odor produced by the body after ingestion of the garlic. Providing that the jail is not located in an Italian area, then the trail of the fugitive should be distinctly marked even above and beyond its ordinary scent.

I once had the occasion to make a related recommendation to the Israeli Army. There was a small village across the Lebanese border which was thought to house several members of a terrorist group and a large cache of arms. Information was available that these terrorists were planning some sort of activity during the following week. Parts of the village were easily observable from our side of the border, as it was located on top of a small treeless hill. But one side was completely obscured. Nor could the goings-on within the village be observed. The plan was to infiltrate several members of a scouting party into the surrounding countryside. At night, the activities in the nearby fields ceased and there was little likelihood of being detected. There was, however, the ever present problem of the local dogs. That the problem was real had been verified during several mock operations on similar villages in Israeli-held territory. Each time the small force was met with an accolade of barks from the untrained chorus of guards. To some degree this could be circumvented by approaching the village from an upwind direction. This, however, was a treacherous solution, too much dependent on the whim of the weather.

The suggestion was made that the members of the scouting party eat the same food, seasoned in the same manner, as the inhabitants of the village for several days prior to the operation. If one could also steal several sets of clothing from the village and then outfit the scouting party in those garments, that too might be useful in making the strange new odors of these foreign bodies less salient.

The strangest suggestion for changing the natural balance of odors in the environment came to me from a completely different direction. Many people come knocking on my office door at the university. Not only students but also book salesmen, parents and insurance salesmen. So when I found Mr. Schein sitting in front of my desk with a stack of six shoe boxes, I merely expected him to whip out the slide rule of his trade, order me to stand up—straight, please—try on a few models—walk over to the mirror there, please, and see how nice they look. We would then have a short discussion on how they felt, how they looked, whether they were the latest design from Italy or England or Thom McAn, and that would be it. But his opening gambit was quite different.

He gently, with both hands, lifted the cover from one of the shoe boxes, carefully unwrapped the noisy tissue paper and then lovingly held high before me, in the palm of his hand, a new white sneaker. I expected him to announce triumphantly:

"And with this super-shoe we will capture the world's entire sneaker market. We will make Adidas and Puma into the Hudsons and Studebakers of the feet."

But no, he first looked at the sneaker, and then at me, glanced at the door behind him to make sure that it was closed, and finally whispered:

"Smell this."

I was, if nothing else, convinced that the sneaker was new, and therefore not worried that his next hoarse command might be: "Find the man that wore this."

To my delight, instead of smelling from an acrid athlete's foot, it was pure vanilla.

"It has a very nice odor," I commented. Mr. Schein was examining me seriously. I was obviously looking at the creation of a man of talent, and was expected to react accordingly.

"That's really something," I added. I had no idea as to the purpose of this exhibition of exotic footwear. Somewhere in my reading of Krafft-Ebing I vaguely remembered a few words about shoe fetishes. Perhaps this was a new twist.

"Yes, I have also got them in cinnamon, wintergreen and oregano. In fact, I can impregnate the rubber soles with almost any odor. It's done through a process of microencapsulation. I spoke to Colonel Jarvik last week and he suggested that I speak to you about an evaluation of the idea, for use in prisons."

The proposal was to add a dose of odorant to the shoes during the manufacturing process. Odorant molecules, enclosed in very small capsules, would be embedded throughout the sole of the sneaker. When the sneakers are worn, each time they touch the ground several of the microscopic envelopes are broken, releasing the odorous molecule. In this way, he suggested, it would be relatively easy to use dogs to track a fleeing prisoner.

What he wanted from me was some endorsement for the idea. Although it seemed quite reasonable, I suggested an evaluation study to determine the amount of savings, if any, that would be gained by employing his technique. Unfortunately, the size of a research project to evaluate even such a simple suggestion as Mr. Schein's is such as to dissuade most administrators from pursuing any novel approach, except for a sure thing, which does not have to be evaluated anyway. It's a pity. In this case, it might well have been worth pursuing.

The idea of artificially odor-marking objects or people that one might want to trace in the future has been successfully applied in other contexts. For example, the flight recorder in airplanes, which transcribes onto tape all of the actions of the pilot and the plane, is one of the most useful instruments in uncovering the cause of an accident. As a result, the recorder is encased in a damage-proof box so that it can survive a crash. However, because of its relatively small size, and the fact that some crashes result from midair collisions or explosions such that the debris may be spread over several square miles, the recorder frequently may be difficult to find.

One solution to the problem of recovery of the flight recorder is to scent the box with squalene and then use trained dogs to find the odor source.[2] Squalene was chosen as the odor to be used because dogs appear to be keenly sensitive to its presence, even though to humans it is odorless. Squalene is an oily compound that is one of the constituents of sweat. It is produced by the sebaceous glands of the skin and is a by-product of the production of cholesterol. It can be found in larger quantities in shark liver.

Once the squalene is dabbed onto the box it retains its ability to produce a significant amount of odor for the dog for many days. It has even been suggested by related work of the U.S. Army that the odor-producing capability can withstand several weeks of weathering, and if applied to clothing can go through one or two good washings without being disturbed.[3] These data are supported by some convincing evidence from the more controlled conditions of the laboratory.

In one study,[4] the stimulus materials consisted of glass slides of the type used with microscopes. The slides, always handled with clean stainless-steel tongs, were either lightly fingerprinted or left completely untouched. Four untouched slides were prepared for every fingerprinted slide. Scores of slides were prepared in this manner and then divided into two categories: those to be weathered outdoors and those to be stored indoors prior to the testing. We will only examine the outdoor case. In addition to the fingerprinted versus clean slide, a major variable was length of time that the slides were left to weather before the test. Weathering durations of 6, 12, 24, 48, 72 and 96 hours and 1, 2 and 3 weeks were employed. Weathering was accomplished by placing the open flat trays of slides on the roof of the laboratory, "exposed to blown dirt, direct sunlight, wind and rain."

Two dogs, a mongrel fox terrier and a Weimaraner, were used for the testing. Both dogs had been previously trained, off-leash, to move in a circle around the laboratory floor, to inspect several station points along the way and to sit at that place where a human odor was detected. A correct response was rewarded with a piece of meat; an incorrect response resulted in the animal merely being led away from the problem area to await the next trial.

For the test trials with the slides, five slides were placed randomly in a circle around the room. The positive, or fingerprinted, slide could thus appear in any one of five positions. Over the course of trials the experimenters ensured that the position was equally distributed among all five positions. Each dog received 200 to 350 trials with each of the time delays. Although the animals did not perform as well on the weathered material as compared to the indoor material, nevertheless they were surprisingly accurate. The fox terrier performed significantly better than at a chance level on all of the durations of weathering up through one week. The Weimaraner was somewhat better and did the same thing up through two weeks.

When one considers the minute amount of material deposited on the slides, the performance is quite remarkable. Is it any wonder that dogs can be successfully used to find flight recorders that are literally painted with scent?

Squalene has been contemplated for other uses too. As part of a counter-terrorist operation, it has been suggested that border areas be sprayed with squalene. An intruder who crosses through the area would pick up the oily substance and then be more easily tracked by the dogs as he penetrates into the neighboring countryside. The U.S. Army has evaluated such a proposal and found that the material could be sprayed from airplanes in much the same way as crops are dusted.[5] Furthermore, they found that, like the fingerprinted slides, the material will remain active for many days and through a diversity of weather conditions. It would certainly appear to be a viable approach for improving the tracking ability of the dog, particularly through densely populated areas. The major concern would be to ensure that the investigating patrol does not become contaminated with the material and spread conflicting tracks of squalene all over the area to be explored.

Perhaps the most bizarre use of an odor-tagging technique involves cockroaches and sex odors. The basic paradigm is structured around the use of a highly volatile substance that the female cockroach exudes and which causes a flurry of sexual activity in her male counterpart. Such substances are called pheromones.

Pheromones are powerful sources of communication by means of chemical signals transmitted from one member of a species to another. Frequently the information is conveyed in volatile molecules that are exuded by the sender and picked up by an olfactory sensor on the receiver. What characterizes pheromone communication systems is their exquisite sensitivity and the complete specificity of the information that they convey. Only the most microscopic amount of the pheromone has to be released in order for a detection to be made. Once the detection is made, it triggers off a chain of species-specific, survival-related responses. Most pheromone systems are intimately related to sexual and reproductive behavior, though there is also evidence for fear pheromones, alarm pheromones, as well as others.

A classic example of the operation of a pheromone-behavior system is seen in the mating behavior of the silk moth.[6] The male silk moth has a relatively huge pair of bushy antennae, almost resembling a set of hairy wings. These structures make up the olfactory network of the moth. What is most peculiar about this network is that 70 percent of the thousands of receptors are sensitive to one, and only one, volatile chemical. This substance, officially known as 10-trans-12-CIS-HEXADECADIEN-1-OL, but thoughtfully shortened to bombycol, is produced by the female silk moth.

When the virgin female moth is ripe for fertilization, she waits on some comfortable leaf and dispenses minute amounts of her attractive perfume. The molecules of bombycol are carried downwind. When, by chance, they are caught in the antennae of the male moth, they cause a pattern of neuronal activity which stimulates the male moth to fly upwind. Studies of the electrophysiological activity of this extraordinary sensing system indicate that one molecule of bombycol is sufficient to produce a neural reaction. Thus, the male moth may receive his first clue of the presence of a potential mate when she is still several miles distant from him. Traveling upwind in response to continued stimulation by the pheromone eventually brings him close enough to the waiting female so that he can begin responding directionally on the basis of differential gradients of concentration of the pheromone.

The sexually attracting pheromones of insects have been used in various programs for pest control.[7] The war against the gypsy moth, a particularly destructive pest, has been successfully waged by using pheromone-baited traps. The gypsy moth was introduced into the New England region of the United States in 1869 in an attempt to produce a hardy new breed of silkworms by crossing it with the silkworm moth. Unfortunately, some of the eggs or caterpillars escaped, and the gypsy moth population grew at an astronomical rate. The hairy caterpillars devour huge quantities of green leaves and, unchecked, would result in millions of dollars of damage each year. After thirty years of extensive investigation at the U.S. Department of Agriculture, the chemical structure of the gypsy moth attractant was identified. The abdomens of a half million female moths produced less than one thousandth of one ounce of the substance. In further laboratory tests it was found that as little as a trillionth of a microgram of the substance would cause the male moth to curve his abdomen and to respond with copulatory movements. Once having isolated the pure subst͟ a very similar product could be synthesized in large enough ͏ so that it could be used in the field to bait thousands of tr͟

The female cockroach, like the gypsy moth, secretes a chemical substance which excites and attracts the male of the species. The presence of a very small quantity of the pheromone in a room is enough to cause the male cockroach to very noticeably increase his activity. In fact, if the cockroach is kept in a small cage, he exhibits severely agitated behavior in the presence of the female pheromone.

The sex attractant pheromone of the American cockroach proved to be difficult to obtain. In the laboratories of the U.S. Department of Agriculture, ten thousand virgin female cockroaches were placed in an empty milk can. A continuous stream of air was passed through the can, and the output distilled. Over a nine-month period, only 12.2 milligrams of the attractant was obtained.[8]

The story has been told to me that the CIA, at least once, used this pheromone. Whether they used some of this small output or had their own stable of cockroaches to milk was not revealed.

According to the story, they were interested in discovering whether a particular individual, let's say a Mr. Green, was visiting the Fifth Avenue apartment of a prominent New York socialite who was believed to be serving as a drop-off for a group of foreign agents. A CIA agent followed Mr. Green into the subway and, while being crushed against him in the rush-hour crowd, deposited a small smear of the "cockroach perfume" on his jacket. Thereafter, the agents stopped following him. On the following day, however, when the socialite was away from her apartment, the CIA entered it with a cage of virile male cockroaches. The caged roaches stampeded, and the agents had their "proof" that Mr. Green recently had been in the apartment.

Conceivably one also could employ this technique in reverse. Instead of being interested in trailing the behavior of one individual, one might ask a broader question, such as which one of several people attended a Ku Klux Klan meeting at the local Grange Hall in Smithfield, North Carolina. Prior to the meeting, or during the meeting itself, the hall could be sprayed with the pheromone. Afterward one could go, one by one, to the list of possible attendees and apply the cockroach activity test. The same technique can be employed with the common bedbug, a species more suitable for a white-sheeted KKK environment.

I I

The Training of Mine Dogs

In the years 1967–68, the American involvement in Vietnam was escalating. From several thousand advisers in the early 1960s, the United States was well on its way to deploying a half million soldiers in Southeast Asia. The televised newscasts nightly reported the grim results: 403 North Vietnamese killed, 934 wounded; 220 Viet Cong killed, 615 wounded; 275 South Vietnamese killed, 812 wounded; and 39 Americans killed, 110 wounded. Pictures of the dead, the dying and the maimed accompanied the statistics and gave witness that for each cold number there was a human tragedy.

Most of the American casualties came not from direct frontal fighting, but were the result of an intensive guerrilla campaign whose most effective weapon was the mine and booby trap. No place was safe from the terror of an unexpected explosion. On a routine patrol through a quiet rice paddy with only the sound of the wind blowing against the reeds, or in a wooded thicket, occasionally ringing with a bird's cool whistle, or even in a friendly village filled with the daytime voices of work, at any moment there could be a shattering blast, a second of quiet when the Fates consult in conspiratorial whispers where to point the bone of destruction, and then the shrieks of anguish, the whimpers of helplessness, and for the lucky ones, sighs of relief. Such was the music for this Oriental Dance Macabre.

There were many variations to the basic theme. One misstep on an unmarked path, and a wide-eyed trooper plunged into a punji pit where sharpened bamboo stakes capped with feces, like rotting teeth, eagerly waited to tear into clean flesh. The resulting gangrenous wound often led to amputation of the leg. No less treacherous were booby-trapped doors with shrapnel-encrusted explosives, some mounted head high, others aimed at the groin. A disfigured face, and even blindness, were not the most feared injuries. The specter of brain damage and of spending the rest of one's life as a vegetable, or of loss of sexual function, these were the terrors that the guerrilla tactics had successfully instilled into the American soldiers.

With each new casualty the demoralization increased. Every excuse was found by the soldier not to participate in even the most seemingly innocuous mission. Anxiety, superstitious behavior, fights, drugs, alcohol and simple military insubordination all were grown from the fertile earth of fear and helplessness.

Against that background, a variety of agencies within the Department of Defense frantically searched for adequate countermeasures to the mine, the booby trap and other such devices. The problem was to rebuild the confidence of the soldier. This could only be accomplished by removing the element of the unexpected, the anguished fear of an explosion, of being fired upon from an ambush, of dropping into a pit.

It is well known today, from animal research, that unsignaled, uncontrollable noxious events are important variables for producing stress, ulcers and even helplessness. One very elegant set of experiments illustrates this point.[1]

Three groups of rats served as the subjects. One animal from each group was placed in one of three small adjacent boxes. Facing each rat was a small hole into which he could poke his nose and press a panel. At the other end, the rat's tail was extended through another aperture in the chamber wall and firmly clamped to a board. Two shock-delivering electrodes were attached to the tail.

So far, the conditions for all three animals were exactly the same. However, during the twenty-one hours that the animals were kept in these boxes, they were treated differently. One rat was given intense shocks at the rate of one per minute. The shocks were preceded by a ten-second warning signal. In addition, the rat could terminate the shock by simply poking his nose through the hole and touching the panel. The animals in this group can be described as having control over a signaled shock. The animal in the adjacent chamber was wired in such a way as to receive the same warning signal and shock. When the first rat turned the shock off, it was also turned off for the second rat. This second rat can be described as receiving signaled but uncontrollable shock. The rat in the third chamber did not receive any shocks, but spent the same amount of time in the apparatus as his two partners.

After this long twenty-one-hour session, the rats of all three groups were sacrificed and their stomachs examined for lesions (similar to the kind of damage of the stomach lining found in humans suffering from ulcers). The animals that could not control the shock had about three times the amount of stomach lesions as those that had contro[l] of the situation.

In other experiments of this type, it was shown that remov[ing a] warning signal further increased the amount of ulceratio[n. It is] quite clear that predictability and control are two ke[y factors that] affect the amount of stress.

Studies using milder shock of shorter dura[tion demon-] strated that lack of controllability can h[ave an effect] on all sorts of behavior, even when [shocks are not rein-] troduced.[2] Similar results have [been obtained with human] subjects.

In one experiment,[3] for i[nstance, two groups of college] students. One group w[as exposed to loud noise that] they could not co[ntrol, and the other group, inde-] pendently of an[ything they did. The control sub-] jects receive[d the same amount of noise, but] they co[uld control it ...] unli[ke ...]

[...]

[...] of [...] word[s ...]

The [...] fewer pr[oblems ...] the student[s ...] noise. This [...] variations,[4] sug[gest ...] even impair perfo[rmance ...]

How mild are these situations as compared to those faced by the soldier in Vietnam. Is it any wonder that guerrilla warfare, which has, almost as its hallmark, the conditions of unexpectedness and lack of control, should prove so disruptive to the American forces?

The immediate causes of these terror-producing events were easily identified. First of all, there were the mines that were planted under the earth and which could be detonated either by the pressure of a footstep or that of a vehicle running over it, or by the snapping of a trip wire, or even remotely by someone sitting in a tree and waiting for the appropriate time to set off the charge. Secondly, there was the danger of ambush, either from behind some protective screen or, more often and more dangerous, from a "spider hole." These small holes were dug deep into the soil and could hold one and sometimes two or more men. They were carefully camouflaged; a patrol could walk by several of these without knowing it. Once bypassed, with eir backs to the holes, a single Viet Cong with an automatic apon could annihilate an entire platoon of soldiers.

one could get some early warning of the presence of any of these tions, then the element of surprise, so important in guerrilla tac- uld be removed and the number of killed and wounded re- st knowing that he possessed a reliable device to detect the d to detect explosives would be a tremendous boost to the ale of the harried foot soldier.

968 we were given a contract to develop a dog-based detection of mines, booby traps, trip wires and tun- vas to come up with a set of procedures for producing, specialized biosensors. The research and develop- awarded to Behavior Systems Inc. by the U.S. are Laboratory, whose major task was to look for uld be effective in the peculiar environment of e of their first animal contracts was with the for developing a scout dog,[6] they chose to ing with a relatively new organization, BSI. l experience had been with pigeons, and ry or was part of a paper-and-pencil ex- out to be awarded a large contract to d in a real-life operation. I had never only furry animal with which I had as the white rat. My partner, Gene

Bernard, was in no better shape, although he claimed to have once had his picture taken while sitting on a horse.

The official Request For a Proposal (RFP) was exactly what we had expected. As was the case with many specialized projects, the decision as to whom to award the contract was taken well in advance of the official competition. It was not unusual for the scientists who would receive a contract to take an active part in drawing up the specification. Indeed, Bernard and I had spent several sessions at the Limited War Laboratory discussing the future program with the people of the Biological Sciences Division, John Romba, Max Krauss and Milton Cutler.

At the time of these meetings, we were not aware that we would have the inside track of the project. Only when we read the official RFP and saw some of our own words did we realize that all of our talking would be put to a test. It's one thing to say, "Yes, there should be no problem to train a dog to detect explosives. It's just a question of the judicious application of principles of reinforcement," and another to provide conclusive proof that it is a feasible system; that is, to show not only that the dog has the capability in question, but that it can be made to work reliably, in the field, using soldiers as trainers and handlers. That was a far more complex task than a laboratory demonstration.

But that was only one concern that we had. Could we do it? There was also the practical problem of putting together a staff. Both Bernard and I were full-time faculty members in the Department of Psychology of North Carolina State University. We could write the procedures, the reports, give technical advice, but neither of us had the time to do the actual training. Nor, considering the scope of the project, would all of our efforts have been sufficient. Dozens of people would be required. Where to find them?

There were two types of workers that we needed. The first group, with knowledge of laboratory training techniques, we acquired easily from among our own graduate students. These students, such as Elizabeth Carr-Harris and Lynne Siebert, became the backbone of the newly founded corporation and eventually owned a considerable part of the company stock. The second group that we needed required no particular technical qualifications but would have to like to work outdoors, with big dogs.

We found that in and around the college community there was an unexpected manpower resource for this work: college dropouts, members of the local drug culture, non-drug-using hippies, all looking for a non-routine, non-office, non-factory job; a job that was not identified with Western industrialized urban ideals. What could be better than working with dogs in the beautiful, green North Carolina countryside? Although the work was clearly defensive in nature, it still was related to the war in Vietnam. On this basis we had expected a considerable problem in recruiting personnel from the available population. However, to our surprise, the anticipated difficulties never materialized.

Another problem that we faced in trying to start the research and development program was that of financial resources. We would need kennels and a training area, money to buy equipment and to pay personnel. Most of this would, of course, come from the contract; but those payments came after some specified amount of work had been completed. Neither Bernard nor I had any capital of our own to bankroll the interim period, so we decided to approach a bank.

We both thought it quite farfetched that a respectable North Carolina bank would loan money to two university professors with a wild idea for training dogs. We may even have been hoping, just a little, that the bank would give a definitive no to our request and thus end this adventure into military research and development which seemed to be carrying us beyond our economic depth. If business acumen would be one of the criteria of success in this program, then we certainly had every right to fear a financial disaster. Perhaps the bank, trained to be objective in these matters, would blow the whistle and tell us straight out that we were amateurs mixing in affairs of which we knew nothing.

Much to our astonishment, after only several weeks, the bank agreed to extend to our company a line of credit that was sufficient to remove any financial barriers. They only needed an official government letter of intent to award the contract and our personal signatures.

We were finally committed. The contract was awarded and we immediately set out to put together the necessary facilities. The main ingredients were kennels and land. Bernard and I spent several days on the back roads around the Raleigh area. Finally, in Apex, we found some land and a willing seller, the same acreage that we used for training the tracker dogs. The land was ideally suited for our purposes. It was located in a quiet untraveled area. There were several acres of open fields which were suitable for obedience training, and the remainder consisted of open pine forest which would be ideal for marking out the necessary training trails.

Within two months, we had the kennels and the support facilities constructed, most of the trails laid and the personnel hired. We then set ourselves directly to the task of showing that it was indeed feasible to train dogs in large numbers to detect mines, booby traps and trip wires (mine dogs, for short) and to detect tunnels.

In the following pages I will describe in considerable detail the procedures that we employed for mine-dog training. The reasons for the details are twofold. Firstly, these procedures provide the basis for most of the training that is currently conducted for producing bomb- and explosive-detecting dogs as well as narcotic-detecting dogs. To understand our procedures is also to understand the operation of these other bio-detection systems, and indeed many new ones that might be created. (How about creating a dog for detecting oil?) The second reason for the detail is to give the reader an appreciation of the tremendous efforts of planning and coordination that are required to produce a mine dog.

Much of the information that follows is taken from the training and operating manual that we prepared at the end of the contract.[7] This manual was intended as a guide for nonprofessional people to train mine dogs. As such, much of the theoretical material is omitted. However, the reader should be acquainted with the general principles from earlier chapters.

It is amusing to note to what extent we professed, at the time, to be dealing with a "black box" system. In the most stringent of behavioristic tradition, we were concerned with only the stimuli and the responses, the input and the outputs. Thus, much like what one would expect to find on the back of a television or hi-fi set, we wrote in our introduction to the potential user: "Only individuals fully cognizant of the underlying theoretical structure should be permitted to alter it [the system] in any way. Changes in either the substance or temporal relationship of any of its parts could seriously jeopardize training goals and produce an unreliable or inadequate system."

Such cautionary notes were also placed in the manuals for handlers and trainers. Had we hoisted a red flag on the dog's tail, we might have had fewer difficulties. One of the persistent problems that dogged us throughout this work was that of getting nonprofessional people to follow instructions exactly as prescribed.

To begin with, let's describe the finished system, the trained mine dog. He was a nonaggressive war dog, trained to detect and respond to various types of ordnance items. The dogs were routinely trained to detect ordnance buried under six inches of overburden, elevated up to five feet in the air or located up to ten feet off to the side of the trail or road or route of travel on which they were working. When they detected the presence of a target item, they, unless otherwise directed by the handler, approached it and sat (usually within two feet) beside it. The distance at which the dog must be from the target in order to make the detection varies considerably with wind and terrain conditions. Under the worst conditions, i.e., a brisk crosswind with the dog upwind of the target, the animal may have to approach within one to two feet before making a detection. Under ideal conditions, i.e., a steady breeze with the dog approaching from the downwind direction, detections may be made up to 100 to 200 feet away. The dogs were trained to work either on-leash or off-leash. However, to maximize their efficiency, they usually were worked in the off-leash mode; they could work up to 300 feet in front of the handler, frequently out of visual contact, around bends in the trail, etc. If the man-dog team was equipped with a harness-mounted radio transmitter and helmet-mounted receiver, the handler could recognize that a sit response had been made even though he could not see his dog. These dogs could, therefore, be used either on point, for units traveling on winding footpaths, or over fields, or on road-sweeping operations. Typically, the dog would move out at a trot, sweeping the path from side to side. The rate of his overall forward motion was thus somewhat limited by the width of the path to be covered. Most dogs were capable of an overall forward motion of at least one mile per hour, even on very wide roads.

The first stage of the program was that of obedience training. All working dogs underwent some form of this training. The three most relevant reasons were: (1) The variety of situations, both on and off patrol. Under these conditions an unruly, undisciplined dog would impose an undue strain on the handler. An adequately obedience-trained dog, on the other hand, would follow quietly, stay where he is told and not require constant supervision and attention from the handler. (2) In order to use his dog most effectively while on patrol, the handler must have control over the animal at all times. Such control was absolutely necessary if field missions were to be conducted with maximum safety for all concerned. It was particularly vital for animals such as the mine dog that were to be worked in the off-leash mode. (3) Perhaps the most important reason for obedience training was that it put the dog in the proper "set" for working in cooperation with a handler. This was especially crucial during training, and for animals, such as the mine dog, that were required to be transferred easily from one handler to another.

Whether on-leash or off-leash, whether the command is given by voice or hand signal, every mine dog had to learn to respond promptly to the commands of heel, down, stay, come, move out. In addition, upon hearing a silent whistle, he had to check immediately with his handler for further commands. When reaching a choice point in his route he had to promptly follow directional hand signals given by his handler. The mine-detection dog was never taught the "sit" command. A sit response was to be elicited only by the presence of a target stimulus.

During the initial six weeks or so of the detection-training cycle, each dog was given up to two hours of obedience work per day. This training was designed to provide the control necessary for initial detection work as well as to lay the proper foundation for later control requirements. Obedience work was cut back to a maximum of one hour per day during the second phase of the training cycle. During the third phase of training only twenty minutes of obedience was needed, and even this was integrated with the detection work. After the training cycle was completed, approximately ten minutes per day of such work was administered in order to maintain adequate control.

The next phase in the program was that of response training. The aim was to make the stimulus (mine) significant to the dog, and to teach him to reliably make the proper sit response in the presence of a mine. A second goal was to teach the animal to work at a distance from, and independently of, the trainer.

Response training required a wide trail or unpaved road, 800 to 900 feet in length. This trail could be between six and eight feet in width with all underbrush removed so that the mines placed on it were easily visible along its entire length.

The day preceding the first day of response training, all food was withheld from the dog. This deprivation ensured an adequate motivational level, and it allowed the trainer to reinforce correct responses.

On the first day of response training, fifteen mines were placed randomly along the length of the road, neither in a straight line nor at equal intervals. The mines were in open view. The animal's daily ration was divided into equal portions (as many portions as there were to be trials per day), and one portion was placed on top of each mine. This method of placement brought the dog into direct contact with the mine as he ate.

After the trail was laid, the trainer brought the dog to the starting position at the head of the road. He removed the dog's collar, put on the harness and attached a short leash to the harness. The trainer then gave the "move out" command and hand signal, and proceeded down the road, allowing the dog to set the pace.

The trainer usually assisted the dog to notice the food on the first mine. The animal then approached the mine and was permitted to eat the food. Each time the dog finished eating, he was given another "move out" command. The same procedure was repeated at the next mine.

If the dog ran past the mine without taking note of it (miss), a correction procedure was used. The trainer allowed the dog to move five feet past the mine, then led him back around in a semicircle so that the dog had to make another approach to the mine. The trainer then forced the dog to stand facing the mine for a moment, but prevented him from eating the food. If the dog attempted to leave the road, or to defecate, or to urinate during his run, or if the dog attempted to circle around behind his trainer, then the correction was a sharp "no" followed by another "move out" command.

During this phase of training, the trainer measured the amount of time that the dog required to get from the head of the road to the end of the road. In addition, the number of mines that were missed was recorded.

Each dog ran on a series of no fewer than 48 trials (mines) per day. The run was usually divided in half, with an hour or more of rest between the halves. By the end of this stage, the dog was moving briskly down the trail, going from mine to mine, and eating without hesitation. When the dog's speed (time from head to end of road) stabilized—less than one minute variation on four consecutive runs— he was promoted to the next stage of training. Most dogs took from four to eight days to reach this criterion.

This next stage was exactly the same as the previous one except that the dog's ration was divided into half as many portions as there were mines, and these portions were placed on only a predetermined half of the mines. The schedule of which mines were to have food on them was randomized, with two exceptions: (1) There could be no more than three mines in succession without food, and (2) the last mine in the run always had food on it.

It was extremely important at this point for the trainer to be able to distinguish a miss from a response to a mine without food. It was not uncommon for a dog to see that there was no food present, and to continue to the next mine without slowing down. In general, the correction procedures were similar to that of the preceding stage. However, if the dog ran past a mine with no food on it, without taking note of it, the dog was allowed to continue on to the next mine without any correction. The miss was recorded on the score sheet.

The most frequent problem at this stage was that the dog began to miss an unacceptable number of mines. If he missed six of twelve mines on two consecutive runs, or three of twelve mines on four consecutive runs, he was put back to an earlier stage of training.

Again, when the dog's time from the beginning to the end of the road showed little variability (to within one minute of each other on four consecutive runs), he was promoted to the next stage of training. Typically, this stage required one to three days.

The next stage—the forced sit response—was designed to train the dog to give an unambiguous indication that he had made a detection. It was required so that the system would not be dependent on the trainer's subjective interpretation of whether or not the dog had made a detection. This not only increased the overall reliability of the system but set the stage for allowing different handlers, without experience with a particular dog, to work with that dog.

As previously, the fifteen mines were set out, clearly visible, on the road. Now, however, the dog was no longer permitted to eat from the mines themselves. Instead, the trainer carried the dog's daily ration with him in a feed bag and reinforced the dog only when he was in the proper response position.

In apportioning the dog's food, the trainer divided the total amount by the number of mines to be encountered during that day's work (48), and fed the dog one portion (1/48 of his ration) at each mine. For instance, if the dog did not respond properly at one fourth of the mines, then, at the end of the day, the trainer had one fourth of the dog's ration in his feed bag. The dog received only three fourths of his normal ration that day.

The dog was worked in harness and was permitted to set his own pace. When the dog reached the mine and saw that there was no food on it, the trainer pushed the dog into a sitting position. No verbal command was given. The trainer attempted to accomplish the positioning of the dog as quickly and smoothly as possible. Once the dog was placed in the sit position, the trainer fed him the equivalent of one portion of his daily ration. The trainer fed the dog as close as possible to the mine and did not allow the dog to leave the sit position until commanded to "move out." Feeding in this manner helped strengthen the association between the mine and reinforcement. After several trials, the dog made the association between sitting at the mine and being reinforced. He began to sit voluntarily.

When the dog missed a mine, went by it without stopping, the correction procedure described previously was employed. This time, when the dog was brought next to the mine, he was forced to sit and maintain the sit position for one minute before he was given the "move out" command. He was not fed.

Sometimes during this stage, dogs became overly conscious of the trainer. The animals would walk down the road constantly looking around at the trainer, paying absolutely no attention to the mines; or they might approach the mine and then try to maneuver away from the trainer. The first usually occurred because the dog, now, was receiving the food from the trainer. This, by itself, was not a problem, and disappeared with practice. But sometimes the first, always the second, and always the two occurring together indicated a problem originating with the trainer. If the trainer was unsure of the act of forcing the dog into the sit position, or was too rough, the dog paid all of his attention to the trainer and to a means of getting out of his reach. This was corrected by having the trainer practice positioning a spare dog into the sit response.

A second problem which occasionally arose in this stage was that of a complete lack of voluntary responses after five to six days. It could happen that a dog would sit only if the trainer cued him (stopping, reaching toward the dog, bending over the dog, etc.). In this case, it was suggested that the cuing be overlooked in terms of advancement. The problem would be dealt with in the next stage of training.

After the dog had made six voluntary responses within a run, he was immediately advanced to the next stage, even if this occurred in the middle of a run. Most dogs took from three to five days to reach the criterion. If after six days the criterion was not reached but the dog was otherwise behaving according to schedule, he also was advanced to the next stage—the voluntary sit response.

This stage was a simple continuation of the procedures employed in the forced-sit stage, with emphasis on getting the animal to make voluntary sits within two feet of the target mine, and on removing cues for this response that might be generated by the handler.

If the dog sat further than two feet from the mine, he was reseated within the correct distance before being fed. In addition, the dog was now allowed only five or six seconds after he had approached the mine to give a voluntary sit. If he did not do this within the appropriate time, the same correction procedures as those employed for misses were used. Namely, the dog was brought to the sit position, made to maintain this position for one minute, and not fed.

The first problem which cropped up in this stage was that of having advanced the dog too quickly. If an animal had one run in which he did not make at least one voluntary sit, then he was recycled through Forced Sit Response Training.

The rest of the problems were directly connected with cuing by the trainer. This was extremely difficult to control while the dog was still on a short leash because of the closeness between the trainer and dog. Nevertheless, it had to be eliminated. The first indications were false positive responses (dog sitting with no mine within ten feet). If this occurred it was likely that the dog was responding to some detail of the *trainer's* behavior. The dog was given a "no," then a "move out" command. Another indication was the dog going up to the mine and sitting only after the trainer was next to him. To correct the cuing problem, the trainer had to be aware of every detail of his own behavior and had to try to eliminate any part of it which might be acting as a cue. It was at this point that the dog began to control the trainer's rate of forward movement. This control remained in effect during the rest of training and in actual operations. If the dog slowed down, the trainer also had to slow down.

It took from four to eight days for most dogs to reach the criterion for successful mastery of this stage: nine voluntary sit responses out of twelve opportunities on two consecutive runs.

For the next stage, the dog was switched from the short five-foot leash to a long twenty-five-foot one. The purpose of this stage was to gradually fade out the trainer, to physically remove him from the dog so as to reduce the possibility that the dog was using cues that were not inherent in the mine itself. The procedures for the long-leash training were exactly as in the previous stage.

When the long leash was introduced, there were several special problems that could occur. One was that of the dog continuing to be reluctant to move out away from the trainer. If this happened the trainer started the dog with only five feet of free leash. When the dog was not paying attention to the trainer, he let out another foot or two while continuing to move forward very slowly. This was continued until the dog was working confidently at least twenty feet ahead of the trainer.

A second problem was that of the dog waiting at the mine for the trainer to approach him before he would make the sit response. When this happened, the trainer slowed down and gave the dog a "move out" command. If the dog moved away from the mine, it was treated as a miss. If the dog did nothing, the trainer quickly moved up to the dog and forced him into a sit, thus treating it as a forced sit (i.e., without giving food).

A third type of problem might be that the dog approached the mine and then returned to the trainer, without ever sitting. If this occurred, the trainer gave the dog a "no," then a "move out" command. He continued this until the dog moved out or sat where he was. The latter possibility was treated in the same manner as the next problem.

If the dog sat at the mine and then broke the sit and returned to the trainer, or if he approached the mine and sat any place between the mine and the trainer, he was guided firmly to the mine and forced to sit within two feet of it. This was treated as a forced sit.

It required twelve out of fifteen good responses on two consecutive runs to successfully complete this stage. For a trial to be scored good, the dog had to approach the mine vigorously, using the full length of the leash, make an immediate sit within two feet of the mine and maintain the sit position while awaiting the trainer's approach. The average dog completed this stage in seven days.

At this point, the dog had a reliable response to the mine, but detection only involved an easy visual identification. The aim of the next phase of training was to define for the dog the dimensions of the concealed stimulus to which he was required to respond, and to gradually increase the difficulty of the detection task, forcing a change from the visual to the olfactory mode.

Detection training was carried out on wooden trails or footpaths between one and three feet in width, and from a quarter to a half mile in length. These trails were staked at thirty-foot intervals with numbered wooden sticks. This was done in order to guard against the possibility that mines might be placed in the same positions day after day, and once concealed, the possibility that they might be lost. Before the trail was set up for the dog, a list of random mine locations was constructed. The locations were identified by indicating the stake number on the trail plus one, two, etc., feet. In order to avoid inadvertent cuing, the trainer was not informed of the location of the mines. Someone other than the trainer concealed the mines and then, working several feet behind the trainer, scored the dog's responses.

In order to systematically transfer the dog from a completely visual task to an olfactory task, a graded system of concealment was used. Basically, there were six grades of concealment. Grade One was a continuation of the previous stage of training. Twelve mines were placed on the trail, visually obvious. Grade Two used twelve mines which were still visible but were no longer in the center of the trail. This gave the dog experience in visually locating mines which were in holes, beyond the boundary of the trail, in and around natural objects, and above the ground level (hanging). Grade Three reduced the amount of visibility of the mines by about half. If aboveground, they were covered lightly by rock or brush from the surrounding area. If they were placed in a hole, the hole was covered so that only half of the mine was visible from above. Grade Four used twelve mines which themselves were no longer visible, but with concealment such that the location of the mine was still visually detectable. Grade Five used twelve mines which were, again, completely concealed visually, but allowed for fairly easy olfactory detection. This was accomplished by placing the mine in a hole, but instead of refilling it with earth, covering it with a loosely woven burlap mat on top of which earth was sprinkled and brush added. Grade Six maintained the visual concealment and added complete burying of the mine in the normal field condition. Jeep tracks and dirt roads were introduced, and the length of runs was increased up to four miles. In addition, the number of mines on any run was varied from zero to ten.

This phase required that the dog's performance on the trail and at each mine be scored in the following manner:

1   **Good Response**   The dog approached the mine and made a sit response within two feet of it. He maintained this position until told to move out.

2   **Bad Response**   This included any response to the mine which did not meet the requirements of a Good Response. The category included sitting more than two feet from the mine, standing at the mine, lying down at the mine, etc.

3   **Miss**   If the dog passed by the mine without making any type of response to it other than sniffing, it was scored as a Miss.

4   **False Positive**   If the dog sat anywhere along the trail and was more than five feet from a mine, it was scored as a false positive. The location was recorded on the score sheet, and it was noted if there was any possible explanation for the response, such as a metallic object at the location or a mine placement from a previous run.

As before, the trainer carried the dog's daily ration with him in a feed bag, and reinforced the dog only for Good Responses. The dog was *never* fed for a Bad Response, a Miss or a False Positive.

Before the dog started his run, he was given an opportunity to drink some water. He was then taken to the head of the trail using a leather collar and leash. The collar was removed and the harness put on. On the first run of the first day of trail adaptation, he was worked using a long leash, but thereafter he was run in the off-leash mode.

At the head of the trail, the dog waited until the trainer gave a "move out" command and then started out down the trail. The trainer paced himself so that he remained about twenty feet behind the dog until it was necessary to reinforce or to correct him. When he made a correct (Good) response, the trainer walked up rapidly and quietly, fed him one portion of food and gave verbal and physical praise while at the same time making an effort to bring the dog into direct contact with the mine. During the grades in which the mine was concealed, the trainer uncovered the mine, showed it to the dog, concealed it again, and finally uncovered it and placed it in the middle of the trail so that the mine would not be lost. At the end of the trail, the dog was given a "stay" command and the trainer then removed the harness, replacing it with the leash and collar. The dog was again offered water.

The dog received two runs of twelve mines each and every day. These runs were separated by at least a one-hour rest period.

To correct a Bad Response, the dog was guided firmly to the mine and placed in the proper position within two feet of the mine. He did not receive any food reinforcement or any verbal or physical praise. The trainer uncovered the mine, showed it to the dog, placed it back in the concealment again, and finally uncovered it and placed it by the dog. Then the trainer moved approximately four feet from the dog, making certain that the dog did not break the sit position. He remained in this position for one minute before the next "move out" command was given.

If the dog missed the mine, the trainer walked approximately three feet beyond the mine and gave the dog a recall command. As the dog approached, the trainer grasped the dog firmly and led him around in a semicircle such that the dog reapproached the mine. When he was within two feet of the mine, the trainer put the dog into the sit position and showed him the mine.

As in the previous training stages, each stage had a specific, objective criterion of performance that the animal had to reach before graduating to the next stage. For Grades One, Two and Three, the dog was required to make 9 out of 12 Good Responses on two consecutive runs. For Grades Four and Five, the criterion was raised to 10 out of 12. For Grade Six, the last grade before being advanced to Tactical Training, the criterion to be reached was no more than one Bad Response to a mine on two consecutive runs. Most dogs completed the first five grades in 14 to 30 days, and Grade Six in from 2 to 3 weeks.

At the end of this phase of training, the dog was moving out eagerly and working at least 20 feet and up to 300 feet from the trainer, depending on the terrain and frequency of the mines. When the dog made his detection, he sat and waited for the trainer.

Once again, there were a number of special problems that could be encountered during this phase on the way to reaching the desired behavior described above. The first problem was that of off-leash control.

After one run on Grade One, the leash was taken off the dog. Usually there was no problem here, but if one did occur it would most likely be that the dog ran too quickly down the trail. One method of correcting this was to recall the dog when he got too far ahead of the trainer and then to give another "move out" command. This was repeated until the dog was working at a satisfactory distance. Another method was to leave the leash attached to the harness and to let it drag on the ground. As soon as the dog began to move ahead too far, the trainer stepped on the leash.

Once the mine was concealed visually, beginning at Grade Three, the dog might begin to dig at the place where it was buried. The most successful method of stopping this was to call out the dog's name loudly when he began to dig. This seemed to startle him and he usually stopped digging. If he sat, he was reinforced. If he just stood looking back, he was given a "move out" command. This procedure was continued until the digging behavior ceased.

As the concealment of the mines increased, it became more and more difficult for the dog to pinpoint the mine's location. Sometimes it appeared that a dog would lose confidence. He would search a small area for long periods of time. The trainer forced the dog into making a decision by giving him a "move out" command. If the dog then made a Good Response, he was fed. If the dog moved out, it was treated as a Miss.

Tactical Training, which is a continuation of Grade Six training, lasted from four to six weeks. This training was designed to simulate, as closely as possible, the actual field conditions that might be encountered during a military operation.

During Tactical Training, the trainer had several options once the dog had made a detection. When the dog first made a detection under average or good weather conditions, the trainer was frequently able to spot a change in the animal's behavior before the dog had finished his search for the source of the mine smell. Either at this point in time, or after he had made the sit response, the trainer could: (1) allow the dog to follow the scent to the source, make a sit response, and then recall the dog; (2) give the dog a "stay," whereupon the animal would stop and stand waiting for further commands; (3) give the dog a "stay" and "down"; (4) give the dog an immediate recall, in which case the dog would break his search pattern and return to the trainer until told to move out again. Practice on these procedures helped to integrate obedience into the detection task and to prepare the dog for situations in actual field operations.

During the course of training, these same dogs were also taught to detect booby traps and trip wires. The booby traps were hung at various heights off the side of the road, carefully camouflaged so as to be invisible from a dog's-eye view. These were introduced into training during Stage Two, and proved to be even more easily detected than the buried mines. This is not surprising since the odor molecules emanating from the hanging explosives are more freely available to the dog than those from beneath the ground.

Trip-wire training was incorporated into the program at about Stage Three. This training was quite different from the others in that it was based primarily on a classical conditioned fear response rather than on an operant response with food reinforcement, although that component was present. The first step consisted of pairing the sound of a bell with a noxious electric shock to the dog's leg. The bell was sounded for five seconds and a sharp jolt of shock was delivered. After two or three trials the bell alone elicited struggling and agitated behavior. This procedure allowed us to punish incorrect responses in the field by presenting just the bell. In an actual training trial, a thin piano wire or nylon fishing cord was stretched across a path. At the beginning of training the dog was put into a forced sit in front of the wire, and then reinforced with food when he made voluntary sits. If, however, he tripped the wire, a circuit was completed and the bell was sounded. These procedures, systematically applied, proved quite effective in training the dog to detect the trip wires.

By the end of the program, seven months after we started, we had trained 14 dogs to be experts at mine, trip-wire and booby-trap detection. An additional 14 dogs were trained to detect tunnels. The finale was a demonstration to the U.S. Army at Fort Gordon, Georgia. If the demonstration was successful, then BSI would be awarded a half-million-dollar contract to produce 56 dogs for deployment in Vietnam.

12

The Mine Dog at War

July 18, 1968, was a scorching-hot, humid day, the kind that makes a Georgia peach shrivel. With the help of Army personnel, who also accompanied us to see that there was no cheating, we laid several trails for the test. One trail, on which several mines were placed, skirted around a stagnant pond, ran through sand and dense underbrush and ended up in a garbage dump. Another went through thinly wooded pine forest. It was on this one that we built a punji pit, but without the sharpened bamboo and without the feces. The trail ended near a large clearing. Off to one side, we had created a tunnel in which one of our employees had hidden himself. On the other side of the clearing was a dilapidated shack, probably once a tobacco smokehouse. On the door, concealed behind a loose board, was a booby trap.

The usual contingent of observers from the Limited War Laboratory was there (Romba, Krauss, Cutler) and in addition the LWL commander, Colonel R. W. McEvoy, several colonels from Fort Gordon and a few unidentified civilians from the Department of Defense and other government agencies. One of the fears that we had was that this large group of a dozen people traipsing behind the handler might upset the dog's behavior. We tried to prevent this from occurring by giving a number of practice sessions at our Apex field station under these same conditions. Nevertheless, we were concerned, and this was further accentuated by having the demonstration in a new environment and in temperatures that would be close to 100 degrees.

In addition, at least part of our audience was hostile to the program. Fort Gordon had its own small training program, mostly for scout and tracker dogs, and the officers resented having a civilian company doing work that they felt should be under their jurisdiction. That the training was supervised by professors, and that the handlers were long-haired hippies, added to their discomfort. Only our German shepherds, straight and sleek, ears at attention, gave any semblance of military order.

That day we demonstrated six dogs. Their behavior was superb, briskly moving out on command, working well ahead of the handler, sometimes even out of sight. With each sit response the twelve spectators would gather around the panting dog and wait for the man who planted the mine to announce that it was a correct detection. He would then confirm this by digging the mine up and showing it to the expectant dog and his followers.

As the day progressed, the BSI and LWL personnel became more and more relaxed, enjoying the performance as much as the director of a Broadway show who knows that he has got a hit.

The highlight of the day occurred when one dog sat at the edge of the very carefully concealed punji pit. One of the Fort Gordon colonels ordered the group to stay put. He wanted to examine the concealment *before* it was opened and displayed to the observers, hoping no doubt to find some telltale sign to which he could attribute the dog's outstanding performance. With eyes focused on the ground, he approached to within four or five feet of the dog. He then proceeded to get down on his hands and knees and to explore the ground even more closely. When he was almost nose to nose with the dog, he stood up and announced that this was a false response, there was no pit in the area. Poor colonel, as he started to walk around the dog, he fell through the camouflaging into the pit.

Shortly after the in-field evaluation, Behavior Systems Inc. received a contract for about $625,000 to train 28 mine-detecting dogs for the U.S. Army and 28 for the U.S. Marines. There was also an unwritten understanding that if this production contract was satisfactorily executed, we could expect continuing work producing mine-detecting dogs. On this basis, we expanded our facilities and created a new training site in Shotwell, North Carolina, also just outside of Raleigh. We purchased about 25 acres, leased another 1500 acres, built new kennel facilities for the dogs, an ammunition storage house to hold the mines, and personnel support buildings. Our main field headquarters was located in a gracious old homestead, part of the lease of the landlords, the Bailey brothers, which was said to have been occupied by General Sherman during his march toward Atlanta. Our bearded, long-haired hippies might well have been mistaken for Sherman's troopers of another era.

At the peak of our efforts to train these 56 dogs, we employed about 150 people. In addition to the project director, who was responsible for the overall organization and execution of the plan, and a training director and staff to train the trainers, there were dog procurers, data clerks, veterinary technicians, a kennel manager, kennel laborers, a field foreman and a staff to cut and mark the hundreds of trails, and of course the trainers and the trainers' aides, the latter of whom were used for laying mines and scoring runs. Is it any wonder that the cost per dog ran a bit over $10,000? For this price we even sent some of our people to Okinawa to give more advanced training to the dogs in an environment close to that of Vietnam, and later to Vietnam itself, to help overcome some of the new problems that were arising in the combat field situation.

We completed the training of both the dogs and the Army dog handlers within the time limits specified by the contract. The system was ready for operation.

On April 22, 1969, the 60th Infantry Platoon (Scout Dog) (Mine/Tunnel Detector Dog) landed in Vietnam for the final test of the dogs. The 60th IPSD was made up of one officer, three headquarters enlisted personnel, two mine-detector dog squads and two tunnel-detector dog squads. Each squad, in turn, consisted of six enlisted men and six dogs. There were four extra dogs assigned to the platoon, bringing the total strength to twenty-eight men and twenty-eight dogs.

The evaluation was divided into two phases, three months with the 25th Infantry Division, and two and a half months with the Americal Division. After each mission, questionnaires were filled out by dog handlers and tactical-unit commanders. In addition, there were interviews with appropriate personnel, on-site observation by the project officer and a review of the 60th IPSD unit records.

At first, the platoon was stationed at a central location at Cu Chi, and later at Chu Lai. From these sites dog units were sent out in support of various missions. Although it was desirable to receive a twenty-four-hour notice before deploying a team, if necessary this could be done within an hour. In general the mine-dog team was used with platoon-sized units, although on occasion with a squad- or company-sized unit.

The missions were classified according to several types: reconnaissance in force, sweeps, search and destroy, land-clearing and road sweeps. Before each mission the handler was briefed as to the nature of the mission, the type of terrain, the duration of the mission, the type of enemy forces to be expected, the types of enemy mines, booby traps, etc., usually found in the area and their typical method of emplacement.

The dog unit was taken by jeep or small truck as far forward to the site of action as possible. When the unit moved out, the dog assumed the point position. He was the leading element. The handler followed the dog about fifteen yards to the rear and was flanked by two riflemen. In this relatively secure position the handler could concentrate all of his attention on the behavior of the dog.

Road-sweep operations, designed to clear roads of all mines before allowing a convoy of vehicles to pass, were performed somewhat differently. Usually this was done accompanied by division engineering personnel. The mine-dog teams, sometimes in pairs, were again the lead element. These frequently were followed by security elements and by two sweep teams using the traditional metal-detecting "carpet sweepers." Occasionally, trucks pushing heavy sand-filled rollers were also used to explode any devices left undetected by the earlier search teams. In this operation the dogs would often work fifty yards in front of the handler and could cover as much as nine kilometers of hard-surfaced road in a day, seven hours of very strenuous work.[1]

During the period of evaluation the 60th IPSD suffered a 25 percent casualty rate:

Two mine dog handlers were killed in action. Neither was actively working his dog at the time. One handler was killed by an unknown type explosive while his unit was taking a rest break. At the time he was alone at the unit's perimeter. It was believed that he detonated a booby-trap located in a hedge row. The other handler was killed by mortar fragments when his unit was subjected to an attack while in a night bivouac. . . . One stepped on an M14 antipersonnel mine while walking his tunnel dog in a passive role with the supported unit. . . . The other handler was wounded by fragments from an M79 round which was accidentally discharged by a friendly force. Three mine dog handlers received minor wounds from enemy action. One was injured by grenade fragments and another was injured when the truck in which he was riding detonated a mine. The other handler was injured on his first support mission. His mine dog had responded correctly on three occasions to trip wire devices. The dog made a fourth correct response and as the handler approached the dog he [the soldier] fainted from heat exhaustion, falling on the trip wire. A grenade was exploded wounding both handler and dog.[2]

Of the 28 dogs, two died, neither of them from enemy action. One died from heat stroke and the other from pneumonia and congestive heart failure. Three dogs were wounded in action.

Records of the unit, summarized by John Romba, the project officer for the U.S. Army Limited Warfare Laboratory, indicated:

The mine dogs made 76 positive responses on ordnance and trip wires; 21 positive responses on tunnels, punji pits, caches and spider holes; 6 alerts on enemy personnel; and 14 alerts that were not checked by the supported unit. There were 12 confirmed cases where mine dogs missed an artifact. Several misses were on ordnance and explosives that had been emplaced for a long period. Two misses were 30 pound plastic mines of ammonia nitrate. Three misses were anti-tank mines. Two of the three misses occurred after heavy rains. Both were also missed by mine-sweep teams.[1]

Not only were the mine-detecting dogs considered to be successful in achieving their goal, but they made a number of operationally useful responses for which they were not specifically trained. The mine dogs, for instance, were not given training to detect tunnels, pits or ambushes, yet such detections often were made. How can we account for this extra dividend?

During the course of training the buried mine is always associated with the scent of both overturned earth and the odor of the strange human that emplaced the mine. These scents, probably more intense than that of the explosive, may reach the dog just before the explosive odor. As a result of the association of the overturned earth odor, the human scent, the explosive odor, and the food reinforcement, the dog learns that the first two odors may be used as a cue to aid in finding the mine. The handler that is familiar with his dog will be able to notice an orienting response, which consists of a generally alert body posture, ears pricked up, head leaning forward and increased sniffing, before the animal comes close to the mine and before the sit response occurs. It is quite possible that this orienting response is triggered by either one of the two precursors of the explosive odor.

The orienting response can be likened to the turning on of a radio, while the subsequent searching is an analogue to the tuning function. Very often, of course, especially in the field, either of the two precursor odors may appear without an explosive in the area. The careful handler, noting that the dog made the alerting response, explores the area much more carefully, and will be more sensitive to unusual disturbances in it.

Another surprise, at least for the military people, was the fact that the dogs responded to a variety of explosive objects to which they had not been trained. We, on the other hand, had fully expected this. The original training had used a mine simulator which had incorporated many of the elements that would be found across a diversified range of mines. The simulator's case was a cricket can (a small wire-mesh cylinder) in which were placed plastic and copper scraps, nails, patches of unwashed Viet Cong clothing, a couple of drops of gun oil, pieces of bamboo, lumps of concrete and, last and most important, several grams of different explosives. The "mines" that were used in the later stages of training included claymores, grenades and artillery shells.

In spite of this relatively limited training sample, the Army reported that the following types of mines were successfully detected by the dogs: Chicom TNT (Chinese Communist manufacture), artillery rounds of 40-mm., 90-mm., 105-mm. and 155-mm. shells, an ammunition can filled with AK-47 rounds, small-caliber-ammunition rounds, a 750-pound bomb as well as claymore mines, antipersonnel mines and hand grenades. In one case a 105-mm. shell, buried three feet, with a release-type detonator was uncovered. In another case, one of the dogs made a sit response alongside a haystack. Careful examination of the stack uncovered several 90-mm. shells.[2]

The tunnel-detecting dogs were equally successful, finding 108 tunnels, bunkers, spider holes, punji pits and caches. In addition they responded to 34 mines, booby traps, trip wires and unexploded ordnance.

Quite clearly, from an objective point of view, the program was a success. How did the people using the dogs feel about it? Ratings were obtained for the effectiveness of the dog on the security of the supported unit. Eighty-five percent of the patrol leaders reported that patrol security was enhanced by the presence of the dog team; 12 percent reported no effect and 3 percent reported that the dog hindered patrol security.

In typical military-style understatement, it was concluded that: "The mine and tunnel dogs are suitable for use by U.S. Army units in RVN (Republic of Vietnam)."[2]

When Lieutenant General William R. Peers was conducting his investigation of the My Lai massacre to determine whether field commanders had participated in the cover-up, he decided to visit the South Vietnamese hamlet.[3] The area was still heavily populated with Viet Cong and North Vietnamese soldiers. During the several days immediately preceding General Peers's visit, an Americal Division task force, assigned to clear the vicinity around My Lai, suffered at least five casualties from booby traps. As heavy rains fell one day in late December 1969, Peers, together with Army personnel and one of the mine-detector dogs, made a house-to-house search in the hamlet. Although no detections were reported to have occurred on this trip, it was a measure of the official Army trust in the detection dogs that one was included in that delicate mission.

In March 1970, 14 more mine dogs, this time with the Marines, were landed in Vietnam. The dogs were used with 18 different unit commanders. The after-action reports indicated that 17 of the unit commanders completely endorsed the use of mine-detection dogs, while only one did not.[4] The April 1970 monthly report[4] by the Marine Corps project officer indicated that between March 18 and March 30, 1970, the following detections were made by Marine handlers using BSI mine-detecting dogs: The dog Prissy, handled by PFC Williams, on a road-sweep operation detected a command-detonated rock mine tunneled underneath the road; the dog Devil, with

PFC Stacy, found three M-79 duds in the open; PFC Daves, with Duke, on a road-sweep operation, detected an M-26 hand grenade rigged for pressure release, a rock mine buried in the shoulder of the road and a 60-mm. mortar round under rocks on the shoulder of the road; PFC Brady, on patrol with Blackie, detected, but did not inspect, an off-trail mine and a trip wire. On a second patrol they discovered a cross-trail trip wire connected to an M-26 grenade; PFC Yarrington, using Michele on patrol, found a buried 4-Deuce wired to a pressure-release device, a trip-wire-attached buried mine of unknown description and a trip-wire-connected Chicom fragmentation mine.

In the final report[5] of the Commanding General of the Marine Corps Development and Education Command, it was concluded that:

a) The Mine Dogs demonstrated the ability to locate mines, improvised mines and surprise firing devices. b) The Mine Dogs are operationally suitable when used to supplement the other preventive measures . . . c) Positive acceptance of the Mine Dog concept was indicated in 99 percent of the employments.

There was no doubt that the mine-detection dog that we had developed was operationally useful. It would save lives and reduce injuries to a greater extent than any other device that was then, or is now, available, either in the vast storehouse or on the research drawing boards of the Department of Defense.

However, our success was not rewarded with continuing contracts. Behavior Systems Inc., which was instrumental in developing the training procedures for mass-producing these biological detection systems, and in demonstrating, to even the most skeptical observer, that the dog could be used as an efficient, reliable explosive detector, was gradually forced out of business. The Department of Defense decided that, in the future, the Army would train its own dogs. Nor were we even graced with those small research and development contracts that provided the intellectual stimulation that fed the production work.

With the success of the mine-detecting dogs in Vietnam, it was suggested that a few additional dogs be trained on mines that had been buried for a long period of time in order to determine whether it was feasible to deploy such a system.

After the peace settlement in Korea, the American troops, before leaving, seeded the treacherous slopes around the demilitarized zone with thousands of antipersonnel mines. These mines, encased in plastic and about the size of a golf ball, were designed to cause injury to intruding forces crossing the border from North to South Korea. This was in 1953. After more than ten years, for reasons still unexplained to me, it was decided that these mines should be removed. However, being somewhat small and light, with the heavy rains and shifting soils, their exact locations were no longer known. The first indication that BSI was out of favor with the Army occurred when our proposal to do the study was rejected, and instead was awarded to Animal Behavior Enterprises in Hot Springs, Arkansas[6]—an earlier LWL contractor that had worked on ambush-detection problems using pigeons and on load-carrying capabilities of different organisms. They were given six months to demonstrate that M-14 mines, buried up to four months, could be reliably detected. If this turned out to be true, then it would be a reasonable guess that mines buried for much longer periods would also be detected.

The study began with five dogs, two golden Labrador retrievers and three basset hounds. For a variety of reasons the three hounds were dropped from the program very early in training, leaving only the two retrievers, Son and Pearl.

The basic training techniques were similar to the ones already described. Now, however, the animals were trained to go down lanes which ensured that a given area was systematically covered. These lanes, marked by white stripes, varied from 3 to 6 feet in width and were from 40 to 90 feet in length.

Training began indoors using buckets of sand, one of which contained the mine. At first, the mine was visible on top of the sand, then it was buried in the bucket. Eventually training was moved to the outdoors, where entire buckets, some with mines and some without, were buried. Concealment was gradually increased until fields were used in which mine depth varied from one quarter inch to five inches. The time since burial ranged up to four months.

The results were not encouraging. At a one-inch depth, Son made 64 percent correct responses, but also had a false-alarm rate of 24 percent, while 12 percent of the trials were incomplete. At a four-inch depth there were only 17 percent correct detections, 47 percent false alarms and 36 percent incomplete trials. Pearl gave a similarly poor performance.

At the Aberdeen Proving Grounds, home base of the U.S. Army

Limited Warfare Laboratory, they had prepared aged minefields on which to conduct further tests of these dogs. The fields were mined before the contract was signed, and on the day of testing were about sixteen months old. On the basis of the earlier tests in Arkansas with four-month-old minefields, it was not surprising that the dogs' performance was now considerably poorer. Even at a half-inch depth, the rate of detection, for both dogs, did not exceed 10 percent.[7] No wonder that the project officer recommended that "the two Specialized Mine Detector Dogs . . . delivered to USALWL by the contractor should *not* be offered to a field unit for evaluation."[7]

Although BSI did bid on it, I am pleased that we were not awarded the contract. I suspect that had we trained the dogs, the results would have been much the same. There is the tendency, even when doing a feasibility study, to assume that the task can be done, and to simply put on the contractor the burden of proving it. Failure is often interpreted as a failure of the contractor rather than the confirmation of the fact that feasibility is not possible.

In retrospect, it is easy to see why it would be impossible to train a dog to detect a mine that has been buried for a long period of time. Indeed, there was evidence already available that such a detection would be problematic. Both the field reports on the mine dogs in Vietnam and our own casual observations indicated that there were problems in detecting mines that had not been recently emplaced.

To sweep an old minefield requires that the dog be in a continuous state of alert, ready to detect the very minute vapor quantities emanating from the ground. One can safely assume that the amount of odorous materials from a buried mine which reaches the surface decreases with the amount of time that the mine has been buried. But even more important, the stimuli for turning the dog onto the explosive search mode—namely, that of the overturned earth and the human odor in the area—probably decay even more rapidly, leaving, after a while, a relatively homogeneous olfactory surface with perhaps the trace of a few molecules from the explosive. To find this, the dog must be searching continuously. I doubt that he is capable of doing this. The search behavior must also be under some stimulus control.

Consider, for example, a human observer in a movie theater lobby where he is supposed to meet a friend. His search behavior is triggered by every new person that enters the lobby. It is not constantly

engaged in action. This is even more obvious when the human is engaged in olfactory search, a behavior that we rarely exhibit. Try hiding a perfumed handkerchief in your living room and then ask one of
your guests to find it using only his nose. You will notice that, after
constantly sniffing, he will give up this tactic and substitute a strategy
based on hypothesizing where the handkerchief might be. He will then
go to sniff in that spot. For the human, these hypotheses are based
on a variety of past experiences. With the dog, these hypotheses are
governed by the more immediate stimulus environment. Although also
a function of their past training, some of these stimuli may, in fact,
have significance even without training. Human odor for the domesticated dog, or overturned earth for an animal bred for ferreting out
prey, may well be in that category. The recent literature in the experimental psychology of learning indicates that, indeed, there are stimuli
which have special biological significance for which different species
are prepared to learn more or less easily.[8] I would argue that the
same must, almost necessarily, be true for stimuli that alert the organism and tune in its detectors.

To the best of my knowledge the steep slopes along the South
Korea–North Korea border are still very dangerous places to go
hiking. The last suggestion that I heard for solving the problem was
to drive herds of sheep back and forth across the area. A most inelegant biological solution.

In spite of this small failure, the evidence of the successes in Vietnam compelled an international acceptance of the dog as an explosive-detection system. Work was continued with mine detection both
in the United States and in Israel; and with the upswing of indigenous
urban terrorist activity, bombing of banks and offices of the large
multinational companies, hijacking, etc., the dog was now being developed by local police forces to search for hidden explosive packages
in a variety of environments. To this was also added the use of the dog
to detect narcotics.

All of these applications stemmed from the initial successes of
mine dogs in Vietnam. These extensions of the mine-dog concept will
be discussed in the next several chapters.

13

Men, Machines,
Dogs, Bacteria
and Other Animals

The off-leash mine dog, as employed in Vietnam, was an exquisitely designed, supersensitive explosive-detecting organism. He was quick and reliable. The system was the product of the application of a highly sophisticated laboratory technology. The manufacturing process was under the constant supervision of professional personnel, trained in experimental psychology. As a result, the final product achieved a standard of quality control that was comparable to that obtained in the production of inorganic electromechanical systems.

What would happen if automobiles, which in general we consider to be reliable systems, were turned over to a public that was trained to drive but not trained to repair cars, with no professional repairmen available. When new, just off the production line, the performance would be excellent. Then, with continued use, the performance would deteriorate, the deterioration accelerating at an increasingly rapid pace as mechanical failures went unrepaired and precipitated other breakdowns, until the automobile either stopped running altogether or was demolished in a self-inflicted accident.

The mine-detection dog, a dynamic, organic system, faced a similar problem in Vietnam. The difficulties were exaggerated even further because the dog was capable of learning—bad responses as well as good. Quite early in training, when we were working with the Army people, teaching them to handle the dogs, we recognized that there would be difficulties once the handlers were sent to Vietnam and separated from their professional supervisors. Together with the LWL staff, we prepared a number of different manuals which were designed to help the handlers maintain the proficiency of their dogs.[1] As an example, we gave detailed instructions for setting up mine-detection exercises for those quiet periods of time when the dogs would not find explosives during operational use.

One of the differences between a man and his dog is that the dog, if given properly designed instructions to execute a task within his capability, will respond as required. Man, bringing with him his experience and his ego, tries to improve upon the dry instructions of the manual. The results were similar to that of the automobile breakdown. The mine-detection systems worked exceedingly well, but with continued use the performance became poorer. Eventually we sent some of our own civilian personnel to Vietnam to apply first-aid. Even though this was successful, we could not keep part of our professional staff in a combat area. After they were withdrawn, the same problems reappeared. Reinforcement was not given rapidly after detection responses, and added cues were given during maintenance runs, so that instead of responding to explosive odors the dogs were using the more salient cues.

Clearly, the nonprofessional Army handler was a liability to good system performance. With the explosive-detecting dogs used in urban and airport areas, the handler is even more critical. He must work with the dog, directing him to respond to certain features of the environment. Dr. Max Krauss, who was involved in most of the dog-explosive programs sponsored by the Limited Warfare Laboratory, concluded:

> It should be obvious . . . that handler selection is a critical factor in the ultimate success or failure of the explosive detection dog concept. The man-dog interface is an extremely delicate area in which the slightest, most subtle variations, even in the handler's mood, may be reflected in his dog's performance.[2]

Improving the selection and training of the handler is one way to increase the overall system performance. Another way is to design a system, either organic or inorganic, which minimizes the contribution of the human element. The first attempt at removing the handler completely was in a study by Behavior Systems Inc. for the Israeli government on detection of weapons carried by passengers boarding airplanes.[3] The most recent research of this type was concerned with the development of a biosensor system for detecting envelopes with explosives in a post-office environment.[4]

Another way of minimizing the influence of the man in the system is to use man's ability to design a machine which itself, once built, does not require his supervision. Indeed, there have been a variety of devices that have been developed specifically for the task of detecting explosives. There are the two types of portable electric mine detectors used by the Army. One is a metal detector which responds to the metal case around the explosive, if present. The other detector responds to changes in the density of the ground, and as such is subject to a high rate of false alarms from rocks, roots, etc.[5] Neither detector is sensitive to the explosive material itself. In both cases the operator wears a headset and receives the information via an auditory signal or changes in a visual indicator. In Vietnam, we had the opportunity to directly compare the dog mine-detector system with the standard Army mine-detecting systems. The informal evaluation indicated that the dog was superior in all respects, being faster and more reliable.

More sophisticated detectors are designed to respond to the specific vapors that are emitted by the explosive material. In general, the greater the rate of vapor emission, as expressed in terms of vapor pressure or volatility, the easier the substance is to detect. A good detection system, whether it is detecting vapor emissions or radar reflections, has to rate high on three fundamental properties: sensitivity, selectivity and specificity. In the case of a vapor-detection system, sensitivity refers to the lowest level of concentration of the vapor which the system is capable of detecting; selectivity refers to the system's ability to collect and concentrate vapors other than those contained in air; and specificity refers to the ability of the system to respond uniquely to the different vapors. This latter property is reflected in the false-alarm rate. A system giving a high response rate to nonexplosive materials is, by definition, low in selectivity.

The electronic sniffer vapor detectors have been, for the most part, modified gas chromatographs or electron-capture detectors. Recently, a comparative analysis was made of several of these electronic sniffers and the dog.[6] Although the overall conclusion was to recommend a particular electronic sniffer (the Model 58 Explosive Detector), there was not enough information presented to endorse this choice as being unequivocally superior to the dog. For instance, the electronic device and the dog were compared for sensitivity to EGDN (ethylene glycol dinitrate), the principal vapor emission from dynamite. The electronic sniffer was reported to be able to detect as little as 0.1 parts per billion of EGDN in air, while the minimum concentration that the dog could detect was in excess of 100 parts per billion.

In spite of the government's own data, there seems to be considerable sentiment within federal agencies favoring the superiority of the dog over the machine, as well as over man.

Despite the use of such sensitive analytical instruments as the gas chromatograph and mass spectrometer, the trained dog remains perhaps the most sensitive odor detector known . . . the detection reliability of the K-9 odor detecting teams exceeds 95%, with at least a 40% better chance of locating a bomb than a man searching for the same device.[6]

Our own work with an electronic device, not too dissimilar from the Model 58 Explosive Detector, and the dog illustrates how simple comparisons can be misleading, particularly when measuring sensitivity. The rationale for comparing a machine sniffer with a dog biosensor was to define a division of labor between the two systems, to investigate the possibility of using the two systems in conjunction with each other and finally to improve the design of either system from information obtained from the other system.

On June 30, 1972, we undertook a direct comparison of the sensitivity of Dog A with the electromechanical sniffer developed by Hydronautics, Inc. The specific machine employed was that used by the Israeli Police Laboratories. A test concentration of 1 part, by volume, MNT dissolved in 1000 parts of liquid paraffin was employed. The sniffer was run at minimum sensitivity with its "nose" in the stimulus tube (the same containers used with Dog A). A random order of presentations of positive and negative (paraffin only) stimuli was used. The stimuli and order of presentation were identical in all ways to the ones used with Dog A. The sniffer operator was run "blind." For any given presentation, he did not know whether it was MNT or paraffin. However, he was informed beforehand as to type of stimulus being employed, and did some calibrations on known samples before beginning the test runs. The criterion response was a verbal one from the operator, who, after inspecting the sniffer printout, said "explosive" or "not explosive." Under these conditions the system achieved 100 percent accuracy with five correct positive responses and five correct negative responses.

When the sniffer's "nose" was moved three to five inches from the stimulus container's opening, simulating the observed distance of the dog's nose on test trials, the machine could not discriminate between positive and negative stimuli, even when set at maximum sensitivity. The comparison of the dog and machine indicates that, as one might expect, there is an interaction between distance of observation and performance. At the same observation distance, the dog is more sensitive than the machine (at least for the distance employed), but overall the machine is capable of better performance because it can be placed closer to the stimulus source.

Partly as a result of these data, we began to consider the design of systems that would maximize the amount of stimulus material available to the dog's nose. Taking a cue from the design of the electronic device which actively pulls air into the odor-sensitive detector, we switched from a "passive" presentation to an "active" one, in which the vapor from the material being inspected is blown into the dog's nose. At the same time, we almost completely removed the man from the system. This procedure, utilized in the development of a letter-bomb detector for the post office, will be described in Chapter 15.

In addition to the various machines designed by man, and the dogs trained by him, there is yet another biological sensor system that has been developed and tested as an explosive detector. This system uses bioluminescent bacteria. As might well be imagined, the system is highly portable. The operator holds a probe which contains thousands of the special marine microorganisms. These have been selected and bred for ability to change the amount of light emission from their bodies as a function of particular vapors in the atmosphere. In addition to the probe containing the cartridge of bacteria, there is a control box with meters and a power supply. The inside of the probe contains a light-sensitive sensor which, in effect, reports on the light-emitting behaviors of the bacteria. This is then translated into a visual signal, a pointer deflection on a meter.

The same evaluation as employed for the electronic sniffers and the dogs concluded that the bioluminescent system, although low in specificity, had sufficient sensitivity and selectivity to be operationally useful—and because of its small size would be particularly valuable in covert operations.

The lowly bacteria has joined another unit in the Army of War Animals, no longer only in the employ of the Biological Warfare Service.

In the continuing search for better explosive detectors, many different animal species have been investigated. The most far-ranging of these studies was performed by the Southwest Research Institute, which examined the olfactory acuity of the domestic pig, javelina, coyote, cat, fox, raccoon, skunk, civet, deer and ferret, as well as various breeds of canines.[7] They used a variety of commonly encountered explosives, including C-4, C-3, composition B, tetryl, PETN, TNT and RDX.

The basic technique for evaluating sensitivity was to vary the depth of sand in which the explosive material was buried. Many of the exotic animals exhibited better sensitivity than the dog. However, because of either great variability in performance or problems in handling wild animals, the researchers concluded that many of the species would have to be dropped from consideration as useful biosensors. Of course, if a biosensor system is designed in such a way as to minimize handling, then this latter consideration is eliminated, leaving only olfactory acuity and reliability as criteria for choice of animals.

Of the many different canine breeds and crossbreeds that were compared, the Rhodesian ridgeback–Weimaraner mix, rabbit hound mix and beagle mix proved to be best. Although all of the dogs made detections at six-inch depths, these crossbreeds proved to be the most reliable. However, of the different species of animals that were tested, the best of all proved to be the domestic Red Duroc pig, detecting explosives buried up to twelve inches.

The domestic pig has been used successfully for many decades to search for that culinary delight, the Frenchman's favorite fungus, the truffle. The truffle, a relative of the mushroom, grows deep in the dark, moist soil of the Périgord oak forests, as much as a foot from the surface. The pig, with its capable snout, if not too selective palate, is trained to root out these very expensive appetizers.

But what policeman worth his salt would dare expose himself leading a pig to the scene of a suspected bomb plant?

14

Narc Dogs and Dream Rats

One of the consequences of lowered morale among the American soldiers in Vietnam was an increase in the use of drugs. Of particular concern was the rising incidence of heroin addiction. This problem was considerably aggravated by the relative ease with which heroin could be obtained in Southeast Asia. Whether the ready availability of the drug was part of the overall Viet Cong–North Vietnamese strategy, or simply the work of local entrepreneurs who recognized a good marketplace, has not yet been fully revealed. No matter what the source, the problem existed and it approached epidemic proportions.

The success of the mine-detecting dogs prompted the U.S. Army to request information from the Limited War Laboratory on how to train dogs to detect heroin.[1] The first question, of course, was: could dogs detect heroin? Heroin is usually described as a white, odorless powder. However, in converting morphine into heroin, acetic anhydride is employed as a reagent. This results in the heroin taking on a barely noticeable acetic acid, or vinegary, odor. Thus, there were two problems that the investigators faced. The first one was concerned with determining the ability of the dog to detect pure heroin; the second one with training the dog so that he did not respond to the secondary odor associated with heroin—namely, that of the acetic acid. If this latter behavior could not be developed, there would be an intolerably high incidence of false alarms. Such a common household item as aspirin might be just one of many irrelevant items to which an acetic-acid-detecting dog might respond.

The first series of investigations aimed at developing a heroin bio-sensor were conducted by John Romba at LWL.[1] He used a standard laboratory discrimination procedure, starting with a two-choice task, then a six-choice task, eventually moving out to room and field searches. The basic techniques were quite similar to those employed for explosive detection, relying on food reinforcement of an appropriate indicator behavior, again a sit response.

Working with two Labrador retrievers, it was quickly demonstrated that, indeed, the dogs could detect heroin, and that they would discriminate between heroin and the odor of acetic acid. A follow-up study by the Southwest Research Institute indicated that, in addition to highly odorous marijuana, hashish and opium, and the heroin, dogs could also detect cocaine.[2,3] The heroin detection capability of dogs was also confirmed in two other evaluations, one using six Royal Canadian Mounted Police dogs[4] and the other continuing the work with the Southwest Research Institute dogs.[5]

This narcotic-detection ability added a powerful weapon to the armamentarium of law enforcement personnel who were involved with narcotics control. Indeed, even before the availability of these data, dogs were used to search for contraband drugs. German shepherds, for instance, have been employed extensively by the Israel Police for detecting commercial quantities of marijuana and hashish.

In the United States, the U.S. Customs Service has employed narcotic-detecting dogs since 1970. As of January 1976, their canine corps consisted of 128 members.[6] According to the FBI, these narcotic-detection dogs

. . . save untold man-hours by locating narcotics in vehicles, mail, unaccompanied luggage, and cargo shipments. In contrast to the previous time-consuming task of lawfully opening and closing certain mail parcels, a dog and his handler can check 500 packages in 3 minutes. At border points, a dog can inspect a vehicle in 2 minutes, where a customs officer would take half an hour. With an unparalleled productivity and cost effectiveness return of 85 to 1, Customs detector dogs last year participated in 4000 seizures of illicit drugs. They searched 168,000 vessels, aircraft and vehicles, 7 million units of mail, and 7 million cargo shipments.[6]

Even with the dogs' apparently amazing efficiency at inspecting individual items, such as described in the FBI report, it would require a vast army of canines to effectively examine all of the packages, envelopes, crates, automobiles and people entering the United States each day. A more productive method of narcotics control, of course, is to try to find the source of the drug at its highest level of concentration, before it is distributed. As in combatting a mosquito plague, it is easier to pour oil on the breeding site, destroying millions of eggs, than to swat each insect after it has left its stagnant homestead. In the past, narcotics-control actions aimed at the central sources of production have relied heavily on information gained from standard police intelligence sources. A uniquely different approach recently was presented to me by the High Commissioner of Police of Hong Kong. He was interested in using dogs to find the local factories that were engaged in converting poppy morphine into heroin. The conversion process uses acetic anhydride, which, upon being exposed to normally moist air, turns to acetic acid, producing a very pungent aroma of vinegar. Could dogs be trained to find these factories? Or could they be trained to detect the acetic anhydride itself, before it arrives at the factory? Normally the material is imported into Hong Kong. If it could be identified at the Customs station, then it could be tracked to the eventual user.

A local Hong Kong dog specialist attempted to train a few animals to detect acetic anhydride. The High Commissioner reported that the training was unsuccessful. Apparently the dogs could not detect the material. What was my opinion? I was rather astonished. First of all, the odor is, to say the least, exceedingly strong—to the human perceiver. However, it is possible that a particular odor can be sensed by one species and not by another. As an example, from a different sense modality, bees are sensitive to the ultraviolet portion of the visual spectrum but humans are not. Likewise, in the auditory modality, dogs are capable of hearing tones that are well over 25,000 cycles per second, bats even higher, but humans only much lower. However, I was certain that this was not the case with the acetic acid odor. Quite for another reason, we had been using the acid in an olfactory test problem with dogs as subjects. They had no difficulty in acquiring the discrimination.[7, 8] Other investigators had also employed acetic acid in a discrimination task without running into any problems.[1, 2] I suspected that in Hong Kong they were using the raw acetic anhydride as a training stimulus. When the vapors came into contact with the wet nose and/or the damp epithelium within the nose, a 100 percent acetic acid solution was formed, which, at best, may have been a strong irritant, and conceivably could have burnt out the odor-sensitive nerve endings. It is no wonder that a dog could not be trained to approach this noxious material.

The general idea of using a biosensor to discover the heroin factories remains an intriguing possibility. Let us consider a more sophisticated approach, one that is dictated by the fact that the high-concentration acetic acid odor is noxious, and that the closer one approaches the source of the acid, the more aversive the odor becomes.

In all of the previous investigations that we have examined, the animal was trained to approach the stimulus of interest. Typically, the information about the presence of the target and the location of the target were indicated by the same response. For example, when the dog sat, he informed the handler both that there was an explosive present and that the explosive was close to the area in which he was sitting. Alternatively, one can train an animal not to approach, or even to avoid, the stimulus of interest. This is particularly easy when the stimulus is noxious. A baby that once touches a hot stove will usually avoid touching that stove again. But now there remains the logical problem of making an inference about whether or not the stove is hot on the basis of the baby's not touching it. This easily acquired avoidance response would not provide the observer with information about either the temperature or the location of the stove.

Likewise, with little effort, we can train a dog to avoid acetic acid; but this simple achievement, brought into field use, will not provide a single clue to the presence or the location of the target. Suppose, however, that we trained the animal to make a distinctive response to the presence of the noxious odor, and that this response also served to *turn off* the source of the odor. There is considerable evidence that animals can be taught to make responses to terminate an unpleasant state of events as well as to achieve positive reinforcement. The literature of experimental psychology is filled with demonstrations of rats and dogs running from one side of an elongated compartment to another in order to escape shock, and of rats pressing a bar in Skinner boxes for the same purpose.[9]

Considering the noxious quality of the acetic acid odor, it would not be difficult to train an animal to press a bar in order to escape from the odor. A Skinner box could be modified by placing an air duct just above the bar. The duct would be connected through a series of valves to a flask containing acetic acid and from there to a source of compressed air. When a valve, controlled electrically, is opened, the compressed air is forced through the flask, carrying the acetic acid vapors. The stream then continues into the animal chamber. If the organism, a rat or a dog, presses on the bar, the valve is closed and the acetic-acid-laden air stream ceases to flow into the box. After several seconds, during which time the air in the animal chamber is refreshed by exhausting the fumes and blowing in fresh air, the acetic acid again is forced into the chamber and again stops only when the animal presses the bar. With a high-intensity odor, the animal will very quickly learn to press the bar to escape from the smell. With this as a beginning, it is possible to train the animal to make a number of bar presses before the odor is turned off. For instance, he can be required to give ten responses before receiving the reinforcement. This type of reinforcement schedule, called a fixed ratio, has an interesting property.[10] As the number of required responses increases before reinforcement can be obtained, the animal's *rate* of responding increases. Thus, for example, a rat that is being reinforced for every 10 responses might respond at the rate of 30 bar presses per minute, while a rat that is being reinforced for every 20 responses might respond at the rate of 50 bar presses per minute. The situation is not unlike the piece-rate procedure sometimes employed in factories. The worker gets paid, or reinforced, for the number of telephones he assembles, or the number of sacks he stuffs. This technique used to be a standard practice in the garment industry. A seamstress might be paid for the number of hems that she completed by the end of the day. The procedure frequently served to increase productivity and, as a result, the wages that were paid to the employees. However, some unscrupulous employers responded to the increased wages by thinning out the schedule of reinforcement. Where previously the seamstress might have had to complete 50 hems in order to earn five dollars, she would now be required to complete 60 of them for the same pay.

Within the garment industry, this was one of several abhorrent practices that led to the development of labor unions. Fortunately for experimental psychologists, their animal subjects do not have the capability for organized resistance. Even so, many of my colleagues will offer testimony that they have encountered individual opposition from recalcitrant rats, exhibiting itself in nasty bites of the experimenter's fingers, or even worse, in not behaving according to the prediction of the hypothesis.

Different rates of responding, then, are a by-product of different schedules of reinforcement. However, it is also possible to directly control response rate by differentially reinforcing only the desired one. If one wants the animal to respond with ten responses per minute, then rates above and below this are not reinforced.

Using what the operant-conditioning specialists call concurrent schedules of reinforcement, it is also possible to get the same rat to respond at different rates under different circumstances. At least theoretically, we might train a rat to make 1 response in a 5-second period to escape from a low-concentration acetic acid odor, 3 responses in 5 seconds to escape from a middle-range concentration odor and 5 responses per 5 seconds to escape from a very strong acid odor. It might even be possible to elaborate this into ten different rates, each rate corresponding to a different strength of odor.

Now imagine the following scenario. A small police van is cruising down a back alley in the Hong Kong warehouse area. On top of the van, poking out through the roof, is a small device that looks like a periscope. The head is constantly turning at a slow but steady rate. One is reminded of the World War II films with the German radio-detection vans passing down a wet Paris street at night. The illegal operator is tapping wildly on his telegraph key while his beautiful girl friend peers out from behind the blackout curtains. She sees the van with its ominously rotating antenna. We are given a flash of the operator inside the van surrounded by sophisticated electronic equipment, and then hear the beep-beep-beep which he is picking up on his headset. We all know it's over. The game is up. The spies have been caught.

In place of the antenna scanning for radio signals, our van has a sniffer. Operating like a vacuum cleaner, it sucks in air from different directions around the compass, first from the north, then east, south and west. Each time it pauses to inhale for five seconds. With every breath, the air is funneled to the trained rat sitting in his chamber. Most of the time the rat sits quietly; the air blowing into the chamber is devoid of acetic acid. But then the monitor-device begins to click, one click for each bar press, and the human operator is alerted that a detection may occur imminently. He takes over control of the vehicle's and the snorkel's movement. The driver is ordered to stop. The operator then moves the snorkel over its four compass positions, listening to the bar presses, like a Geiger counter, indicating the direction from which the odor is strongest. The vehicle is ordered to take the next right turn; another sample is taken. If the system is correct, then at one of the new points the response rate should be higher than at any of the previous points that were sampled.

The procedure is carried out according to plan and the system finds the area of maximum response rate. The operator radios headquarters, and assuming that no one has been bribed beforehand, the police descend on the heroin factory, smashing stills and arresting the surprised and frightened criminals.

15

The War Against Terror

In the late 1960s, explosive detection was the focus of a new set of problems. There was, to begin with, the first ripple in what was to become a wave of hijackings. Individuals carrying guns, grenades or explosives boarded aircraft and threatened to destroy planes and passengers unless either a ransom or a political debt was paid. After the initial hijackings, BSI contacted every major airline with a proposal to train and supply dogs that would be capable of detecting explosives and weapons either on the passenger's body or in luggage.

The responses that we received were noncommittal and evasive. Most were concerned with the image that might be created for the airline. It would be difficult enough to countenance any type of passenger search activity, but to do this with a dog would bring about disastrous publicity. It was quite clear that the introduction of any type of countermeasure would have to be initiated by the Federal Aviation Agency.

We arranged a meeting with Lt. General Benjamin Davis, head of Federal Aviation Agency, and spoke extensively about the possible use of dogs in the airport environment. We were encouraged to submit a proposal. Nevertheless, the U.S. Army Limited Warfare people, now being the government experts in the field of dog use, were invited into the project. With funds provided by the Law Enforcement Assistance Administration of the Department of Justice, LWL awarded a contract to the University of Mississippi.[1,2]

Using standard techniques, five dogs were successfully trained to detect a variety of different explosives—commercial dynamite, black powder and the plastic explosives C-3 and C-4. By the end of training the animals were capable of detecting quantities of less than a half ounce of each of these substances, concealed in a variety of different packages, and hidden in several different environments, including the football stadium, a warehouse and some vacant dormitories at the University of Mississippi.

The final training took place at the Naval Ordnance Disposal Center at Indian Head, Maryland. Realistic pipe bombs containing from a quarter pound to a half pound of black powder and packages containing from three to five sticks of dynamite were concealed in several different buildings. The dogs exhibited an overall detection rate "of the order of 70 to 80 percent."[2]

In regard to the problem of continuous search, it is interesting to note that during training the verbal command "search" was delivered when the dog entered the room containing the explosive, and was subsequently given each time that the animal came close to the target. As a consequence of these frequent pairings, "the dog immediately intensified his sniffing and searching behavior when given this command."[2] The auditory stimulus "search" now served the same priming function as did the odor of overturned earth and humans for the mine dogs. While providing the necessary cuing function, however, it also introduced the handler as a key element in the search. As this system is currently designed, the handler must be the one to provide the hypotheses for the dog to test, at least for stimuli that are not very salient. Putting the man back into the system has some disadvantages. These will be discussed later.

Four patrolmen from the New York City police force and two soldiers from Fort Gordon were given several weeks of training to operate the dogs in search activities. On May 1, 1971, two of the dogs, Brandy, a German shepherd, and Sally, a Labrador retriever, were delivered to the New York City Police Department. Although other police departments, such as those in Baltimore and Washington, D.C., had been using dogs for a variety of tasks for many years, these two dogs were the first in twenty years to be used in New York.[3]

In September 1971, the Federal Aviation Agency contacted the New York Police Department to inquire if the dogs could be worked in an airport environment, searching hangars, storage areas and airplanes for hidden explosives. The first tests were conducted aboard a

Boeing 727 and in a U.S. Customs warehouse. When these proved to be successful, eleven different training-evaluation exercises were conducted jointly with the FAA. These exercises took place aboard a 707, DC-7 and 747, and in the airport terminal facilities of different major airlines at John F. Kennedy International Airport and La Guardia Airport. In all of the exercises, simulated explosive devices were used. These training aids were carefully hidden in many different locations—behind passenger ticket counters, in luggage and storage rooms, in stored aircraft, aircraft being repaired, aircraft receiving final preparations for flight and aircraft in the final boarding process.

A number of problems were faced, including scraps of food on the floor and limited space for search movements and the sit response. Each one was countered with specific training. As an example, since the dog had no room to make the sit response on the floor if the explosive was on one of the inner seats, he was trained to sit in the passenger seat itself.

William Halligan, chief of the Air Security Field Office at John F. Kennedy Airport, who was present at these exercises, wrote:

> The dogs performed well and improved markedly, from a shaky nervous beginning to an assured acceptance and adaptability to aircraft and airport environment. They located each specimen quickly, were not distracted by the many noises and odors of airport activity and proved themselves to be a valuable tool or aid in the detection of this type of sabotage or threat to aircraft and airport security.[4]

Parallel with the efforts in the United States, the British also undertook a series of investigations to determine whether the dog could be used to detect explosives in an airport environment. Their first study[5] showed that a dog could detect nitroglycerine, the most common explosive used in England for criminal purposes between 1964 and 1967. A second study[6] used two RAF German shepherds, Rex and Jenny, and two Metropolitan Police Labradors, Max and Blue. All four dogs had received explosive-detection training. The evaluation of their ability was conducted in a most admirably controlled manner. Two types of explosive were used, TNT and dynamite, placed in one of two types of containers, tin boxes or polyethylene bags. Blank containers were also employed and different packers were used for each sample. The blanks were filled with an inert material, glass balls, and were handled and hidden in exactly the same manner as the packages containing explosives.

In general, the results indicated that the dogs were capable of detecting these substances. However, the overall performance was too low to be the basis for recommending immediate operational use of the dogs. Similar conclusions can be drawn from a later study at the Southwest Research Institute in Texas. Dogs were capable of making reliable detections of concealed Composition C-3, Composition C-4, TNT and nitroglycerine dynamite. However, when tested in Dulles Airport, their performance was not acceptable.[7]

The poor performance is not surprising. The dogs had not been given specific training in the airport or aircraft environments in which they were tested. The experience of the New York police, faced with a similar problem, is summed up by them as follows: ". . . a dog must be trained to search in *each* [italics added] particular configuration, i.e., airplanes, airline terminals, ships, etc. Each configuration must be treated as a new training experience for the dog."[3] When explosive-detecting dogs are supplied with proper training, they can be remarkably successful, as illustrated in the following incident.

On March 7, 1972, a fully loaded Boeing 707 took off from JFK Airport. A few minutes after it was airborne, an anonymous phone call was received. The caller warned that a bomb had been placed aboard the plane. The 707 pilot was contacted by the control tower and ordered to return immediately to the airfield. Brandy, the German shepherd, and her handler were quickly brought to the area. Within one minute from the time that she was introduced into the airplane, she gave the response indicating the presence of an explosive. The response, made in the cockpit area, was next to a briefcase which had an airline tag indicating that it belonged to a member of the crew. The briefcase was carefully removed to a secure area. Upon examination, it was found to contain four and one half pounds of C-4, a plastic explosive, attached to a sophisticated timing device.

Twelve hours later an identical device exploded in an aircraft cockpit in Las Vegas causing $1,500,000 damage. That plane had also departed from JFK. It had been checked visually by airport personnel, but not by the dogs.

The situation was duplicated on March 10 by the FAA personnel. Two pounds of C-4 was placed in the first-aid kit which was hanging on one of the cockpit walls. Both Brandy and Sally discovered the explosive within seconds of entering the cockpit.

During the summer of 1972 Brandy and Sally were employed by the Secret Service to cover the Democratic and Republican National Conventions in Miami Beach.

In the two years since the dogs became operational, about January 1, 1972, they have been deployed on 1,098 occasions under the greatest possible variety of circumstances. They have been used in subways and on ships, in vehicles and in hotels, for Presidential or other V.I.P. security, at the national political conventions and elsewhere. In the course of the foregoing they have alerted to 21 concealed explosives or bombs. In short, the dogs have done everything they were asked to do. This is not to imply that they must not be used judiciously and with full understanding of their capabilities and limitations. They most definitely must be so used. But if this is truly understood then it may be said that more often than not it is not the dog who will fail, but rather their human masters.[3]

The Federal Aviation Agency and the Law Enforcement Assistance Administration now have about twenty dog teams at different airports scattered about the United States. The twenty airports were selected so that no in-flight aircraft is more than an hour's flying time from one of the facilities.[8] The twenty-one-week training program is carried out at the Department of Defense Canine Center at Lackland Air Force Base. The Law Enforcement Assistance Administration has estimated that this program "saved 120 lives, hundreds of thousands of dollars in potential property loss, and has resulted in 300 arrests."[9]

In the early 1970s, urban guerrilla warfare in general, and Palestinian terror activities in particular, took a refined course. Once, the standard practice, in addition to hijacking, was to throw bombs through restaurant windows, as in Northern Ireland, or to leave timed explosives to detonate in the middle of a crowded marketplace or in a bus, as in Israel. Men, women and children were killed indiscriminately, even some who might be sympathetic to the terrorists' cause. With the advent of the letter bomb these killings could become more directed. The letter bomb was like a guided missile of the utmost precision. All that had to be done was to put the name of the target on the envelope. One could be reasonably certain that it would arrive at the appropriate address, to be opened by the intended victim.

What type of countermeasure could be taken to combat this new source of injury and death? The first step, of course, was to alert the public to the dangers of opening letters or packages that were not expected or which were in other ways suspicious-looking. In Israel, citizens were advised to bring those items to the nearest local police station. After each new letter-bomb incident, the numbers of people who called on the police to investigate letters and packages grew enormously. Each item was examined carefully, taking into account size and weight. Letters that remained in the category of being potentially dangerous were investigated with X rays, electronic sniffers, and other sophisticated equipment.

Meanwhile, at the post office itself, a preliminary screening procedure was introduced. Mail clerks and people specially hired for the job sat for hours inspecting each piece of mail for certain preselected signs that might indicate the presence of an explosive device.

This time-consuming, boring and sometimes not very reliable method of examination, akin to the quality-control procedures on an assembly line, reminded me of the earlier attempts to introduce animals to replace quality-control inspectors.[10] This, together with our own work on explosive detection with dogs, suggested that it might be possible to use animals to screen incoming mail for explosive odors.

The first question was: could the dog detect the type of explosives normally used in letter bombs? Fortunately, in earlier investigations we already had determined that the dog was capable of detecting a whole range of explosives, including PETN, RDX, TNT, ammonia nitrate, potassium chlorate and dynamite.[11] With the exception of the potassium chlorate, which had not been tested elsewhere, this ability had been confirmed in other laboratories.[12] Ethylene glycol dinitrate has also been identified as being detectable by the dog.[13]

Nevertheless, to be on the safe side, we decided that the first step in developing a biosensor to detect letter bombs would be to use real items. We were furnished with a sample of detected letter bombs that had been sent through the mails. Only the detonating device was removed before we were given the letters with which to conduct our experiments.

The system design was based on the need to reduce the role of the handler and to provide a strong cue that would serve to initiate the search process by the dog. The basic apparatus consisted of a Skinner box, large enough to hold a full-grown German shepherd, a system of tubes, valves and compressed air so that we could blow into the dog's face one of several different odor streams from cylinders containing the appropriate stimuli, a lever that the dog could press with his nose and the inevitable food dispenser for reinforcing correct responses.

Using the standard techniques for discrimination training that were described in previous chapters, the mildly hungry dogs were taught to press the bar six times during the presence of an air stream containing one odorant, and to withhold bar-pressing during the presence of an air stream containing a different odorant. Once the dog learned the general task requirements—to discriminate between two different air streams—he was switched to the odors that were of interest to us. Within one session the dogs learned to discriminate between the air stream from the cylinder containing a letter bomb and the one containing an ordinary letter. Our first questions were answered affirmatively. Dogs could smell the odors of explosives used in letter bombs, and they could detect an explosive in the relatively small quantities employed, even when it was placed inside an envelope.

But, given all of the above, we were still many steps away from proving the feasibility of the biosensor letter-bomb detector. When one considers the number of letters and parcels that daily pass through a post-office system, even in a small country like Israel, it becomes quite obvious that one cannot have an efficient detection system that is based on examining individual items. If one could take a larger unit of inspection, say a mail sack full of envelopes, and have the dog indicate which sack contained a letter bomb, then we would be well on the way to achieving a useful explosive-detection system.

This was our next task—to find out in how many letters we could bury the target envelope and still have the dog detect its presence. The procedures were the same as before, except that with each new session of training we added more and more neutral envelopes to both cylinders. First 5 new envelopes to each cylinder, then 10, 50, 100. We continued doing this until we reached the limit of the physical capacity of the cylinders, 500 envelopes in each. Even then the dogs were able to tell us which cylinder contained the letter bomb. They did this with such facility that we decided it would be unnecessary to continue further testing of this type. We were convinced that, given a standard mail sack, the dog had the olfactory acuity necessary to provide reliable explosive-detection information.

However, before making our final recommendation to the government, we had to face one other potentially serious problem. You probably never browsed through one of the large canvas sacks in which mail is transported in bulk, and if you did, you certainly did not do it with your nose. Can you imagine the cornucopia of odors that would meet the especially sensitive nose of the dog? How many different-smelling glues, licked by how many different-smelling saliva-coated tongues. But this we already knew would not cause any problems. After all, we had been using real envelopes that had gone through the mails. These we collected regularly from the secretaries' offices at the university. However, our envelope-sampling procedure would not allow us to generalize to the contents of an average mail sack.

First of all, the envelopes were empty, the contents removed. Secondly, there are many types of materials that might well be found in the "average" mail sack that would not likely appear in college campus letters addressed to professors and opened by their secretaries. Perfumed love letters and packages of salami would be only two examples of odor sources that might interfere with the olfactory detection of an explosive and normally would not be found in the samples of mail that we were using in our tests.

We decided to attack the problem directly, concerning ourselves not only with these "natural" odors but also with the more general question of countermeasures. Once the terrorist becomes aware that a dog is being used to sniff out explosives, is there anything that he can do to hide the odor from the dog?

In the context of a different, but related, set of problems, we had already done some considerable investigation of countermeasures.[14] We trained dogs to make four separate odor discriminations. Each discrimination was between two distinctly different pairs of odors. After they had learned all four pairs, we took each combination of two positive odors, and each combination of two negative odors, and retested the animals. For example, the dog learned one discrimination between alcohol and gasoline, with responding to the alcohol being reinforced and responding to the gasoline not being reinforced. In a similar fashion he learned a discrimination between acetic acid (vinegar odor) and acetone (nail-polish-remover odor). On the critical tests, for example, a small beaker of acetic acid and a small beaker of alcohol were placed together in a large container so that the vapors were mixed. The same procedure was followed with the two nonreinforced odors.

The question posed was basically this: when two odor sources are combined for the dog, is the resultant odor perceived as a new one with the identity of the individual constituents being lost, or are the individual components still perceived? In other words, is the olfactory system of the dog analytic or synthetic? Human vision, for example, has the characteristics of both an analytic and a synthetic system. It is analytic in that a human observer can report seeing a triangle shape in one case and a rectangle shape in another case. If the two shapes are superimposed on one another, he still will be able to see both a triangle and a rectangle. The individual forms retain their perceptual identity even though they are simultaneously presented to the sensor. On the other hand, a similar mixing of two separate colors, as in mixing two different paints, or two differently colored lights, results in a phenomenal experience that cannot be broken down into its component parts. When yellow and blue pigments are mixed, the resulting perception is that of green. When the observer sees the green, he cannot tell you that it is the result of a blue and yellow pigment mixture. A new visual sensation is synthesized.

Now what about odor perception? Is it analytic or synthetic? If the latter, then we would have to anticipate a number of troublesome problems in making our biosensor system effective. The critical odors might easily be masked by other odors.

The results of our first studies were encouraging. The dogs responded to the combination of odors in the same manner that they responded to the individual odors. Not only was there no increase in number of errors, but the reaction time with the "compound" odor was almost identical to that with the individual odors.

With this information we proceeded to carry out some more realistic tests, ones that closely simulated what we might expect to find in the post-office mail sacks.[15] In one cylinder of our test apparatus we placed a letter bomb, and to this we added other letters which, on different occasions, were heavily scented with a variety of perfumes, after-shave lotions, spices, tobacco and foodstuffs. These same odorous letters, with the exception of the critical letter bomb, were introduced into the second chamber. All in all, we examined the effects of over twenty different substances.

The results were quite clear. For all practical purposes, the ability of a dog trained to detect the odor of an explosive cannot be readily jammed by the addition of other odors.

To the above information, plus the data that we accumulated on the sensitivity of the system, we added our calculations on the system's reliability. What percentage of true explosive envelopes would it detect? How many false detections would it give—responding to a nonexplosive envelope as though it contained an explosive? In addition we determined the rate at which it could inspect and report.

In our final report, we completely endorsed the biosensor approach to letter-bomb detection. There is no system in existence that can match its speed, sensitivity and reliability.

16

Body-Recovery Dogs

Finally, when all else fails, the bomb explodes and the building collapses, or there is some catastrophic natural disaster, dogs might be of value in finding the wounded and recovering the dead. In July 1970, the Lancashire Constabulary began a program to train dogs to recover bodies.[1] The aim was primarily directed at finding the victims of murder or accident. They reasoned, quite correctly, that a dog would be an efficient instrument for covering large areas of land in which a corpse might presumably lie. The search for a possible murder victim is quite costly both in time and in the use of manpower. One source has estimated that it requires 500 man-days to reliably cover one square mile.[2]

The program started with two dogs, Tess, a Border collie bitch who was picked up as a stray and evidently had considerable experience in foraging for food, and Carl, a German shepherd police dog. Tess was ten months old and Carl five years when training commenced.

The general technique was quite similar to that used to train mine-detecting dogs. First the dogs were trained to find small pieces of minced meat clearly visible on the surface of the ground. Although the authors do not report the procedure, it is reasonable to assume that their search and detection behavior was reinforced by allowing them to consume the target. After this stage was successfully completed and the animals responded reliably and rapidly to the meat target, the samples were buried at increasing depths down to a maximum of two feet of overburden. The dogs, working off-leash, responded to the presence of the meat target by digging. The training program lasted for a surprisingly long eighteen months and was completed in the spring of 1972.

The evaluation trials were all conducted with pig meat or whole pig cadavers serving as the simulated corpse. The pig, evidently, was also the source of the original training stimuli. In addition to the general ability of the dog to detect the target, a number of variables which were thought might possibly influence the detection performance were investigated; these included: weather, soil condition, soil type, depth of burial, age of burial and size of burial.

For each trial, a four-by-four-meter grid was laid out such that there were sixteen possible target locations within the area. Each target was approximately identical, with an average weight of three kilograms. For each of the sixteen points, it was decided by random choice whether to bury a sample of meat or not.

In general, the performance of the dogs was excellent. At any given point the overall probability of success for Carl was between 70 and 80 percent, and for Tess between 65 and 80 percent. Jason, a "normal police dog" known for "a good nose," was also run over the course to see if the specific training invested in Carl and Tess was the cause of their success or whether this type of performance can be exhibited by even an untrained dog. As one might expect, Jason's performance was considerably poorer than that of either Tess or Carl, although he did make some detections.

In regard to the other variables that were investigated during the course of evaluations, the authors conclude that the results showed the following tendencies:

"(1) A greater possibility of success at low levels of humidity. (2) A higher success rate at warm air temperatures. (3) No significant difference between normal and wet soil conditions. (4) Age and size of burial have little effect on detection, but, as expected, deep burials gave a lower probability of success." (Some of the detected burials were as much as four months old.)

It is interesting to note that, although this research preceded the Yom Kippur War, many of the variables have a direct implication on what these animals would be asked to do in only several more months. Low levels of humidity, warm air temperatures, bodies buried for several months are an eerie prognostication of the grisly Sinai death scenes that would soon face the dogs.

In order to make the evaluations more realistic, trials were conducted under "normal" corpse-recovery conditions. Pigs weighing between 20 and 40 kilograms were used as the "victims." The depth of the graves, from top of the pig to the surface, was varied between 15 and 50 centimeters. In addition, care was taken to conceal the grave as much as possible.

Nineteen sites, each between two and five acres, were chosen. These varied in terrain and included "woodland, scrub, thick shrubs, rough grass and marshland." Burials were made in fourteen sites and five were left clear. Sixteen weeks were allowed to pass between the time of burial and the search.

The two handlers and their dogs were brought to the sites and allowed to devise their own method of search. The handlers were neither apprised beforehand of the location of the target nor told whether a particular site contained a target. Even the total number of burials was unknown to them.

Of the seventeen trials that were used for evaluation (two of the areas had been disturbed by wild animals who dug up the cadavers), "8 burials were discovered, 5 areas were correctly declared clear and the dogs were unsuccessful in detecting the burials in 4 areas." On the average they covered approximately two and one half acres an hour. However, in open terrain it was expected that they would achieve as much as four acres per hour.

Overall, this small program seemed to promise success. The major question mark was whether these animals could generalize their detection response from a target composed of the odor of decaying pig meat to that of a human corpse.

Parallel, and apparently independently, procedures to train body-recovery dogs had been developed in the United States. It is reported that in June 1972, following the disastrous flood in the area around Rapid City, South Dakota, the Military Dog Detachment of the U.S. Army Infantry School in Fort Benning, Georgia, was alerted for possible deployment. This group had been used for such a purpose once before, in Mississippi in the aftermath of the 1969 Hurricane Camille.

These attempts were evidently made more with goodwill than with a reliable, serviceable system. For in August 1973, only a few short weeks prior to the breakout of hostilities in the Middle East, the U.S. Army Limited Warfare Laboratory and the U.S. Army Infantry School undertook a four-month study to evaluate the idea of a dog-based system for body recovery.[3]

The Limited Warfare Laboratory had been active for many years in promoting the use of biological detection systems. Under the pressures and needs of the Vietnam War they had been involved in such projects as the development of scout dogs, mine-detector dogs, tracker dogs and a variety of other animal-based systems, most of which have been discussed in previous chapters. With the end of the war the Laboratory was looking for a way to re-employ some of its dogs as well as trying to find a rationale for its own continued existence. One such program centered on the body-recovery-dog concept, an idea which obviously had possible implications in peacetime disasters, such as floods, hurricanes, tornadoes, earthquakes, avalanches and explosions, as well as in wartime.

From an original group of sixty dogs, four German shepherds which had previously received scout and mine/tunnel training and three Labrador retrievers with combat tracker training were selected. Of these seven animals, only the German shepherds successfully completed the intensive four-month program. Whether the failure of the retrievers was due to a breed difference or because their previous training was different from the shepherds' is impossible to determine.

The training procedure was standard, based primarily on food reinforcement of the correct response, and the establishment of a strong secondary reinforcer, the word "good," so that the animals could be quickly reinforced for the correct response even though they might be at some distance from the handler.

The dogs entered the new lessons already trained to make a sit response in the presence of a mine or a tunnel. As part of this previous training they were also obedience-trained and were under good handler control, on- and off-leash.

However, because of the unusually difficult conditions in any disaster area it was deemed worthwhile to give the animals intensive exercise in order to increase their stamina and endurance, as well as to simply acclimatize them to the unusual demands of their new task. The physical fitness program included daily marches, some of which were ten miles, daily runs of one to three miles and practice on a confidence course twice daily.

It was anticipated that the rough environment of a disaster area, with splintered wood, broken glass, debris and mud, might cause some problem with the dog's foot pads. Standard military dog boots (which look like small leather string-drawn pouches) were tried as a protective measure, but proved to be unsuitable and, indeed, unnecessary. No special foot problems were reported for the dog.

Training was divided into several phases: free feeding, food reinforcement, shaping the moving-out response, developing the detection response (sit) and integrating it with the search behavior. The procedures employed in each of these phases were based on those developed for training the mine-detection dog.

One of the most critical decisions in a program such as this is the type of stimulus materials to use in training. The materials should have the same odor as a human, either healthy and trapped, or wounded, or decomposing.

Considerations of ethics and sensibilities, as well as the law, preclude the use of human cadavers. The experimenters in this project also felt that the use of animal flesh would result in a stimulus which would not allow the dog to generalize to the human odor. Several substitutes were tried: one was worn and soiled clothing (which proved to be quite effective in the tunnel-dog program); the other, used for most of the training and evaluation, was a mixture of macerated monkey meat with the addition of some "chemicals added to cause it more closely to resemble the desired odor. The material proved to be effective, particularly as it decayed in use. A principal drawback with its use was that the decay rate was quite rapid under the training conditions. Its odor, even when fresh, was so unmistakable that the dogs were able to distinguish it from decaying mess hall garbage, commissary meat and dead animals found in a sanitary fill." Since this potent material was used in both the training and the evaluation, it was still to be determined whether the dogs would be capable of finding human victims of disasters or just dead monkeys.

The detection training began by placing a container of this awesome-smelling stuff in clear sight of the dog, but several feet away from him. If the dog made any movement in the direction of the target material, he was reinforced by the handler proudly announcing "good," followed by a small portion of food. Movement of the dog toward the target was shaped in small increments, like the shaping of any other response, until the dog quickly moved out and headed for the target regardless of where it was placed.

Thus, by gradually concealing the container, the dog was forced to rely more and more on the olfactory stimulus emanating from it. Concurrently with this, the dog was required to make a sit response when he came close to the target. At first it was necessary for the handler to push gently on the dog's rump and to withhold the reinforcement until the sit response was made. But very quickly the odor itself, and the distance from the odor source, gained control over the response and the dog sat within a foot or two of the smelly containers. The sit response was rapidly acquired, since it had been used by these same dogs as the indicator for the detection of explosives and tunnels in an earlier training course.

Was the dog detecting the target odor, or the odor from the container or from the handling of the container? How does one ensure that the animal is responding to the critical stimulus, the stimulus that is the signature of the target of interest, rather than to some unreliable, accidental stimulus accompanying the critical one? In general, this question is common to all training procedures of this type. We have encountered it before in discussing discrimination training of pigeons for man-made objects versus non-man-made objects, and of dogs in discrimination training for mines, explosive letter bombs and tunnels.

Let's look at an example of what can occur if the animal has learned to respond to an extraneous stimulus and the experimenter has failed to detect and correct it. In the training procedure described above, suppose that the smelly containers were always placed in their position in the field by the trainer's assistant, Joe. The containers would then have both the odor of interest and the odor of Joe. It could very well be that the animal is making all of the associations between odor–sit response and reinforcement on the basis of Joe's smell and not that of the critical odor. This would become increasingly likely if Joe had also been the one feeding the dog. The training procedures could have created a dog that was a Joe detector rather than a generalized body detector.

On the other side, since the odor containers are buried and the act of burying, turning over earth and debris, also creates unique odors, there is the danger that a turned-over-earth detector will be created.

This situation will lead to a large number of false positives. That is, the dog would sit wherever earth had recently been turned irrespective of whether the target odor was present or not.

Both of these problems are countered by specific discrimination training. Joe plants the containers with the target stimulus, and he also plants the containers without the target stimulus. In a standard discrimination experiment these two stimuli would be referred to as the positive stimulus and the negative stimulus. When this is done and the dog sits at the positive stimulus, the usual reinforcement is administered. If, however, he sits at the negative stimulus, there is no reinforcement forthcoming. Typically, with this procedure, it is indeed found that early in training there is a high false-alarm rate. The dog makes many errors of the sitting-at-the-negative-stimulus type. With continued discrimination training these errors gradually disappear while the sit response to the positive stimulus maintains its high reliability. In other words, discrimination has been achieved, and the animal is now responding only to the critical target odor.

With the completion of the discrimination training the focus of the program turned to simulating disaster environments and to training dogs to work in these environments with speed and reliability. Debris training was conducted in a junkyard and in a sanitary-fill area, and thus allowed the dogs to be exposed to both inorganic debris (cars, tires, refrigerators, furniture, etc.) and organic debris (dead animals, food materials, etc.). On many of the trials, hand-to-hand combat dummies, made of rubber, were used, but always in conjunction with the special training odor. The dummies were at first partially hidden and then completely buried; the type of trash covering the dummy was varied as much as possible. Occasionally scraps of old clothing, only partially concealed, were used as the training stimulus instead of the smelly dummy.

Mud training, designed to simulate the aftermath of a flood or hurricane disaster, was conducted along a creek. Again, dummies or clothing were concealed either along the banks of the creek or in the mud of the shoreline, sometimes buried as much as six inches under water and mud of varying densities. In early November the program was shifted to the fish hatcheries at Auburn University, where an unused pond was drained. The bottom of the drained pond contained as much as three feet of mud and therefore provided excellent simulation of post-flood conditions.

Collapsed-building training was required in order to capture the effects of earthquake and explosion. Needless to say, it requires a rather expensive training environment. How many buildings can one go around blowing up so that they can be used for training dogs—no matter how good the cause? The experimenters had to wait for "targets of opportunity" in order to pursue this aspect of the program. When such a building became available, then procedures similar to the ones described for debris and mud training were employed.

This relatively short program, lasting only four months, underwent extensive evaluations in the many different environments. The four German shepherds that completed the course—Cricket, Heidi, Joe and Wolf—performed extremely well. Only one of the tests of the final evaluation will be described, for although the environments were different, the procedures and the results were remarkably the same. The test described by the experimenters was conducted in the Sand Hill sanitary fill:

The test area consisted of a red clay plateau about 700 meters by 400 meters bounded by embankments on three sides. At three corners were gullies with deep washed-out areas. At the edges of the plateau were three distinct belts of debris, from ten to fifty meters wide. The largest belt contained dead trees and brush, piled as much as twenty feet high. Adjacent to this was a belt of mainly inorganic wooden debris, with some organic trash. The third belt was mainly inorganic concrete, metal and plastic materials. Near one end of the plateau was a trash pile about 15 meters in diameter and one to two meters high, containing fresh organic trash. Twenty positive targets were emplaced around the perimeter, in four five-target lanes. The targets, emplaced about four hours before the test, were totally concealed in locations that required the dogs to negotiate obstacles. The trash pile provided the most significant demonstration of the dogs' ability to discriminate the target odor from other strong odors. In the center of the pile was a large quantity of hospital trash, including used bandages, sheets and miscellaneous materials. A target containing about two ounces of training odor was buried twelve inches deep in the center of this mass. The behavior of one dog in particular in this situation is worth noting. When the dog reached the trash pile, it investigated the area for fully fifteen minutes. Several times it stopped, as if to consider the situation, started to sit, but then changed its mind. After much encouragement from its handler, the dog finally dug down to the target and dragged it out with its teeth before sitting.[3]

Summarizing all of the evaluation data, the authors report that, of 128 targets, 92 percent were detected. Only 17 times did the dog give an incorrect detection response, sitting where no target had been buried.

The major concern, as indicated earlier, was whether these animals would generalize their excellent capabilities for detecting the artificial odor of the training stimulus to the real-life (perhaps, more appropriately, real-death) situations.

When the training was completed, the four dogs were placed on standby status at Fort Benning, available to be employed by either civilian or military authorities in the event of a disaster.

Several interesting comparisons between the American and British program are noteworthy. Both groups achieved a considerable degree of success, demonstrating high rates of target detection and low rates of false alarms. However, the British program conducted by a local constabulary was eighteen months long and the American program only four months. I have been told that a similar Israeli program was accomplished in only four weeks! How can we account for these discrepancies? Or how could I answer the question that was posed to me right after the Yom Kippur War: how long would it take you to train a body-recovery dog?

There are a large number of variables involved in addition to the type of training system. It would be spurious to conclude that the American training system is better than that of the British, or that the Israeli one is better than that of the American, simply on the basis of length of training program (assuming, of course, that all reach the same criteria of performance). Of particular significance is the total number of training hours per day per dog. This can be maximized only with a rather large number of trainers and auxiliary personnel. The question then can only be answered in the context of the budgetary and manpower allotments for a particular program. Given unlimited freedom in those areas, and a dog that is already obedience-trained, and considering the powerful odor of the stimulus and the fact that the dog is a foraging carnivore, it would not surprise me if the training could be accomplished in only several days. This estimation is not one that I would have ventured without first seeing the data from the British and American projects.

Finally, in comparing the two programs we must return again to the problem of stimulus generalization. The British trained a pig detector, the Americans a monkey detector. What evidence is there that these dogs, each trained to a very specific odor, will be able to generalize to the real-world human body odor task?

The problem of generalization, in its broadest form, is one that concerns all scientists, and behavioral scientists in particular. In the experiments discussed above, the problem centers on the assumption that monkey odor and pig odor share a common stimulus attribute with human odor *and* that this attribute will come to control responding with continued training.

This assumption is not different in kind from the one made, for example, by the psychologist in the laboratory studying the effects of stress on problem-solving. He may operationally define and manipulate stress by varying the intensity of shock administered to the subject. But what is the relationship between this stress and that incurred by a wife watching her husband die of cancer or a soldier in a bunker listening to the artillery rounds falling closer with each shell burst?

Sometimes the scientist is fortunate in that he can take his laboratory hypotheses into the world outside and determine if they are in fact applicable to real-life situations or are only a product of some complex interaction between his manipulated variables and the artificial laboratory environment. Sometimes he wishes that, for his special problem, the opportunity to test it in the field did not arrive.

But the war did come. The Yom Kippur War. And several weeks after its end, the dogs were called out to find the still missing dead.

The sand blew through the deserted streets and was sloped up, in gray indifference, against the ruined walls. The ghost town of a spent gold mine, a tumbleweed crazily bouncing across the track, presaged the appearance of a tired cowboy, bent in his saddle, winding his way through the main street searching for someone he had left behind a long time ago.

This was what used to be the town center of what used to be the town of Cantara, on the westerly edge of the Sinai Desert, on the eastern bank of the Suez. There was once such a town filling this space. One, which I am told, was inhabited by several thousand souls, many of whom were engaged in the various activities associated with the movements of cargoes and seamen through the canal. If it were a flourishing seaport or a sleepy camel stop probably depended on whether you were from Amsterdam or Addis Ababa. But all would agree that now it was nothing.

A few palm trees rose above the shattered walls and ignored the silence of the *shukh* once noisy with bargaining voices and burdened beasts, where loosely robed men with striped kaffiyehs framing their brown mustached faces, and women kerchiefed in billowing black gowns, their faces screened from intruding eyes, hurried and spoke, and carried on all of the small activities that bespoke of life.

As the small convoy passed through the sand-blown streets of Cantara one wondered how many years it would be before the town was completely blown over with sand, and how many centuries it would be before it was rediscovered, and to what catastrophe the anthropologists and archeologists would attribute its destruction?

This was December 1973, six years since the town was destroyed as a result of the Six Day War. The convoy was on its way to an area several kilometers to the southeast of Cantara where a major and bloody battle had been fought only several weeks earlier during the Yom Kippur War. The task was simple and grim, to try to recover the bodies of Israeli soldiers that were missing in battle and presumed to have been killed in this area.

All possible means had been used to find and identify the fallen soldiers. And yet there were several score who had not returned home again—neither to live nor to be buried. This search for them would probably be the last effort made to shorten the list of "missing in action."

From Cantara it was only a few kilometers to the U.N. base at Rabah, where a U.N. military observer, the British handler and his dog joined the group. At Romani, ten kilometers further, the Israeli liaison officer was picked up, and from there to the Egyptian frontier post where the Israeli searching teams were waiting. It was eight o'clock in the morning and the warming sun was well over the horizon, taking the chill off the night-cooled desert. The Egyptian escort from the other side soon appeared. Everyone was seated in a covered vehicle so that nothing could be seen on the Egyptian side of the new frontier. We were driven to the area that was to be searched.

Typically these areas were in the vicinity of fallen airplanes, abandoned tanks or bunker emplacements. The Israeli body-recovery teams made the first search, removing the exposed bodies, and then the dogs were brought in to continue the search. The dogs worked quickly, sniffing into the wind, sniffing the ground, running nose to the sand, right and left, occasionally backtracking, looking very purposeful as though they were being pulled by some invisible wire attached to their noses. When a body was located, the dog was prevented by his handler from touching it. The Israeli team was immediately called, and the corpse was carefully uncovered and removed.

The searches were continued for many weeks, until the end of March 1974. In all, the British team found 147 bodies or parts of bodies, with additional finds being made by two Israeli dog teams which were hurriedly trained for this task. It was the Israeli team that found the brother of Anwar Sadat.

As each recovered body was prepared to be carried across the line, the Egyptian, Israeli and United Nations soldiers came to attention, each solemnly saluting to honor the dead, and to mark his passing from battlefield-grave to home.

If only that first journey, the other way, were accompanied by such brotherly sorrow and anguish, and the recognition that finally, under the sand, we are all alike, there would be no more War Animals.

Notes and References

Introduction

1. Excellent reviews can be found in:
   Murphy, G., and Kovach, J. K. *Historical Introduction to Modern Psychology* (6th ed.). London: Routledge & Kegan Paul, 1972.
   Boring, E. G. *A History of Experimental Psychology*. New York: Appleton, 1950.

2. Boring, E. G. *History, Psychology and Science: Selected Papers*. New York: Wiley, 1963.

3. Theological fiat: the Pope's car?

4. For reviews of behavior modification techniques see: Kanfer, F. H., and Phillips, J. S. *Learning Foundations of Behavior Therapy*. New York: Wiley, 1970.
   Bandura, A. *Principles of Behavior Modification*. New York: Holt, 1969.

5. Neuringer, C., and Michael, J. L. (eds.). *Behavior Modification in Clinical Psychology*. New York: Appleton, 1970.

6. Raimy, V. (ed.). *Training in Clinical Psychology*. New York: Prentice-Hall, 1950.

7. Hull, C. L. *Principles of Behavior: An Introduction to Behavior Theory*. New York: Appleton, 1943.

8. Tolman, E. C. *Purposive Behavior in Animals and Men*. New York: Appleton, 1932.

9. Guthrie, E. R. *The Psychology of Learning*. New York: Harper, 1935.

10. Watson, J. B. *Psychology from the Standpoint of a Behaviorist*. Philadelphia: Lippincott, 1919.

11. Skinner, B. F. *The Behavior of Organisms*. New York: Appleton, 1938.

12. Skinner, B. F. Teaching machines. *Science*, 1958, *128*, 969–77.

13. Skinner, B. F. *Walden Two*. New York: Macmillan, 1948.

14. Rogers, C. R. *On Becoming a Person: A Therapist's View of Psychotherapy*. Boston: Houghton Mifflin, 1961.

15. Maslow, A. H. *The Farther Reaches of Human Nature*. New York: Viking, 1971.

16. Skinner, B. F. *Beyond Freedom and Dignity*. New York: Knopf, 1971.

17. Bolles, R. C. Species-specific defense reactions and avoidance learning. *Psychological Review*, 1970, *77*, 32–48.

18. Seligman, M. E. P., and Hager, J. L. (eds.). *Biological Boundaries of Learning*. New York: Appleton, 1972.

1.   Some Stories from the Past

1. Levi, W. M. *The Pigeon*. Columbia, S.C.: The R. C. Bryan Co., 1940, p. 3.

2. Ross, Estelle. *The Book of Noble Dogs*. New York: Century Co., 1922, p. 258. Cited in Chapman, S. G. *Dogs in Police Work*. Chicago: Public Administration Service, 1960, p. 3.

3. Livy, *The Early History of Rome*. Books I–V of *The History of Rome from Its Foundation*. Translated by Aubrey de Selencourt. Baltimore, Md.: Penguin, 1971, p. 393.

4. *Encyclopaedia Britannica*. Chicago: Encyclopaedia Britannica, Inc., 15th ed., 1975.

5. Levi, W. M. *The Pigeon*. Columbia, S.C.: The R. C. Bryan Co., 1940.
Much of the material in this chapter is based on Levi's very schol-

arly treatise on the pigeon. A revised edition appeared in 1957: Levi, W. M. *The Pigeon.* Sumter, S.C.: Levi Publishing Co.

6. Hersh, S. M. *Chemical and Biological Warfare: America's Hidden Arsenal.* London: MacGibbon and Kee, 1968.

7. Verhave, T. The pigeon as a quality control inspector. *American Psychologist,* 1966, *21,* 109–15.

8. Cumming, W. W. A bird's eye glimpse of men and machines. In Ulrich, R., Stachnik, T., and Mabry, J. (eds.). *Control of Human Behavior.* New York: Scott, Foresman, 1966.

2. Pigeon-Guided Missiles

1. Skinner, B. F. Pigeons in a Pelican. *American Psychologist,* 1960, *15,* 28–37.

2. Chernikoff, R., and Newlin, E. P. ORCON. Part III. Investigations of target acquisition by the pigeon. *Naval Research Laboratory Letter Reports,* 1951, No. S-3600-629a/51 (September 10).

   Conklin, J. E., Newlin, E. P., Jr., Taylor, F. V., and Tipton, C. L. ORCON. Part IV. Simulated flight tests. *Naval Research Laboratory Report,* 1953, No. 4105.

   Searle, L. V., and Stafford, B. H. ORCON. Part II. Report of phase I research and bandpass study. *Naval Research Laboratory Letter Report,* 1950, No. S-3600-157 (May 1).

   Taylor, F. V. ORCON. Part I. Outline of proposed research. *Naval Research Laboratory Letter Report,* 1949, No. S-3600-157/50 (June 17).

   White, C. F. Development of the NRL ORCON tactile missile simulator. *Naval Research Laboratory Report,* 1952, No. 3917.

3. Lorenz, K. *On Aggression.* London: Methuen, 1966.

   Ardrey, R. *The Territorial Imperative.* New York: Atheneum, 1966.

   Morris, D. *The Naked Ape.* London: Cape, 1968.

3. A Bird in the Bush

1. Holmes, S. C., Colonel, G.S. Commanding, U.S. Army Limited War Laboratory, Aberdeen Proving Grounds, Maryland. Memo dated

January 14, 1964, to Director, ARPA/DOD, Washington, D.C. Subject: Training Birds for Field Surveillance.

Tabor, H. E., Colonel, U.S.A., ARPA, Washington, D.C. Memo dated March 10, 1964, to Major General Wienecke. Subject: Bio- and Chemo-Sensory Reception.

Krauss, M., and Nichols, D. G. Potential Application of Animals in Unconventional Warfare. Technical Note, TN-6. U.S. Army Limited War Laboratory, Aberdeen Proving Grounds, Maryland. May 1, 1964.

General Atronics. Training Birds for Field Surveillance. Phase II. Final Report. Technical Report 65-226. U.S. Army Limited War Laboratory, Aberdeen Proving Grounds, Maryland. April 15, 1965. (Secret.)

Animal Behavior Enterprises. Development of a Pigeon Ambush Detection System. Final Report. Contract No. DA 18-001-AMC-860. January 18, 1967. (Confidential.)

Krauss, M. Ambush Detection by Pigeons: Contractor Studies. Technical Memorandum 67-04. U.S. Army Limited War Laboratory, Aberdeen Proving Grounds, Maryland. October 1967. (Confidential.)

Romba, J. J. Ambush Detection by Pigeons: In-House Studies. Technical Memorandum 67-13. U.S. Army Limited War Laboratory, Aberdeen Proving Grounds, Maryland. November 1967.

Romba, J. J. Problems of Controlled Bird Flight. U.S. Army Limited War Laboratory, Aberdeen Proving Grounds, Maryland. August 9, 1968. AD 837-165L.

2. Herrnstein, R. J., and Loveland, D. H. Complex visual concept in the pigeon. *Science*, 1964, *146*, 549–51.

4. Pigeon Intelligence

1. Lettvin, J. Y., Maturana, H. R., McCulloch, W. S., and Pitts, W. H. What the frog's eye tells the frog's brain. *Proceedings of the Institute of Radio Engineering*, 1959, *47*, 1940–51.

2. Skinner, B. F. Pigeons in a Pelican. *American Psychologist*, 1960, *15*, 28–37.

3. Several symposia on the topic of bionics were sponsored by the U.S. Air Force Avionics Laboratory and the Aerospace Medical Division. The published proceedings include:

Bionics Symposium, 1963. Air Force Systems Command, U.S. Air Force, Wright-Patterson Air Force Base, Ohio, 1963.

Bionics Symposium: Living Prototypes—The Key to New Technology. Directorate of Advanced Systems Technology, Wright Air Development Division, Air Research and Development Command, U.S. Air Force, Wright-Patterson Air Force Base, Ohio, 1960.

Oestreicher, H. L., and Moore, D. R. (eds.). *Cybernetic Problems in Bionics: Bionics Symposium, 1966*. New York: Gordon and Breach, 1968.

Bernard, E. E., and Kare, M. R. *Biological Prototypes and Synthetic Systems*. New York: Plenum, 1962.

4. Orne, M. T. On the social psychology of the psychological experiment. *American Psychologist*, 1962, *17*, 776–83.

5. Milgram, S. *Obedience to Authority: An Experimental View*. New York: Harper, 1974.

6. There is some evidence for what is called a "feature positive" effect. That is, it may indeed be easier to train an animal to make a discrimination when the critical feature that distinguishes the two stimulus patterns is associated with the reinforced response. See:

Jenkins, H. M., and Sainsbury, R. S. Discrimination learning with the distinctive feature on positive or negative trials. In *Attention: Contemporary Theory and Analysis*. D. I. Mostofsky (ed.). New York: Appleton, 1970.

7. The experiments on concept formation in the pigeon have appeared in several places. The fullest documentation occurs in:

Lubow, R. E., Siebert, L. E., and Carr-Harris, E. The Perception of High-Order Variables by the Pigeon. Air Force Avionics Laboratory Technical Report AFAL-TR-66-63. March 1966.

A more easily available and briefer version can be found in:

Lubow, R. E. High-order concept formation in the pigeon. *Journal of the Experimental Analysis of Behavior*, 1974, *21*, 475–83.

8. Herrnstein, R. J., and Loveland, D. H. Complex visual concept in the pigeon. *Science*, 1964, *146*, 549–51.

Mallott, R. W., and Siddall, J. Acquisition of the people concept in pigeons. *Psychological Reports*, 1972, *31*, 3–13.

Siegel, R. K., and Honig, W. K. Pigeon concept formation: Successive and simultaneous acquisitions. *Journal of Experimental Analysis of Behavior*, 1970, *13*, 385–90.

5. Project PAPP

1. Bernard, E. E. Research Planning Program for the Reconnaissance Pigeon. Air Force Avionics Laboratory, AFAC-TR-179, Wright-Patterson Air Force Base, Ohio, August 1967. AD 818-502.

2. General Atronics. Training Birds for Field Surveillance, Phase II. Final Report. Technical Report 65-226. U.S. Army Limited War Laboratory, Aberdeen Proving Grounds, Maryland. April 15, 1965. (Secret.)

3. Bailey, R. Load Carrying Capabilities of Mammals and Birds. Technical Report CR-CIB65. U.S. Army Limited War Laboratory, Aberdeen Proving Grounds, Maryland. April 1967. AD 822-000L.

4. Krauss, M. Ambush Detection by Pigeons: Contractor Studies. Technical Memorandum 67-04. U.S. Army Limited War Laboratory, Aberdeen Proving Grounds, Maryland. October 1967. (Confidential.)

   Romba, J. J. Ambush Detection by Pigeons: In-House Studies. Technical Memorandum 67-13. U.S. Army Limited War Laboratory, Aberdeen Proving Grounds, Maryland. November 1967.

   Romba, J. J. Problems of Controlled Bird Flight. U.S. Army Limited War Laboratory, Aberdeen Proving Grounds, Maryland. August 9, 1968.

5. Ziegler, H., and Wykoff, L. B. Observing responses and discrimination learning. *Quarterly Journal of Experimental Psychology*, 1961, *13*, 129–40.

6. Ridenour, L. N. Doves in the detonator. *Atlantic*, 1947, *179*, 93–94.

7. Lubow, R. E., and Bernard, E. E. The Use of Birds in Selected Military Applications. For Israel Ministry of Defense. January 1971.

8. Lubow, R. E. High-order concept formation in the pigeon. *Journal of the Experimental Analysis of Behavior*, 1974, *21*, 475–83.

6. Sounds from the Jungle

1. Licastro, P. H., Brodnax, L. D., and Byers, H. K. Potential of Ultrasonics to Provide Early Warning. Headquarters, U.S. Army Secu-

rity Agency, Arlington Hall Station, Arlington, Virginia. Combat Developments Study Number CD-29-0-5. August 1, 1964.

2. Tatge, B. Forest Spectrum Analysis. Advanced Technology Laboratory, General Electric Company, Schenectady, New York (Contract
No. DA-18-001-AMC-514). April 20, 1965. AD 618-082. Quotation
from p. 2.

3. Standley, P. C. The Flora of Barro Colorado Island. *Contr. Arnold
Arboretum,* Harvard University, Volume 5, 1933.

4. Zetek, J. Report on the Canal Zone Biological Area for the Year
Ended June 30, 1950. *Annual Report, Smithsonian Institution,* 1950.

5. Eisenmann, E. Annotated List of Birds on Barro Colorado Island,
Panama Canal Zone. *Smithsonian Miscellaneous Collections, 117,*
No. 5, 1952.

6. Barnhart, C. S., Sr., Krauss, M., Cole, M. M., and Mayer, M. S. The
Use of Arthropods as Personnel Detectors. U.S. Army Limited War
Laboratory, Aberdeen Proving Grounds, Maryland. September 1967.
AD 820-550.

7. Sea Mammals

1. Bailey, R. E. Training and Open Release of an Atlantic Bottle-Nose
Porpoise Tursiops truncatus (Montagu), NOTS TP 3838, 1965,
1–18.

2. Norris, K. S. Trained porpoise released in the open sea. *Science,*
1965, *147,* 1048–50.

3. Irvine, B. Conditioning marine animals to work in the sea. *Marine
Technology Society Journal,* 1970, *4,* 47–52. Quotation from p.
52.

4. The same general procedures for training porpoises to work in the
open sea also are used for sea lions. See:
Evans, W. E., and Harmon, S. R. Experimenting with trained pin-
nipeds in the open sea. In Harrison, R. J., Hubbard, R. F., Peterson,
R. S., Rice, C. E., and Schusterman, R. J. (eds.). *The Behavior and
Physiology of Pinnipeds.* New York: Appleton, 1968.

5. Conboy, R. E. Project Quick Find: A Marine Mammal System for
Object Recovery. NUC TP 268 Rev. 1. Naval Undersea Research

and Development Command, San Diego, California, June 1972. Quotations from pp. 1, 27.

6. Seiple, R. E. Quick Find Hardware for the Sea Lion Object Recovery System. NUC TN 492. Naval Undersea Research and Development Center, San Diego, California, January 1972.

7. Bowers, C. A., and Henderson, R. S. Project Deep Ops: Deep Object Recovery with Pilot and Killer Whales. Project Summary Report. Naval Undersea Research and Development Center, San Diego, California, November 1972.

8. Evans, W. E., and Powell, B. A. Discrimination of different metallic plates by an echo-locating delphinid. In Busnel, R. G. (ed.). *Animal Sonar Systems: Biology and Bionics*. Vol. 1, N.A.T.O. Advanced Study Institute, Frascati, Italy, 1966.

9. Johnson, C. S. Discussion of Discrimination of different metallic plates by an echo-locating delphinid. In Busnel, R. G. (ed.). *Animal Sonar Systems: Biology and Bionics*. Vol. 1, N.A.T.O. Advanced Study Institute, Frascati, Italy, 1966.

10. Airapetyants, E. Sh., and Konstantinov, A. I. *Echolocation in Nature:* Parts I and II. *Ekholokatsita v Prirode*. Leningrad, 1974. Translation by Joint Publications Research Service, Arlington, Virginia, October 31, 1974.

11. Airapetyants, E. Sh., Voronov, V. A., Ivanenko, Yu. V., Ivanov, M. P., and Ordovskii, D. L. Physiology of the sonar system in the Black Sea. *Dolphins Zhurnal Evolyutsionni Biokhimii i Fiziologii* (U.S.S.R.), 1973, 416–22. Translation by Joint Publications Research Service, Arlington, Virginia, October 17, 1973.

12. Since the frogman or diver emits air from his lungs into the water and these bubble to the surface, there is also a salient olfactory cue that can be detected against the relatively homogeneous background of the sea. Attempts have been made to use dogs in small patrol craft to detect these emissions. See:
Eisenhower, P. M. Dogs for Swimmer Defense. Report No. NSRDL/PC-C3469. Naval Ship Research and Development Laboratory, Panama City, Florida, September 1971. AD 517-324L.

8.   The Stalking Dog

1. Castle, L. J. Bloodhounds: a tool for law enforcement. *FBI Law Enforcement Bulletin,* May 1972, 1–5.

2. Carr-Harris, E., and Siebert, L. Off-leash Tracker Dog Helicopter Tracking Team: Final Report. Technical Report LWL CR-08B69. U.S. Army Limited War Laboratory, Aberdeen Proving Grounds, Maryland. September 1969. AD 858-987L.

3. One nanometer is equal to one billionth of a meter.

4. Gibson, J. J. *The Senses Considered as Perceptual Systems.* Boston: Houghton Mifflin, 1966.

5. In the same field there are additional gradients to those of texture— for example, a gradient of retinal disparity and, for the moving eye, a motion parallax gradient.

9.   Off the Beaten Track

1. The name is fictional.

2. For a recent review of this very extensive literature see: Schultz, E. F. and Tapp, J. T. Olfactory control of behavior in rodents. *Psychological Bulletin,* 1973, *79,* 21–44.

3. Kimmelman, B., and Lubow, R. E. The inhibitory effect of pre-exposed olfactory cues on intermale aggression in mice. *Physiology and Behavior,* 1974, *12,* 919–22.

4. Penrose, L. S. Human biochemical genetics. *Advances in Science,* 1953, *10,* 56–64.

   That metabolic disturbances may result in the production of significantly different odorous substances is suggested by the fact that in patients suffering from phenylketonuria there is a characteristic odor which is probably traceable to substances found in the sweat.

   Jervis, G. A. Excretion of phenylamine and derivations in phenylpyruvic oligophrenia. *Proceedings of the Society of Experimental Biology.* New York, 1950, *75,* 83.

   Likewise, there is apparently a peculiar odor in the sweat of schizophrenic patients:

   Smith, K., Thompson, G. F., and Koster, H. D. Sweat in schizophrenic patients: identification of the odorous substance. *Science,* 1969, *166,* 398–99.

5. Kalmus, H. The discrimination by the nose of the dog of individual human odours and in particular of the odours of twins. *British Journal of Animal Behavior,* 1955, *3,* 25–31.

6. Galton, F. Anthropological Miscellany: The History of Twins and the Criterion of Their Relevant Powers of Nature and Nurture, 1875.

7. Kalmus, op. cit.

10.   Smelly Sneakers, Squalene
and Cockroach Perfume

1. Castle, L. J. Bloodhound: a tool in law enforcement. *FBI Law Enforcement Bulletin,* May 1972, 1–5.

2. McHaffie, T. A. The use of dogs in searching for pre-scented objects. Undated summary of Royal Air Force work on detection of squalene-scented flight recorders (about 1969).

3. Whitlaw, J. T., Jr., Pratt, J. J., Jr., and Hilchey, J. D. Identification of Squalene by Dogs. Final Report. U.S. Army Natick Laboratories, Natick, Massachusetts. For Advanced Research Projects Agency, Washington, D.C. November 8, 1963.

Whitlaw, J. T., Jr., Pratt, J. J., Jr., and Hilchey, J. D. A Study of the Detection of Chemically Contaminated Persons by Dogs. U.S. Army Natick Laboratories, Natick, Massachusetts. For Advanced Research Projects Agency, Washington, D.C. April 1964.

4. King, E. J., Becker, R. F., and Markee, J. E. Studies on olfactory discrimination in dogs: (3) ability to detect human odour trace. *Animal Behavior,* 1964, *12,* 311–15.

5. Peters, A. C., and Allton, W. H., Jr. The Use of a Marking Agent for Identification by Dogs. Report No. BAT-171-40, RACIC, Battelle Memorial Institute, Columbus, Ohio. For Advanced Research Projects Agency, Washington, D.C. March 11, 1966. AD 378-125.

Schmidt, G. L., and Klenker, L. G. Trip Report, II Corps Headquarters, 19 February 1965–to Chief, OSD/ARPA R&D Field Unit –Vietnam. San Francisco, California, March 25, 1965.

Baker, K. W. Squalene: Marking, Tracking and Identification (August to December 1965). Final Letter Report to Chief, OSD/ARPA R&D Field Unit—Vietnam. San Francisco, California, June 1, 1966.

6. Schneider, D. Insect olfaction: deciphering system for chemical messages. *Science*, 1969, *163*, 1031–36.

7. Jacobson, M., and Beroza, M. Insect attractants. *Scientific American*, August 1964. Vol. 211, No. 2, p. 20.

8. In some insect species the male too secretes a pheromone. Unlike the female-produced pheromone, the odor of the male pheromone may be detectable by the human nose. The odor has been characterized as pineapple, musk, lemon oil, chocolate and others. According to Jacobson and Beroza (note 7, above): "One of these substances, a clear fluid with a cinnamon-like odor secreted by a tropical water bug, has long been used as a spice by inhabitants of Southeast Asia. In 1957 Adolph Butenandt and his associate Nguyen Dang Tom isolated the odorous substance in pure form. . . . They then succeeded in synthesizing the compound, and the synthetic product is now sold as a spice in Asia."

11. The Training of Mine Dogs

1. Weiss, J. M. Psychological factors in stress and disease. *Scientific American*, 1972, *226*, 104–13.

2. Seligman, M. E. P. *Helplessness: On depression development and death*. San Francisco: W. H. Freeman, 1975.

3. Hiroto, D. S., and Seligman, M. E. P. Generality of learned helplessness in man. *Journal of Personality and Social Psychology*, 1975, *31*, 311–27.

4. For example: Miller, W., and Seligman, M. E. P. Depression and learned helplessness in man. *Journal of Abnormal Psychology*, 1975, *84*, 228–38.

5. Carr-Harris, E., and Thal R. Mine, Booby-Trap, Trip-Wire and Tunnel Detection. Final Report. Contract No. DAAD05-69-C-0234. U.S. Army Limited War Laboratory, Aberdeen Proving Grounds, Maryland. January 1970. AD 867-404L.

Thal, R., Thal, C., and Lubow, R. E. Mine Detector Dogs. Final Report. Contract No. DAAD05-70-C-0001. U.S. Army Limited War Laboratory, Aberdeen Proving Grounds, Maryland. August 1970. AD 874-794L.

6. McIntyre, R. W. The Training of Dogs for Field Reconnaissance. Final Report, from Canine Behavior Laboratory, University of Maryland, to U.S. Army Limited War Laboratory, Aberdeen Proving Grounds, Maryland. September 1965.

7. Carr-Harris, E., Siebert, L., Thal, C., and Thal, R. Mine, Booby-Trap, Trip-Wire Detection Training Manual. Contract No. DAAD05-69-C-0234. Behavior Systems, Inc., Raleigh, North Carolina. September 1969.

   U.S. Army Limited War Laboratory. Tunnel and Trip-Wire Detecting Dog-Handler Teams. Operating Manual. U.S. Army Limited War Laboratory, Aberdeen Proving Grounds, Maryland. April 1969.

   U.S. Army Limited War Laboratory. Mine, Booby-Trap and Trip-Wire Detecting Dog-Handler Teams. Operating Manual. U.S. Army Limited War Laboratory, Aberdeen Proving Grounds, Maryland. April 1969.

12. The Mine Dog at War

1. Romba, J. J. Tactics in the Development of Mine Detection Dogs. U.S. Army Land Warfare Laboratory, Aberdeen Proving Grounds, Maryland. 1970. AD 713-577.

2. White, B. W., Jr., Lt. Col. ACTIV 60th Infantry Platoon (Scout Dog) (Mine/Tunnel Detection Dog). Final Report. Project No. ACG-65F, December 1969.

3. Army probers inspect ruins of My Lai Huts. The Evening Star (Washington, D.C.), January 3, 1970.

4. Lucero, D. A. Monthly report of Marine Corps Mine Detection Program, 1 April 1970. Headquarters, 3rd Military Police Battalion, Force Logistic Command, Fleet Marine Force, Pacific, FPO San Francisco, April 1, 1970.

5. Final Report of USMC Project 90-69-01. Dog Detection of Mines/Booby-Traps. From: Commanding General, Marine Corps Development and Education Command, Quantico, Virginia. To: Commandant, Marine Corps (Code Ax), Washington, D.C., May 7, 1971. AD 883-469L.

6. Breland, M., and Bailey, R. T. Specialized Mine Detector Dog. Technical Memo LWL-CR-04B70. U.S. Army Land Warfare Labo-

ratory, Aberdeen Proving Grounds, Maryland. December 1971. AD 736-360.

7. Romba, J. J. Ability of Specialized Mine Detector Dogs to Find Mines in an Aged Mine Field at APG. Technical Note 71-02. U.S. Army Land Warfare Laboratory, Aberdeen Proving Grounds, Maryland. September 1971.

8. Seligman, M. E. P., and Hager, J. L. (ed.). *Biological Boundaries of Learning.* New York: Appleton, 1972.

13. Men, Machines, Dogs, Bacteria
and Other Animals

1. U.S. Army Limited War Laboratory. Mine, Booby-Trap and Trip-Wire Detecting Dog-Handler Teams. Operating Manual. U.S. Army Limited War Laboratory, Aberdeen Proving Grounds, Maryland. April 1969.
Carr-Harris, E., Siebert, L., Thal, C., and Thal, R. Mine, Booby-Trap, Trip-Wire Detection Training Manual. Contract No. DAAD05-69-C-0234. Behavior Systems Inc., Raleigh, North Carolina. September 1969.

2. Krauss, M. Explosives Detecting Dogs. Technical Report No. 71-11. U.S. Army Land Warfare Laboratory, Aberdeen Proving Grounds, Maryland. September 1971. AD 736-829.

3. Lubow, R. E. Weapons Detection Study Using Dogs. Final Report. Submitted to Israel Ministry of Defense, July 1971.

4. Lubow, R. E. Use of Biological Systems to Detect Explosives. Progress Report, 1972–73. Israel Ministry of Police.

5. Department of the Army Field Manual, FM 20-32: Landmine Warfare. August 1966.

6. National Bomb Data Center. *General Information Bulletin* 75-5. Picatinny Arsenal, Dover, New Jersey. June 12, 1975.

7. Southwest Research Institute. Olfactory Acuity in Selected Animals Conducted during the Period June 1972–September 1974. Contract No. DAAK02-72-C-0602 with U.S. Army Mobility Equipment Research and Development Center, Fort Belvoir, Virginia. September 1974. AD 787-495.

14. Narc Dogs and Dream Rats

1. Romba, J. J. Training Dogs for Heroin Detection. Technical Memorandum No. 71-04. U.S. Army Land Warfare Laboratory, Aberdeen Proving Grounds, Maryland. September 1971.

2. Dean, E. E. Training Dogs for Narcotic Detection. Technical Report No. LWL-CR-60 DJ 71. U.S. Army Land Warfare Laboratory, Aberdeen Proving Grounds, Maryland. July 1972.

3. Dean, E. E. Behavior conditioning and training of dogs to detect heroin hydrochloride. *Proceedings of the 1975 Carnahan Conference on Crime Countermeasures,* May 1975, 141–44.

4. Gridgeman, N. T. Trials of the Contraband Screening Abilities of Six Trained RCMP Dogs. Division of Biological Sciences, National Research Council of Canada, Ottawa, 1972, 1–14.

5. Knauf, H., and Johnston, W. H. Evaluation of Explosives/Narcotics (EXNARC) Detection Dogs. Report 2102. U.S. Army Mobility Equipment Research and Development Center, Fort Belvoir, Virginia. May 1974. AD 787-308.

6. *FBI Law Enforcement Bulletin,* January 1976. Quotation from p. 18.

7. Lubow, R. E., Kahn, M., and Frommer, R. Information processing of olfactory stimuli by the dog: I. The acquisition and retention of four odor-pair discriminations. *Bulletin of the Psychonomic Society,* 1973, *1,* 143–45.

8. Lubow, R. E., Kahn, M., and Frommer, R. Information processing of olfactory stimuli by the dog: II. Stimulus control and sampling strategies in simultaneous discrimination learning. *Bulletin of the Psychonomic Society,* 1976, *8,* 323–26.

9. MacIntosh, N. J. *The Psychology of Animal Learning.* New York: Academic Press, 1974.

10. A more appropriate schedule of reinforcement might be that of a variable ratio rather than a fixed ratio. A variable-ratio schedule is one in which the number of responses that precede the reinforcement is not a constant, but varies around a mean. Thus a variable-ratio 10 schedule will, on the average, require 10 responses from the animal before reinforcement is delivered; but sometimes the number of responses will be more or less than 10. The advantage of

a variable-ratio schedule is that it produces a high response rate that is highly resistant to extinction. This is the schedule that keeps the gambler at the card table or the horse track. He only wins some of the bets, and it is not exactly predictable which bet will be successful. The fixed-ratio schedule also has a drawback for our purposes in that this schedule exhibits what is called a "scalloping effect." After each reinforcement there is a relatively long pause in responding. The duration of the pause is a function of the particular schedule. Schedules that require many responses before reinforcement produce longer post-reinforcement pauses than schedules that require a fewer number of responses. If one considers writing as an analogue to the bar press, and the publication of a book as the reinforcement, then one can understand why authors take so much time between the completion of one book and the initiation of the next book.

15. The War Against Terror

1. Phillips, R. Training Dogs for Explosives Detection. Technical Memorandum. No. LWL-CR-01B70. U.S. Army Land Warfare Laboratory, Aberdeen Proving Grounds, Maryland. October 1971. AD 733-469.

2. Krauss, M. Explosives Detecting Dogs. Technical Report No. 71-11. U.S. Army Land Warfare Laboratory, Aberdeen Proving Grounds, Maryland. September 1971. AD 736-829.

3. New York City Police Department Explosive Detection Dogs. Undated memo, pp. 1–10.

4. Halligan, W. A. Evaluation of Familiarization and Training in Aircraft and Airport Environment for Dogs Trained in Explosive Detection Measures. Internal FAA memo to S. Maggio, Chief, Air Transportation Security Division, October 19, 1971.

5. Berryman, G., Churchman, D., and Yallop, H. J. The Detection of Explosives by Dogs—Feasibility Study. RARDE Memorandum 33-71. Royal Armament Research and Development Establishment, Port Halstead, Kent, England. October 1971.

6. Morgan, P. M., Robinson, G. A. N., and Yallop, H. J. The Detection of Explosives by Dogs—Trials in Aircraft. RARDE Memorandum 29/73. Royal Armament Research and Development Establishment, Port Halstead, Kent, England. December 1973.

7. Knauf, H., and Johnston, W. H. Evaluation of Explosives/Narcotics (EXNARC) Detection Dogs. Report 2102. U.S. Army Mobility Equipment Research and Development Center, Fort Belvoir, Virginia. May 1974. AD 787-308.

8. National Bomb Data Center. *General Information Bulletin* 74-4. Picatinny Arsenal, Dover, New Jersey. March 13, 1974.

9. FBI Bomb Data Program. Use of Dogs to Find Concealed Explosives—update. *General Information Bulletin* 76-1. January 1976.

10. Cumming, W. W. A bird's eye glimpse of men and machines. In Ulrich, R., Stachnik, T., and Mabry, J. (eds.). *Control of Human Behavior*. New York: Scott, Foresman, 1966.

    Verhave, T. The pigeon as a quality control inspector. *American Psychologist*, 1966, *21*, 109–15.

11. Lubow, R. E. Use of Biological Systems to Detect Explosives. Progress Report, 1972–73. Israel Ministry of Police.

12. Krauss, M. Explosives Detecting Dogs. Technical Report No. 71-11. U.S. Army Land Warfare Laboratory, Aberdeen Proving Grounds, Maryland. September 1971. AD 736-829.

    Knauf, H., and Johnston, W. H. Evaluation of Explosives/Narcotics (EXNARC) Detection Dogs. Report 2012. U.S. Army Mobility Equipment Research and Development Center, Fort Belvoir, Virginia. May 1974. AD 787-308.

    Phillips, R. C. Training Dogs for Explosives Detection. Technical Memorandum LWL-CR-01B70. U.S. Army Land Warfare Laboratory, Aberdeen Proving Grounds, Maryland. October 1971. AD 733-469.

    Southwest Research Institute. Objectively Evaluate the Performance of Dogs Trained to Perform Various Militarily Significant Tasks. For U.S. Army Mobility Equipment Research and Development Center, Fort Belvoir, Virginia. December 1972. AD 909-955L.

13. Gage, H. M., and Wall, W. A. An Investigation of the Sensitivity of Trained Detector Dogs for Vapors of the Explosive Ethylene Glycol Dinitrate. Technical Note 74-14. U.S. Army Land Warfare Laboratory, Aberdeen Proving Grounds, Maryland. May 1974.

14. Lubow, R. E. Use of Biological Systems to Detect Explosives. Progress Report, 1973–74. Israel Ministry of Police.

The only other formal evaluation of olfactory countermeasures for military dogs that I am aware of is:

Tomlinson, S. E. Field Evaluation of Dog Countermeasure Materials. Report No. 74-53. U.S. Army Land Warfare Laboratory, Aberdeen Proving Grounds, Maryland. March 1974.

15. Lubow, R. E. Use of Biological Systems to Detect Explosives. Progress Report, 1974–75. Israel Ministry of Police.

16. Body-Recovery Dogs

1. Walker, R. W., and Payne, C. D. The Use of Trained Police Dogs for Corpse Detection.

2. Cadaver Detection Study Report. Report No. ERL/R 144U. The Plessey Company Ltd., Havont, Hampshire, England.

3. Quinn, W. L., Jr., and Montanarelli, N. Body Recovery Dog. Technical Report No. LWL-03B73. U.S. Army Land Warfare Laboratory, Aberdeen Proving Grounds, Maryland. May 1973. AD 763-219.

Epilogue

1. Anonymous. Operation Omega: Lancashire police dogs search for war dead in Sinai Desert. *Lancashire Police Journal Commemorative Issue*, 1974.